THE CLIMBERS

CHRIS BONINGTON

·

THE CLIMBERS
A HISTORY OF MOUNTAINEERING

BBC BOOKS

Hodder & Stoughton

LONDON SYDNEY AUCKLAND

To Maggie

Published by BBC Books, a division of BBC Enterprises Ltd,
Woodlands, 80 Wood Lane, London W12 OTT and
Hodder and Stoughton, a division of Hodder and Stoughton Ltd,
Mill Road, Dunton Green, Sevenoaks, Kent TN13 2YA
Editorial Office: 47 Bedford Square, London WC1B 3DP

ISBN 0 563 20918 6

Copyright © Chris Bonington 1992

First published in Great Britain 1992

Designed by Linda Blakemore

Maps and drawings by Alec Spark

Photoset and printed in Great Britain by Butler and Tanner Ltd, Frome, Somerset
Jacket printed by Belmont Press, Northampton

CONTENTS

•

MAPS

●

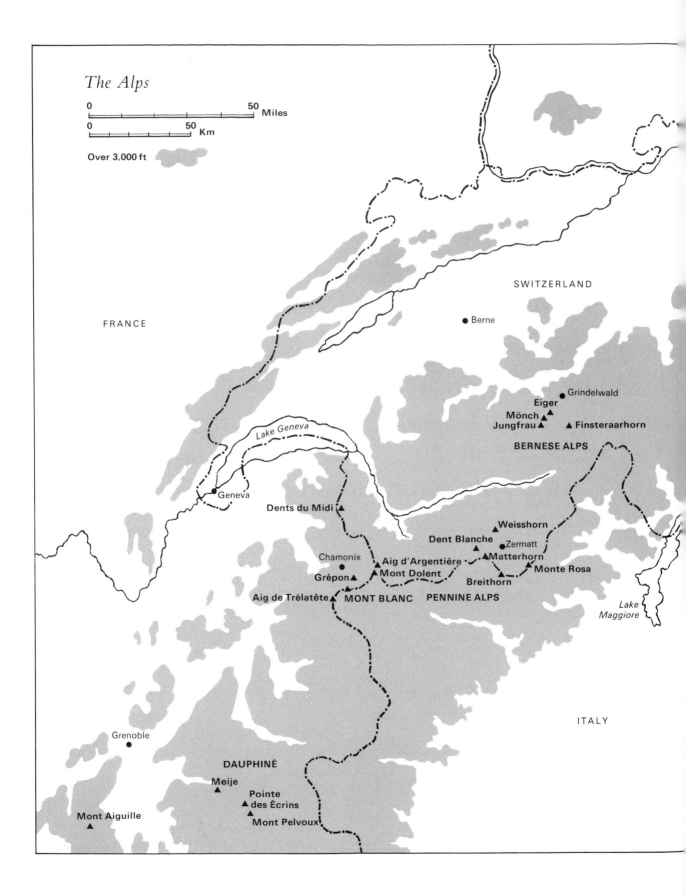

The Alps

0 _____ 50 Miles
0 _____ 50 Km

Over 3,000 ft

SWITZERLAND

FRANCE

● Berne

● Grindelwald
Eiger ▲
Mönch ▲
Jungfrau ▲   ▲ Finsteraarhorn

BERNESE ALPS

Lake Geneva

● Geneva

Dents du Midi ▲

▲ Weisshorn

Dent Blanche
▲   Zermatt ●
Matterhorn ▲

Chamonix
●   Aig d'Argentière ▲
Grépon ▲ ▲ Mont Dolent   Monte Rosa ▲
Breithorn ▲

Aig de Trélatête ▲ MONT BLANC   PENNINE ALPS

Lake
Maggiore

ITALY

Grenoble ●

DAUPHINÉ

Meije ▲
Pointe
▲ des Écrins
▲
Mont Pelvoux

▲ Mont Aiguille

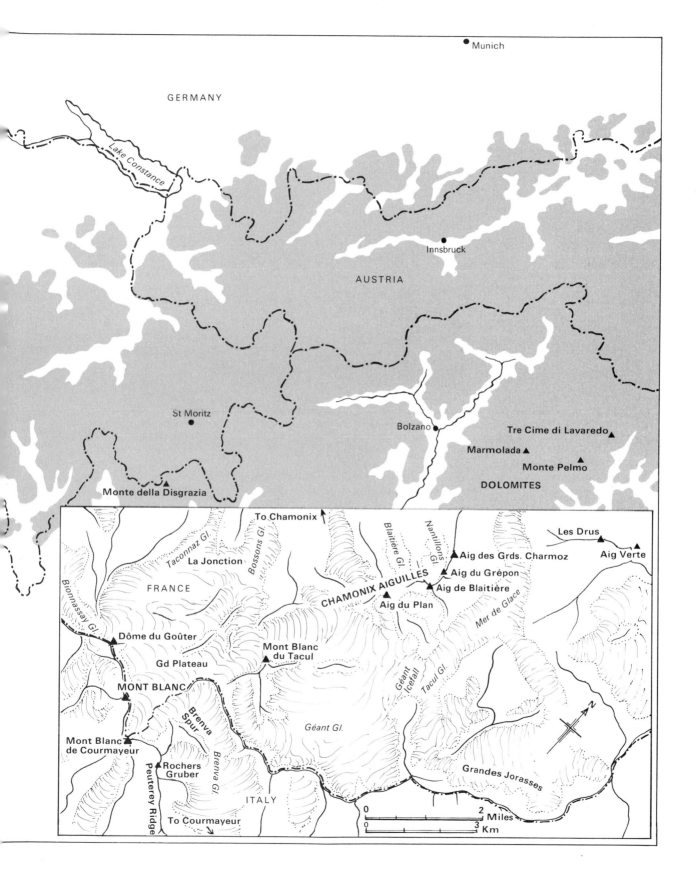

Munich

GERMANY

Lake Constance

Innsbruck

AUSTRIA

St Moritz

Bolzano

Tre Cime di Lavaredo ▲

Marmolada ▲

Monte Pelmo ▲

DOLOMITES

Monte della Disgrazia ▲

To Chamonix

Les Drus ▲   ▲

Taconnaz Gl.   La Jonction   Bossons Gl.   Blaitière Gl.   Nantillons Gl.   Aig des Grds. Charmoz ▲   Aig Verte ▲

FRANCE   CHAMONIX AIGUILLES   Aig du Grépon ▲

Aig de Blaitière ▲

Bionnassay Gl.   Aig du Plan ▲   Mer de Glace

Dôme du Goûter ▲

Gd Plateau   Mont Blanc du Tacul ▲   Géant Icefall   Tacul Gl.

MONT BLANC ▲   Brenva Spur

Mont Blanc de Courmayeur ▲   Brenva Gl.   Géant Gl.

Rochers Gruber ▲   Grandes Jorasses

Peuterey Ridge   ITALY

To Courmayeur

0   2 Miles
0   3 Km

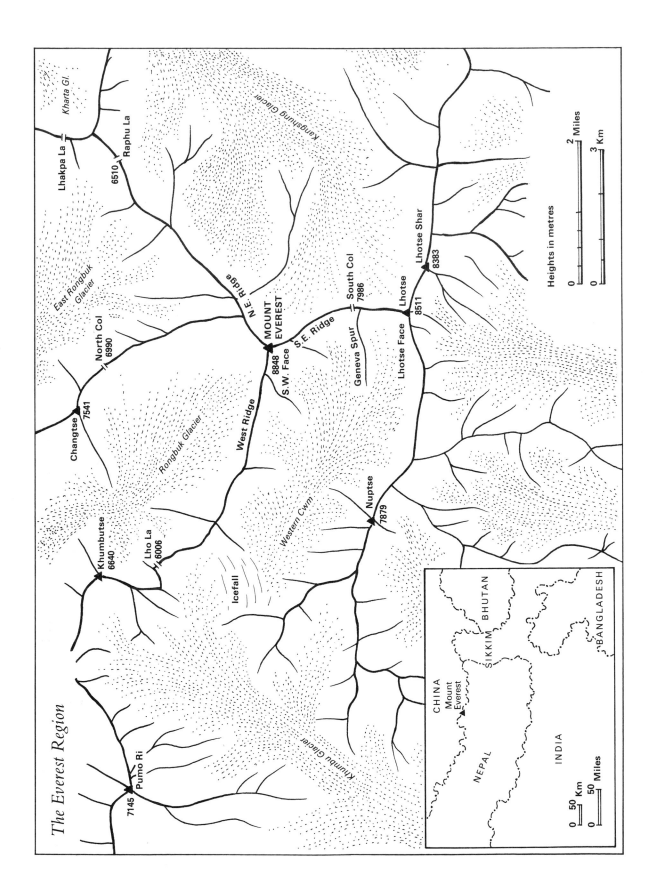

The Everest Region

Kharta Gl.

Lhakpa La
Raphu La
6510

Kangshung Glacier

East Rongbuk Glacier

Lhotse Shar
8383

North Col
6990

N.E. Ridge

MOUNT EVEREST

South Col
7986

Lhotse
8511

Changtse
7541

S.E. Ridge

S.W. Face

8848

Geneva Spur

Lhotse Face

West Ridge

Rongbuk Glacier

2 Miles
3 Km

Heights in metres

0
0

Khumbutse
6640

Lho La
6006

Western Cwm

Nuptse
7879

Icefall

Khumbu Glacier

Pumo Ri

7145

CHINA

SIKKIM BHUTAN

Mount Everest

NEPAL

INDIA

BANGLADESH

50 Km
50 Miles

0
0

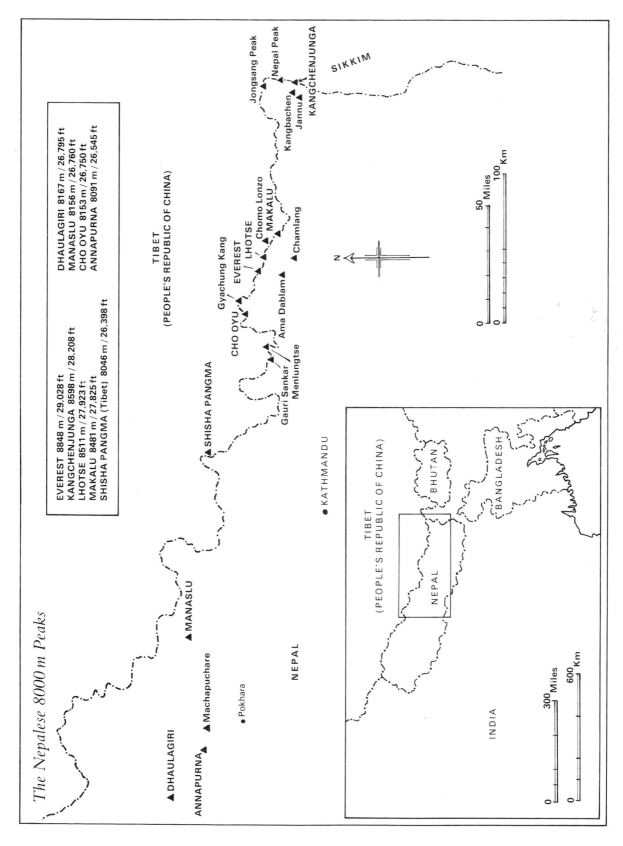

The Nepalese 8000 m Peaks

EVEREST 8848 m / 29,028 ft
KANGCHENJUNGA 8598 m / 28,208 ft
LHOTSE 8511 m / 27,923 ft
MAKALU 8481 m / 27,825 ft
SHISHA PANGMA (Tibet) 8046 m / 26,398 ft

DHAULAGIRI 8167 m / 26,795 ft
MANASLU 8156 m / 26,760 ft
CHO OYU 8153 m / 26,750 ft
ANNAPURNA 8091 m / 26,545 ft

TIBET
(PEOPLE'S REPUBLIC OF CHINA)

▲ DHAULAGIRI
ANNAPURNA ▲
▲ Machapuchare
● Pokhara
▲ MANASLU
NEPAL
▲ SHISHA PANGMA
● KATHMANDU

Gauri Sankar
Menlungtse
CHO OYU
Gyachung Kang
EVEREST
LHOTSE
Chomo Lonzo
MAKALU
Ama Dablam ▲
▲ Chamlang

Jongsang Peak
Nepal Peak
KANGCHENJUNGA
Kangbachen
Jannu ▲
SIKKIM

N

100 Km
50 Miles
0
0

INDIA
NEPAL
TIBET
(PEOPLE'S REPUBLIC OF CHINA)
BHUTAN
BANGLADESH

300 Miles
600 Km
0
0

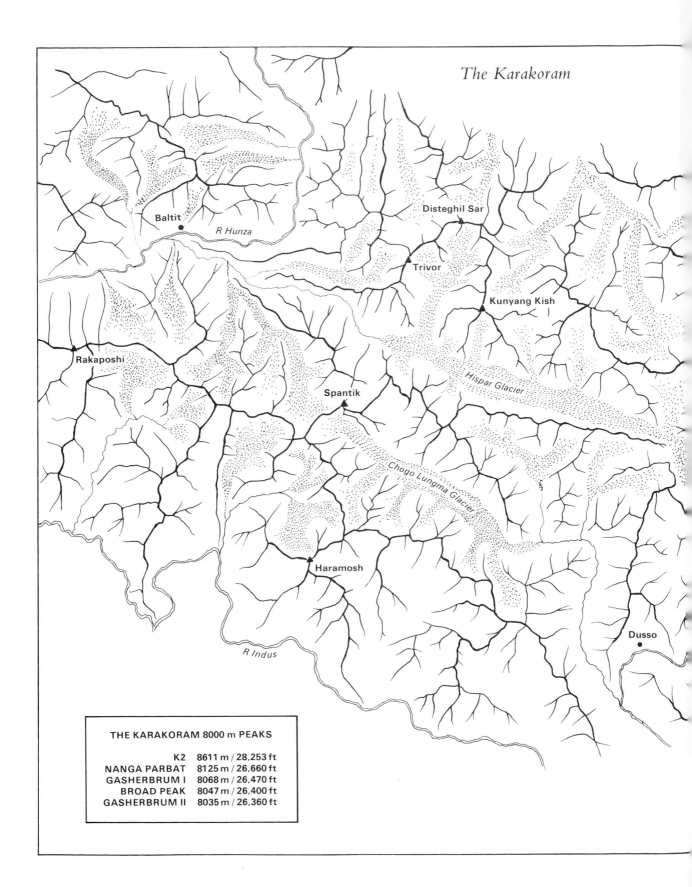

The Karakoram

Baltit

R Hunza

Disteghil Sar

Trivor

Kunyang Kish

Rakaposhi

Spantik

Hispar Glacier

Chogo Lungma Glacier

Haramosh

Dusso

R Indus

THE KARAKORAM 8000 m PEAKS

K2	8611 m	28,253 ft
NANGA PARBAT	8125 m	26,660 ft
GASHERBRUM I	8068 m	26,470 ft
BROAD PEAK	8047 m	26,400 ft
GASHERBRUM II	8035 m	26,360 ft

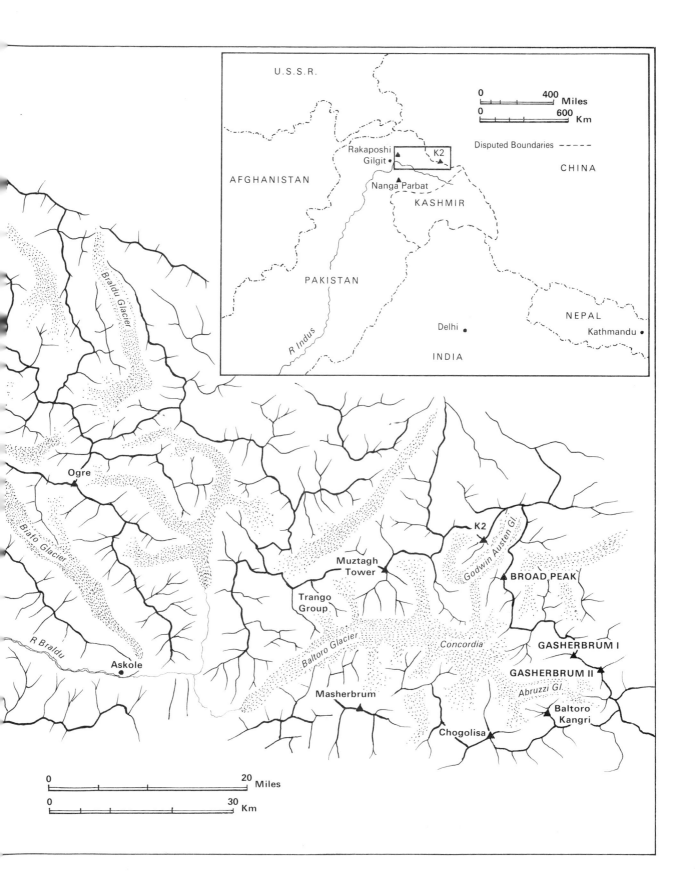

U.S.S.R.

0 ⊢⊢⊢⊢⊢⊢⊢⊢ 400 Miles
0 ⊢⊢⊢⊢⊢⊢⊢⊢ 600 Km

Disputed Boundaries ─ ─ ─ ─

Rakaposhi ▲   ▲ K2
Gilgit •

CHINA

AFGHANISTAN

▲ Nanga Parbat

KASHMIR

PAKISTAN

NEPAL

R Indus

Delhi •

Kathmandu •

INDIA

Braldu Glacier

Ogre

Biafo Glacier

K2 ▲

Godwin Austen Gl.

▲ BROAD PEAK

Muztagh
Tower ▲

R Braldu

Trango
Group

Baltoro Glacier

Concordia

GASHERBRUM I ▲

Askole •

GASHERBRUM II ▲

Abruzzi Gl.

Masherbrum ▲

▲ Baltoro
Kangri

Chogolisa ▲

0 ⊢⊢⊢⊢⊢⊢⊢⊢ 20 Miles
0 ⊢⊢⊢⊢⊢⊢⊢⊢ 30 Km

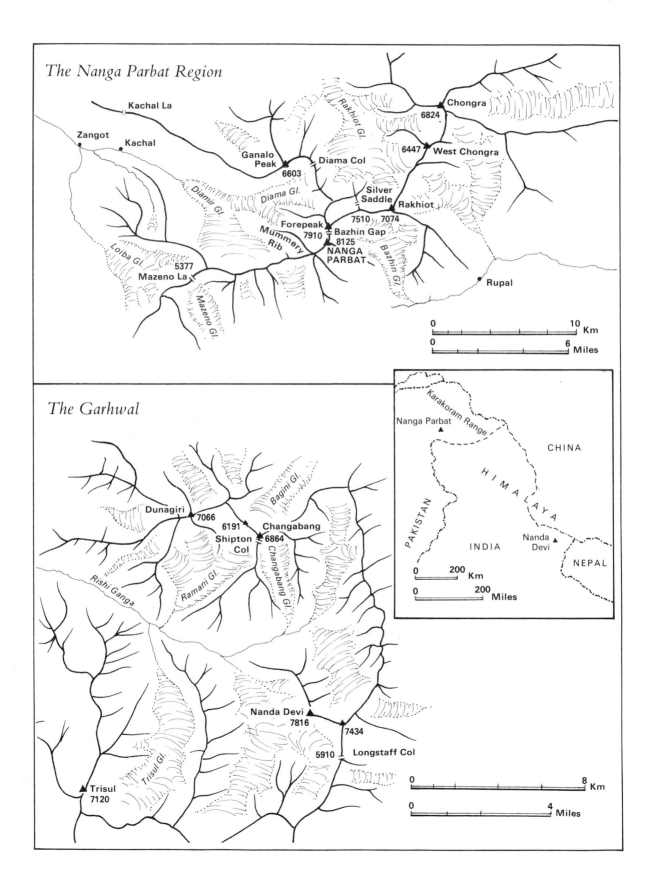

The Nanga Parbat Region

Kachal La

Zangot
Kachal

Ganalo Peak
6603
Diama Col

Rakhiot Gl.

Chongra
6824

6447
West Chongra

Diamir Gl.
Diama Gl.

Silver Saddle
Rakhiot

Forepeak
7910
7510 7074
Bazhin Gap

Mummery Rib

Bazhin Gl.

8125
NANGA PARBAT

Loiba Gl.

5377
Mazeno La

Rupal

Mazeno Gl.

0 ———— 10 Km
0 ———— 6 Miles

The Garhwal

Dunagiri
7066

Bagini Gl.

6191
Shipton Col

Changabang
6864

Changabang Gl.

Rishi Ganga

Ramani Gl.

Nanga Parbat ▲

Karakoram Range

CHINA

PAKISTAN

H I M A L A Y A

INDIA

Nanda Devi ▲

NEPAL

0 ———— 200 Km
0 ———— 200 Miles

Nanda Devi ▲
7816

7434

5910
Longstaff Col

Trisul Gl.

▲ Trisul
7120

0 ———— 8 Km
0 ———— 4 Miles

AUTHOR'S NOTE

In writing a one volume history of mountaineering I have had no choice but to be selective. You have only to walk round the Alpine Club Library to see how much has been written about our sport or way of life, as I think it is. So I have followed what I have perceived as the mainstream development, from its birth in the Alps through to the giants of the Himalaya, leapfrogging past those superb mid-height ranges of the Americas, Antarctica, Scandinavia, New Zealand, concentrating on the major innovative climbs of each era. I have also touched on rock climbing as a foundation for so much of what we do in the mountains.

In biography or autobiography, I have always found the subject's early life the most fascinating; it has a freshness of discovery and provides the foundation for later achievement. The same is applicable in the development of our sport. It starts as a clear tumbling stream that is easy to follow but, as we get closer to the present time, it spreads into a wide delta as opaque as the mouth of the Ganges. It is less easy to pick the main stream, and inevitably I will have left out some ascents or climbers whom my readers might feel I should have included.

It is difficult for me to be completely objective since I have been closely and directly involved with the development of climbing in the last forty years. It has filled my life, given me that combination of joy, excitement, wonder and inevitably sorrow at the loss of all too many friends, but I hope that this has enabled me to empathise all the better with those early climbers who first explored the mysteries of the Alps and trace the course of this serpentine river of ours.

I owe a special thanks to the many climbers and friends who have spoken to me during my research, particularly Charlie Houston whom I accompanied to the foot of Nanga Parbat and with whom I had many long and useful conversations, and to Andy Kauffman who kindly let me see the manuscript of *A K2 Diary*, which is shortly to be published.

I certainly could not have completed this book without the help of my well tried team, and should like to give special thanks to Margaret Body, my editor, who once again has cut and crafted my words with surgical precision, to Audrey Salkeld whose knowlege of mountaineering people, literature and references is the fullest of anyone I know, to Louise Wilson, my secretary, for a first line edit, great patience and advice, to Frances Daltrey who looks after my pictures and to Alison Lancaster who completes my super office team. Also to Andy Fanshawe, who checked my text for accuracy and balance. But if I have made mistakes or got the balance wrong, I accept full responsibility.

I hope I have managed to capture and portray the richness and variety of the story of climbing, where each generation has thrust back the frontiers of what was perceived to be impossible from those first stumbling efforts to reach the summit of Mont Blanc to Tomo Cesen's amazing solo ascent of the South Face of Lhotse.

CHAPTER ONE

A JOURNEY BACK IN TIME

Mummery's first ascent of the Grépon, 1881

•

I was stiff and cold in my tweed jacket and breeches. The polished rock felt slippery under my hands and the clinker nails of my boots scraped on it ineffectually while the rope round my waist dug into my ribs as Jean-Frank Charlet heaved upon it. It was Wednesday, 4th July 1990, 109 years after Albert Frederick Mummery, with the guides Alexander Burgener and Benedict Venetz, made the first ascent of the Grépon, a magnificent peak of serried granite turrets, towering above the town of Chamonix in the Mont Blanc massif. I was dressed as he had been, though my hawser laid rope was made of nylon, rather than hemp, as a concession to our safety officer.

We were trying to re-create for television an ascent by the man who, more than anyone, could be described as the father of modern climbing. A.F. Mummery bridges the approach of the original alpine pioneers, dependent on their guides, and the modern climber, wanting to seek adventure with his peers. He started his climbing with guides, completed some of his finest ascents in partnership with Burgener, but then sought a more complete and fulfilling experience by climbing with fellow amateurs, sharing the lead and choice of route. There had been guideless ascents before those of Mummery, but no-one else of that period had the technical ability on rock and ice, the infectious enthusiasm or the vision that he enjoyed. In donning those heavy tweeds and scrambling on the cold smooth rock of what was to be known as the Mummery Crack, I felt a deep respect for the man.

For most climbers in 1881, however, guides were considered as obligatory as an alpenstock and, even with clients as experienced as Mummery, there was no question about it, the guide did the lead climbing, his *Herr* or *Monsieur* often brought up on a tight rope behind him. In such circumstances partnerships were frequently made which continued from season to season. Mummery had brought his regular guide, Burgener, and Burgener's young colleague, Venetz, from Switzerland, a gaffe which cost him his breakfast in the closed shop of Chamonix. Anxious not to make the same mistake, I was accompanied by two native Chamonix guides, Jean-Frank Charlet to represent Burgener, and Hervé Thivierge, for the smaller and nimble rock climber, Venetz.

Mummery's first attempt on the Grépon was from the southern side. He had seen what seemed a feasible line while making a new route on the Aiguille Verte, the mountain opposite. They managed to cross the bergschrund at the base of the Mer de Glace Face, Venetz, as usual, dispatched out in front, and then made good progress up the deep-cut gullies that penetrate its lower defences. Then the angle began to steepen and the rock became more compact. The climbing certainly sounded as if it was in the modern idiom, as they tried to bypass a formidably steep smooth slab by its overhanging edge: 'We were supported mainly by gripping the lower edge of this slab between our fingers and thumbs, whilst our legs sprawled about on the next slab below in a way which suggested that such useless appendages would have been better left at home.'

This, of course, was in nailed boots with a hemp rope that at best had been passed over a rocky spike, but in all probability with no anchoring belay at all. However, they saw a possible line leading up to the col between the Grépon and Charmoz, which they knew they could reach easily from the other side and so they retreated to Chamonix that afternoon. (The Mer de Glace Face finally succumbed to the trio, H.O. Jones, R. Todhunter and Geoffrey Winthrop Young, with guides Josef Knubel and Henri Brocherel, thirty years later in 1911).

After just one day's rest they were plodding back up the hill to try the Grépon from the north. They set out from Chamonix at 1.30 a.m. by the light of a bottle lantern that could have cast little more than a glimmer on the winding path through the dense pine forest leading up towards the alpine meadows at the foot of the Aiguilles. Even when I first visited Chamonix at the age of twenty-five, I'm not sure I would have had that kind of energy, though at least I walked up to Montenvers, as I was unable to afford the train fare. Today climbers can either catch the first téléférique, to be whisked up to the Plan d'Aiguille or even the summit of the Aiguille du Midi, or they can go up the night before to camp or stay in a hut.

Mummery's party reached the Nantillons Glacier in the dawn and paused to work out the most feasible route. The strongest voice in the

The Charmoz (left), the Grépon (centre foreground) and the Aiguille Verte (in the background), photographed from the Blaitière Glacier at the turn of the century by the Abraham brothers of Keswick, two of the earliest British professional mountain photographers. Mummery followed the left skyline to reach the north summit on his first attempt and two days later returned to traverse the skyline pinnacles to the higher south summit.

discussion would undoubtedly have been that of Burgener, but Mummery would have had his say. They picked a line up a steep tongue of ice that required step-cutting all the way, only to notice another team coming up fast behind by a different route. Mummery commented: 'Our leader exerted his utmost strength, and by Herculean efforts managed to reach the upper glacier simultaneously with the other party.'

Things certainly don't change over the years. I have never been able to resist the temptation of slipping into an undeclared race against other teams or even fellow climbers. They discovered that this was a party led by a well-known Oberland guide who announced he was climbing the Aiguille de Blaitière and advised against any thought of tackling the Grépon. 'For,' said he, 'I have tried it, and where I have failed no-one else need hope to succeed.'

Inflammatory words indeed, enough to ensure that Burgener would go to the limit. They climbed a couloir leading to the col between the Charmoz and Grépon which they had followed the previous year and then struck up to the right to find the foot of the feature that was to be immortalised as the Mummery Crack. Following up the crack, Mummery, who was over six feet tall and had just managed to reach a small protuberance to pull up on, wondered how the much smaller Venetz had managed it. I frequently pondered the same question when climbing with Don Whillans whose reach was a good ten inches less than mine, but who could climb places that had me struggling.

Beyond the top of the crack was a hole in the ridge formed by a huge perched block, dubbed by Burgener the 'Kanones Loch' (Cannon's Breach). An easy gangway led up to it and beyond it there was a comfortable ledge, where Burgener

> proposed, amid the reverent and appreciative silence of the company, that libations should be duly poured from a bottle of Bouvier. This religious ceremony having been fittingly observed (the Western form, I take it, of the prayers offered by a pious Buddhist on reaching the crest of some Tibetan Pass), we proceeded to attack a little cleft overhanging the Mer de Glace.

Bouvier, an Austrian wine, used these days more for blending, was an important part of all climbs, and they didn't take just one bottle. As Mummery tackled a rocky crevasse by bracing back and feet across it,

> Burgener at this point exhibited most painful anxiety, and his '*Herr Gott! geben Sie Acht*' had the very ring of tears in its earnest entreaty. On my emergence into daylight his anxiety was explained. Was not the knapsack on my shoulders, and were not sundry half-bottles of Bouvier in the knapsack?

A sharp rib, now known as the Râteau de Chèvre (Goat's Rake), led up to a platform below the north summit (3478m) which is formed by a spectacular blade of rock. This looks so daunting that, when we reached it during our reconstruction, we were happy to ignore it. Mummery was made of sterner stuff. He shimmied up it, then called upon the others to pass up stones to build a small cairn on its top which he decorated with a red handkerchief.

Mummery, left, on the Mummery Crack on a later ascent of the Grépon with Lily Bristow who took this only surviving picture of him climbing; right, Chris Bonington, as Mummery, tackling the same problem.

They had made the first ascent of the Grépon, whereupon they turned round and went all the way back down to Chamonix. In his account Mummery doesn't even bother to mention the descent – nearly 3000m, reversing the rocky ridge with their elementary abseil technique which involved going hand-over-hand down the rope.

But that night Mummery was consumed with a frustrating worry that I have known all too often. He could not help remembering the sight of the south summit, a great square tower that cut the horizon. Had this been the high point and not the northern summit? There was only one way to find out – go there. Burgener tried to convince Mummery that they had been on the highest point, but Mummery stuck to his guns and so, the very next afternoon, they plodded back up through the woods to an alpine chalet below the Aiguille de Blaitière, spent the night there and set out early the next morning to repeat their route to the top of the north summit, then beyond.

I did something similar in 1981 on the summit of Kongur, a 7719m peak in the Chinese Pamirs. Four of us, Peter Boardman, Al Rouse, Joe Tasker and I, had climbed the mountain alpine-style in eight days, four of them trapped by bad weather in tiny snow caves. We had reached what we perceived to be the summit and dug a snow hole just below it in which to spend the night. But I couldn't get the worry out of my mind that another top, about half a mile away, might be higher. The following morning, like Mummery, I persuaded my companions to trek over and check it out, but in this case our first top proved to be the higher.

Ours had been little more than a walk, though serious enough after eight days at nearly 8000m, with a long and complex descent to come. Mummery's challenge was different, but in its own way just as great. The ridge linking the two summits of the Grépon is a cockscomb of granite blocks and pinnacles, probably steeper and more daunting than anything they had been on before.

It starts with a giddy drop of about twenty metres to a notch in the ridge. Mummery described in a matter-of-fact way how they took out the spare rope, tied two or three knots in it, and descended, one must assume, hand-over-hand. With the prudence of men who had acquired a later skill, Jean-Frank, Hervé and I chose to abseil and I must confess to feeling very exposed. At the start the notch is invisible and you are poised over the sheer drop of the Montenvers Face. Going down hand-over-hand, without the security of a safety rope, would have frightened me. Mummery too, had his moments!

> I brought up the rear in company with the knapsack and an ice axe. I found the first twenty feet very easy, then I began to think that the Alpine Club rope is too thin for this sort of work, and I noticed a curious and inexplicable increase in my weight. To add to these various troubles the axe, which was held by a loop round my arm, caught in a crack and snapped the string. Luckily, by a convulsive jerk, I just managed to catch it in my left hand. This performance, however, greatly excited Burgener, who, unable to see what had happened, thought his Herr, and not merely the ice axe, was contemplating a rapid descent on to the Mer de Glace.

They drank some of the ubiquitous Bouvier to calm their nerves before continuing along the ridge. They now had a pleasant surprise, for an easy scramble led to a broad ledge on the Mer de Glace side, 'suitable for carriages, bicycles or other similar conveyances'. This led in turn to the foot of the final tower. 'It was certainly one of the most forbidding rocks I have ever set eyes on.' The rock was smooth to the touch and seemed impregnable, except for a wide crack that led up to an overhanging capstone perched on the summit. Burgener and Mummery tried initially to throw a rope over the block but didn't succeed. Then Venetz was prodded into the lead and started what was probably the most difficult piece of rock climbing that had ever been attempted at that time.

> Our rope throwing operations had been carried on from the top of a sort of narrow wall, about two feet wide, and perhaps about six feet above the gap. Burgener, posted on this wall, stood ready to help Venetz with the ice axe so soon as he should get within his reach, whilst my unworthy self, planted in the gap, was able to assist him in the first part of his journey. So soon as Venetz got beyond my reach, Burgener leant across the gap and, jamming the point of the axe against the face of the rock, made a series of footholds of doubtful security whereon Venetz could rest and gain strength for each successive effort. At length he got above all these adventitious aids and had to depend exclusively on his splendid skill. Inch by inch he forced his way, gasping for breath, and his hand wandering over the smooth rock in those vague searches for non-existent holds which is positively painful to witness.

When Hervé came to lead it during our reconstruction, he needed help from the ice axe every bit as much as Venetz had and, in addition, had a cheat running belay from a loop of rope hidden in the back of the crack. He struggled and panted just as much as his predecessor and afterwards admitted that he had very nearly fallen. Jean-Frank had declined to balance on the wall like Burgener, but jammed himself down in the notch immediately below the crack while I belayed Hervé. Reading Mummery's description of how the higher south summit of the Grépon (3482m) was achieved, I could not help wondering what security, if any, Venetz had had from the rope or, had he fallen, whether he would have taken both Mummery and Burgener with him to the bottom of the Montenvers Face.

When it was my turn to climb the Venetz Crack, I was able to produce a pair of rubber-soled tennis shoes, which were what Mummery had taken with him for any very difficult climbing. It was a sign of the originality of his thinking, for this surely must have been the first time that anyone had used 'rubbers' for rock climbing.

Mummery described his effort:

> When the rope came down for me, I made a brilliant attempt to ascend unaided. Success attended my first efforts, then came a moment of metaphorical suspense,

promptly followed by the real thing; and, kicking like a spider, I was hauled onto the top, where I listened with unruffled composure to sundry sarcastic remarks concerning those who put their trust in tennis shoes and scorn the sweet persuasion of the rope.

I did no better than Mummery. My hands were cold and I was frozen to the bone from a wind that bit through my tweed jacket and breeches. My two guides, impatient to get the climb over, hauled me up with the same lack of respect as had Burgener and Venetz back in 1881. I imagine that the Venetz Crack is very rarely climbed today and, when Mummery returned ten years later to make the first guideless ascent, he avoided it by climbing the much easier Fissure Z, which is just round the corner. In modern grading the Venetz Crack is only Grade V, but when we were there one of the best rock climbers around Chamonix, with a large number of new routes to his credit, tried it and backed off, largely because of the complete lack of protection.

The first ascent of the Venetz Crack was a tribute to the extraordinary skill of a superb natural climber about whom very little is known. He acted as Burgener's assistant in a series of bold first ascents with Mummery in 1880-1, thrust out in front whenever the going was difficult, and then vanished from the annals of climbing. Perhaps he got married and returned to farming. Burgener, on the other hand, was already established as one of the leading guides of the period and was to continue guiding at a high level late into the first decade of the twentieth century.

The Grépon was just one of an impressive list of climbs by Mummery and Burgener. Mummery's subsequent ascent of the Grépon without the help of guides also represented an important development in alpine climbing which made his contribution to mountaineering even more important. To understand this it is necessary to look at the whole evolution of mountaineering from its beginnings.

CHAPTER TWO

A MOUNTAIN PRIZE

The first ascent of Mont Blanc, 1786

•

People have climbed from earliest times – a Bronze Age hunter left his spear head on the summit of the Riffelhorn (2928m) – but these early venturers went no higher than was necessary for hunting game or perhaps crystals. The alpine passes were routes for trade and invasion, but the peaks were places of fearsome mystery, the abodes of gods, devils or dragons.

One of the earliest recorded ascents of a peak for purely aesthetic reasons was by the Emperor Hadrian, who wanted to view the sunrise from the summit of Mount Etna in the second century AD, whilst the first technically difficult climb was in 1492 on Mont Aiguille, a magnificent limestone peak near Grenoble, guarded like a fortress on all sides by sheer walls. The Emperor Charles VIII passed it on his way to Italy, adopted its image as an heraldic device and ordered his military engineer, Antoine de Ville, to climb it. The result was the first documented artificial climb, using 'sobtilz engins', whatever they might have been, to lay siege to the mountain. I climbed it in 1965 and descended by what was presumably the route of ascent. It must have been quite an adventure.

Conrad Gessner, who made the first ascent of the Gnepfstein in 1555, was perhaps the first mountaineer to express a reason for climbing that could easily be recognised by many a climber today when he wrote, 'As long as it may please God to grant me life, I will ascend several mountains, or at least one, every year at the season when the flowers are in their glory, partly for the sake of examining them and partly for the sake of good bodily exercise and mental delight.'

The eighteenth century saw the development of tourism – the Grand Tour of Europe that so many English gentlemen embarked upon. Chamonix, with its Mer de Glace, was on their itinerary and Mont Blanc, now surveyed as the highest point of western Europe at 4807m (15,770ft), began to beckon. In 1760 Professor Horace-Bénédict de Saussure in Geneva offered a reward to anyone who could find a way up the mountain so that he could then follow it to take scientific observations. No-one took up the challenge. It needed perhaps a higher level of public awareness – that very modern ingredient, publicity. This was provided by the man who could be described as mountaineering's first publicist. Marc-Théodore Bourrit, Precentor at the Cathedral in Geneva, was an enthusiastic painter of mountain landscapes and a prolific writer who first visited Chamonix in 1766 and wrote several books about the valley in which he examined the possibility of climbing the mountain.

Even so, the first serious attempt was not made until 1775, when four local men climbed from Chamonix straight up the forest-clad rocky ridge known as the Montagne de la Côte, which is squeezed between the icy snouts of the Glacier des Bossons and the Glacier du Taconnaz, and on to a spot known as La Jonction. It is fairly flat, but heavily crevassed and the sun was high in the sky, the snow wet and soggy. That day they probably reached the lower part of the Petit Plateau. One of them had nearly fallen into a hidden crevasse; they were tired and almost certainly feeling the effects of altitude. The summit must have seemed very, very distant. Although Chamoniards did venture onto the lower sections of the glaciers on their way to hunt chamois or search for crystals, or show tourists the wonders of the ice structures, they would never have been as high as this before.

It is difficult for us today to understand just what a huge step into the unknown these ventures were. The climbers' clothing and equipment, consisting of homespun jackets and trousers, ordinary working boots, pointed staves and perhaps a wood-chopping axe for cutting steps, were all inadequate. But even more challenging were the psychological barriers. No-one, as far as they knew, had ever been to such heights. In many ways the summit of Mont Blanc appeared to be more mysterious, less attainable than Everest was to be some 150 years later.

That same year, Michel-Gabriel Paccard, a medical student and youngest son of the notary of Chamonix, ventured into the mountains. Interested in botany, he had undoubtedly already explored the wooded slopes above the village, the high pastures around the Brévent and the north side of the Aiguilles de Chamonix. The lower parts of the glaciers were also probably familiar to him. It was the arrival of Thomas Blaikie, a Scottish landscape gardener, keen to find alpine flowers, that encouraged Paccard to the next step in his mountaineering career. He took Blaikie on an adventurous expedition that started at Montenvers and climbed the high alpine meadows to the moraines of the glaciers flowing down from the north side of the Aiguilles de Chamonix. After a night in a cow herder's hut, they crossed the Glaciers des Bossons and Taconnaz to reach the lower rocks of the Aiguille du Goûter, a useful reconnaissance of the approaches to Mont Blanc.

There were two more ineffective attempts in the following years and then, in September 1783, Bourrit and Paccard came together. Bourrit's fascination with the mountain and, no doubt, frustration at the limited progress so far achieved, made him resolve to try it himself. Paccard was now qualified as a doctor and practising in Chamonix. They set out up the Montagne de la Côte with three guides, but, according to Paccard, Bourrit refused to venture onto the glacier, using the weather as an excuse.

Paccard was now fully committed to the mountain. He ventured up the Mer de Glace to investigate the icefall of the Glacier du Géant the following year, then later that same season, pushed on up the crumbling rocky ridge of the Aiguille du Goûter, getting high above the Tête Rousse.

This was enough to rekindle Bourrit's enthusiasm and, a few days after Paccard's return, he followed the same route from Les Houches, armed with his painting materials and supported by four guides and his dog. He got no further than the lower slopes of the Tête Rousse, had a headache, probably felt frightened and decided to halt where he was to sketch – today we busy ourselves with photography when we want a breather. Two of the guides, however, pressed on and made impressive progress, reaching the top of the Dôme du Goûter. This was by far the highest point reached to date and they were convinced they had been higher than anyone had ever been and returned to tell the tale. In doing so they had broken through a major psychological barrier.

It was now twenty-five years since de Saussure had made his offer of a reward. In the intervening years he had watched the progress of succeeding attempts and had pursued his own travels in the mountains. He even joined Bourrit in another aborted attempt in 1785. Bourrit blamed the failure on de Saussure, though his progress, by all accounts, was the slowest of all. On the descent, he had his hand on the shoulder of one guide while another held him by the coat collar.

But much of the mystery had now been removed and success seemed possible. Another attempt was made in early June of the following year by three guides, one of whom was François Paccard, Michel-Gabriel's cousin, who had been on the first serious assault back in 1775. Once again he chose the Montagne de la Côte as an approach, bivouacking on its summit. They were about to set off the following morning when they were joined by an unwelcome companion, Jacques Balmat des Boix, a tough and ambitious young crystal hunter, who had presumably heard of their endeavour. Apparently he was unpopular in Chamonix but they must have reached some kind of accommodation and all four set out, finding a way up past the Petit Plateau, through the crevasses which this time were safely covered with hard frozen snow. They probably went straight up to the Col du Dôme and then turned up the broad ridge leading to the cluster of rocks that is the site of the Vallot Hut today. However, the Arête des Bosses, from immediately beneath, looked all too formidable, with its steep icy slopes dropping away on either side. It is not surprising they retreated.

Balmat pressed on a little higher to search for crystals but the others did not bother to wait for him and started down. It was getting late and cloudy by the time Balmat began his descent, following the line of tracks winding down through the snow-covered glacier, until it was too dark to see them. So he spent a chilly night on the snows and continued down the next day, tired, badly sunburnt, but none the worse for the experience which demonstrated that you could spend a night out on the snows with no long-lasting ill effects. This was the first recorded high mountain bivouac and in itself another important psychological break-through.

In the meantime, Michel-Gabriel Paccard had been taking stock. He had examined the possible routes up Mont Blanc from the opposite side of the valley on the slopes of the Brévent and had picked out what seemed a possible line across the North Face from the Grand Plateau to join the easier-angled North Ridge leading to the summit. In doing this he showed he had the eye of a mountaineer but he was not able to get away to put his theory to the test until nearly the end of the season. On 8th August 1786 he took Balmat with him as a porter and between them they shared the thermometer and aneroid, both heavy items of equipment in those days, as well as provisions, a blanket and their alpenstocks. They had neither crampons nor rope. It was an attempt very much in the modern manner, just two climbers going for the peak. Paccard wanted to carry out his observations on the summit and Balmat wanted to collect de Saussure's reward, but both must have had that fundamental spirit of adventure shared by every climber.

The way was not easy. Being late in the season, many of the snow bridges over the crevasses had melted. They used their alpenstocks as precarious bridges, edging their way over them like tightrope walkers. It took them eight hours to get above the Grands Mulets and they still had a

Summit 4807 m

Les Bosses

Dôme du Goûter

Rochers Rouges

Grand Plateau

Petit Plateau

Glacier du Taconnaz

La Jonction

Glacier des Bossons

▲ Bivouac 7/8/1786

Montagne de la Côte

The first ascent of Mont Blanc. Above left and right, Michel-Gabriel Paccard and Jacques Balmat whose ascent in August 1786 won a prize and fuelled a controversy.

long way to go. Paccard was the driving force, with Balmat now remembering his ailing daughter, whom he had left the previous day. Shouldn't he return to help his wife? But they continued, plodding across the gigantic reflector bowl of the Grand Plateau in the mid-afternoon, and then striking up onto new ground, heading over the snows of the North Face, past a band of rock toward the North Ridge.

By this time it was early evening, but there were no suitable sites for a bivouac and so they kept going, with Paccard reaching the summit at 6.25 p.m., and Balmat a short time after. Everyone in Chamonix who could lay their hands on a telescope was following the ascent. It must have had the same fascination that held us in front of our television sets when Neil Armstrong first set foot on the moon.

The way a successful route evolves out of earlier attempts is mirrored many times on later challenges, like the North Wall of the Eiger, on Everest, K2 or Nanga Parbat. Even the subsequent controversy over whether it was Paccard or Balmat who found the key to the route, who helped whom and who reached the summit first, was to be repeated with sad frequency down the years in the Alps and the Himalaya.

The second ascent of Mont Blanc was made in 1787 by Balmat with two guides in an effort to find a safer and easier route to the summit, but it was the third ascent that attracted the greatest publicity and set the style of subsequent climbs. De Saussure was determined to reach the top and did so with a magnificent entourage of guides, making the obligatory observations on the summit.

Ascents of Mont Blanc became a regular occurrence, but these were not so much part of a developing sport as a piece of adventurous tourism – and the guides of Chamonix were there to cater to it. The first ever Company of Guides was founded there in 1821, with a tariff of charges, the proviso that there should be four guides for every amateur going to the top of Mont Blanc and a roster system forcing the potential client to take whoever happened to be at the head of the list, irrespective of his ability. This might have done for the tourists but it inevitably led to frustration among serious climbers who had developed relationships with particular guides. It also led to guides being brought in from other villages or even Switzerland, as Mummery did with Burgener and Venetz as late as the beginning of the 'eighties. Only in recent times have the guides of Chamonix come to a comfortable understanding with foreign interlopers. Today, British guides operate happily alongside their Chamoniard counterparts.

De Saussure eventually climbed Mont Blanc himself, equipped with ladders, staves, ample provisions and a large number of guides, including Balmat.

Climbing activity steadily built up through the first half of the nineteenth century, though there was still a strong emphasis on the scientific aspect, as if a serious excuse had to be found to make up for an undertaking as frivolous as climbing a mountain for fun or adventure. Thermometers, barometers and plane tables remained essential items of equipment. The first to leave them behind as 'a hindrance to adventurous climbers' were the Meyers from the Oberland, a remarkable family, imbued with a more modern mountaineering spirit. In 1811 they tackled the Jungfrau (4158m), one of the finest peaks in the Oberland, well equipped with 'warm clothing, ropes, a ladder, alpenstocks and a big black linen sheet to act as a tent and also as a flag to be set up on the summit'. With inadequate maps, they experienced the problems Mallory was to suffer in 1921 in his search for the easiest approach to the north side of Everest, or Herzog and the French experienced in 1950 when they tried to find a way to the foot of Annapurna. It is not clear what approach the Meyers took to the mountain, and the map they drew from their ascent is confusing, but there seems no doubt that they reached the summit, even though the flag they displayed was not seen from below in Grindelwald. They continued their climbing exploration, with the youngest Meyer, Johann Rudolph III, crossing many of the Oberland passes and attempting the Finsteraarhorn (4274m). In many ways he could be described as one of the first adventure climbers, embarking on a progressive series of climbs rather than just a one-off.

Mountaineering's first publicist, Albert Smith, has a full house at London's Egyptian Hall for his Mont Blanc magic-lantern show.

By the middle of the century there was a steady traffic of visitors to the Alps, though there was still a strong scientific element in their interest. One of the most important of these adventurous scientists was James David Forbes, the youngest son of a Scottish baronet, who explored the length and breadth of the Alps in the 1840s, investigating the movement and nature of glaciers. The mountains were extolled by enthusiasts as diverse as John Ruskin, who marvelled at their sublimity but deprecated attempts to climb them, and Albert Smith. Albert Smith was definitely a man of the new age. He reached the summit of Mont Blanc in 1851 with no less than sixteen guides and provisions to match, which included cognac, champagne and four packets of prunes. On his return he hired the Egyptian Hall in London and laid on what was probably the first audio-visual mountaineering lecture with a magic lantern, a large screen, girls in Swiss costumes and some St Bernard dogs. Queen Victoria attended one of his shows and he lectured to packed houses for six years. With the possible exception of Captain John Noel, who organised a similar style of show after the 1924 Everest expedition, bringing over a group of Tibetan lamas to provide background chants and dancing, Smith was probably the most succesful lecturer of all time.

The mountains had received their popularist. Now improved railway communications, and the growth of an increasingly affluent middle class, all contributed to the development of mountaineering as a sport.

CHAPTER THREE

THE GOLDEN AGE

The heyday of Victorian alpinism

•

The ascent of the Wetterhorn in 1854 by Alfred Wills is frequently quoted as marking the start of modern mountaineering as a sport in its own right. In fact the boundaries are much more blurred, but certainly the 'fifties marked an explosion of activity, with climbers beginning to go regularly to the Alps for their annual holidays, exploring the passes and tackling the main summits. By the end of the decade most of the 4000m (13-15,000ft) peaks had been climbed, the world's first mountaineering club had been founded and the sport was firmly established in a form that we can recognise today. The British had made comparatively few first ascents before 1850, but made up for this in the latter part of the 'fifties and through the 'sixties.

The early mountaineers on the whole were members of the more comfortably off, newly emerging middle class. Alfred Wills was a judge, Francis Fox Tuckett a landowner, Mummery and C.E. Mathews were successful businessmen, and a high proportion of early pioneers were clergymen, some no doubt with private incomes. Edward Whymper, most famous of all the Victorian mountaineers, had no private means. He was an engraver for Longman's, the publisher, and was to earn his living through his writing.

But it was still a very small group of people who were climbing regularly in the Alps. There was a lot of the region to be explored and certainly a lot to learn about mountaineering, the problems of altitude, avalanches and weather patterns in the next fifty years before climbers began to look to the Himalaya. Today, with the proliferation of *téléfériques* and huts, helicopter rescue services, way-marked paths, crowds of climbers festooned with modern equipment, it is difficult to conceive the scale of pioneering adventure that our Victorian forebears enjoyed. Although a railway system now reached the foothills, onward travel in the lower valleys was by horse and carriage for the wealthy, or a crowded diligence (forerunner of the bus) for those with less money. The journey to the higher villages was made on foot with pack mules for the baggage. In terms of time and cost, it was relatively more expensive to journey to the Alps then than it is to fly to the Himalaya, today.

The early pioneers stayed in inns but these were probably no more expensive, and in many cases a good deal more primitive, than the little Sherpa hotels that are now available in Nepal. Fleas and vermin abounded, the food was plain and often badly cooked, and the rooms were dark and ill-furnished. Above the valleys, the only refuges were shepherd's huts and the occasional simple bothy that had been built for a specific venture. The early climber needed to be a formidable walker and, although labour was cheap and it was therefore easy to hire a porter as well as a guide, there are plenty of records of climbers carrying their own packs over considerable distances. John Ball, first President of the Alpine Club and author of the first guide to the Alps, was a prodigious mountain traveller and usually carried his own rucksack.

Victorian Britain was the era of the gentleman's club. Many of the London clubs date back to this period and it was therefore perhaps inevitable that the little group of alpinists should decide to band themselves together formally, if only to meet and talk over their previous summer's adventures in the long British winter. Being the first ever mountaineering club there seemed no need to identify the club's nationality – 'The Alpine Club' was sufficient description, and reflected the buoyant self-confidence of imperial Britain. The first meeting, chaired by E.S. Kennedy, was at Ashley's Hotel, Covent Garden on 22nd December, 1857. There were just twelve original members listed, but this was increased to twenty-one in a second circular.

The first *Alpine Journal* was produced in March, 1863, though the publication, *Peaks, Passes and Glaciers*, provided a record of ascents before this date. The *Alpine Journal* opened with an account of the ascent of Monte della Disgrazia (12,074ft) by Edward Shirley Kennedy, second President of the Alpine Club, and two other AC luminaries, Sir Leslie Stephen and the Rev. Isaac Taylor, with their trusted guide Melchior Anderegg, and Thomas Cox, their servant. Like so many accounts that followed, their report conveyed the zest of exploration and adventure, combined with a real sense of fun.

The party had travelled down Lake Lugano by steamer and then by carriage, in the blazing afternoon sun, over dusty roads to the village of

Edward Shirley Kennedy, second President of the Alpine Club, left, may have looked every inch an eminent Victorian but the joyfully adventurous spirit of his ascent of Monte della Disgrazia is what still motivates climbers today. Right, his companion, Sir Leslie Stephen with Melchoir Anderegg (left) from Meiringen, one of the most celebrated and successful of the early alpine guides.

Maddelena. The following morning they walked five miles to Chiesa, a mountain village below their objective, and climbed to a viewpoint on the slopes of Mount Nero to spy out a route. Taking in deep lungfuls, Kennedy wrote:

> How free and exultant is the true mountaineer, when he exchanges the warmly glowing atmosphere of the south for the cold and invigorating blasts of the mountain; when he leaves behind him the gentle beauty of the Lakes and glories in the savage grandeur of riven rock and contorted glacier.

That night, they stayed in the local inn and were immediately the focus of attention.

> A council was held. Present, the five travellers, the two Chamois hunters, and the landlord of the hotel, who, joking aside, was a host in himself. In fact we never discovered who the landlord was. The establishment seemed to be conducted upon the principles of a London joint-stock hotel – numerous proprietary, limited liability; for those who made every passage and every room resonant with a Babel of Tongues swarmed around in countless numbers . . . Impossible was pronounced by a hundred tongues and in a hundred tones.

But they were not deterred and set out at three o'clock the following morning, Anderegg, lantern in hand, leading the way. It was a three-hour walk to the village of Chiaraggio, a collection of huts towards the head of the valley. A short distance beyond, round a bend in the valley, they had their first close view of Monte della Disgrazia.

The climbing proved harder than they had anticipated. By the time they had reached the crest of the ridge leading to the top, it was getting late and they discovered that they were on a subsidiary peak. They had no choice but to retreat down steep snow that was softened by the afternoon sun. Fortunately they were near the bottom when retreat was turned into a rout. Leslie Stephen slipped, pulling Kennedy's servant, Cox, off his holds, and then Kennedy himself, so that Anderegg was holding all three.

> He was not aware of the strong pull upon me from below, so that immediately his hold was relaxed I dashed down the smooth and slippery course that the two others had formed. Stephen and Cox averted their gaze as a fellow creature rushed wildly past, but, unable to check him in his headlong plunge, they were almost instantly carried off their legs and hurled into the depths below. Entangled with the rope, and twisted, and tossed, and rolled over in every conceivable way, we were carried,
> > like a swarm of fire flies,
> > Tangled in a silver braid,
> about 90 feet down the ice slope, shooting in our course the bergschrund, across and over which we fell vertically some twenty feet through the air. A short distance below this bergschrund the human avalanche was arrested in the soft snow bed that we had descried from above. Spectacles, and veils, and hats are scattered in every direction; cigars are destroyed, and pipes broken, and pockets and shirts, and clothes, and ears, and noses, and mouths are filled with snow.
> > Regarded in a proper point of view, this little affair was a most fortunate occurrence, for it was a means of saving much valuable time, and was not destitute of enjoyment, inasmuch as it afforded us a new sensation.

I find it difficult to link the solemn portraits of these Victorian gentlemen, frock-coated, immaculate and posed, with their capacity for risk and sheer fun once they were in the mountains. This is perhaps the essence of the reason for their adoption of mountaineering – the contrast between the stately and serious order and purposefulness of the Victorian age and the free excitement and fun of their life in the hills.

They did not get back to the inn at Chiesa until the early hours of the morning and they had to hammer on the locked doors to get in. Next day they took stock. There is a progression of emotions after an epic failure that I suspect is universal – the immediate relief that you're back in one piece, the satisfaction and fatigue from a long hard day, the enjoyment of shared experience and narrow escapes, but this is almost inevitably followed by the niggle of failure.

Their initial plan was to return to Switzerland over the Bernina Pass, but Kennedy couldn't help thinking of the magnificent unclimbed bastion of Monte della Disgrazia, and approached the topic of a return to the fray obliquely:

> 'It is a very hot day, Stephen, would you not like a ride?'
>
> 'Yes I should. I dislike these straight, hot, dusty, in every way detestable, Italian roads. I suppose we can have a carriage up the valley, at any rate as far as the foot of the Bernina Pass?'
>
> 'I suppose we can, Stephen; also, we can have a carriage down the valley to Morbegno.'
>
> 'No! I have been there once; I won't go along that odious road again.'
>
> 'But, Stephen, think of the beautiful vineyards, and Indian corn fields that we shall see.'
>
> 'I hate beautiful vineyards and I hate Indian corn fields.'
>
> 'Also, Stephen, there is another beautiful valley that comes down to Morbegno at right-angles to the high road and near the head of this beautiful valley I find there is a "Grand Ancient Italian Bathing Establishment", at which 140 people of distinction dine daily at a magnificent table d'hôte; and, Stephen, if we start directly after breakfast we shall be just in time.'
>
> 'I don't care, Kennedy. I hate Grand Ancient Italian Bathing Establishments and I hate 140 people of distinction, and I hate magnificent table d'hôte, and I hate being just in time.'
>
> 'Also, Stephen, at the head of this beautiful valley is the foot of the glacier that runs up to a notch not far from the summit of a certain mountain that you know; also, the carriage can wait at the "Grand Ancient Italian Bathing Establishment" until to-morrow evening, and can then bring us back to Sondrio.'

Stephen was persuaded and they set out in two carriages, one for the *Herren* and one for the guide and servant, winding their way up the precarious zigzags of the side road towards the Spa Hotel. By this time Taylor, who seems to have been less adventurous, had gone home.

> Our welcome was cold as the stream of the glacier; we were obviously not invalids, and all other classes of visitors were deemed unworthy of even nitrogenous salt. Of the existence of our mountain every one was placidly unconscious, and mountaineers themselves are a race so entirely unknown that we were regarded as a species of *lusus naturae*.

The weather now became unsettled. They set off three times within the space of twenty-four hours, being turned back on the first two occasions, but rewarded on the third with a fine alpine dawn and they were able to follow the glacier towards the summit ridge, which proved to be both steep and rocky. Some early rope manœuvring followed:

Melchior fastens both ends of the rope around his waist. We three stand, each of us, in the firmest position we can select and allow the doubled rope to pass through our hands as Melchior descends the side of the buttress, and gradually, with scarcely hold for finger or for toe, contrives to wind round its face ... As we three stand there pulling in the rope as we feel him gradually nearing us, it may be believed how thorough is the determination that we all share, to hold on with unflinching grasp should the foot of our trusty guide fail. But the fact is, I believe, that in all these ticklish passages a slip never does occur. The nerves are braced to the utmost, the limbs move slowly and cautiously and the consciousness that there is sufficient power in others to afford the necessary support, in case of necessity, imparts a feel of confidence that materially tends to diminish the risk of accident.

This applies today as directly as it did then. The difficulties eased and a relatively easy ridge led towards the top. Kennedy's feelings on reaching the summit showed that the age of scientific justification for climbing was at an end:

The scientific observation is of the utmost importance, and with most unfeigned satisfaction do I behold others trying to keep their hands warm while they are conducting it. But, to my mind, each and every one of these sources of gratification sink into insignificance when compared with the exhilarating consciousness of difficulty overcome, and of success attained by perseverance.

This was not the most important ascent of the era, but it does capture much of the atmosphere of the time and portrays the relationship between guide and client. The social distinctions were clearly defined and accepted in a completely unselfconscious way. At the same time there is a strong sense of shared experience, mutual respect and a very real friendship. Melchior chose the line and took the tactical decisions, as Burgener was to do in his ascents with Mummery, but these were carried out very much as a team, with the clients contributing their own ideas and taking a full part in the climbing.

Mountaineering was not solely a male preserve and women, admittedly in small numbers, were involved from the very beginning. They had a lot to contend with, not least their skirts. It was only in the later 'seventies that women began wearing breeches under these, abandoning the skirt once they were beyond the last house or hut. Another ploy was to use a length of cord to hitch it up between the legs, like a kind of pantaloon.

Two of the earliest, and certainly most successful, women climbers were Lucy Walker and Miss M.C. Brevoort, whose nephew W.A.B. Coolidge, was to become her climbing partner and go on to be an acerbic pundit on all mountaineering topics. Lucy Walker first visited the Alps at the age

Left, the redoubtable Lucy Walker with her father (seated) and A. W. Moore (behind right). Next to Moore is Melchoir Anderegg, her favourite guide. On the day Whymper climbed the Matterhorn, the men in this picture climbed the Brenva Face of Mont Blanc. Right, Miss Brevoort, with her nephew and climbing partner, W. A. B. Coolidge (left), flanked by their guides, Christian Almer and his son, Ulrich, c 1874.

of twenty-eight in 1859 and then regularly for the next twenty-one years, climbing mainly with her father or brother and the guide, Melchior Anderegg. Homely and inclined to be plump, she never wore breeches, and existed on the mountain on a ladylike diet of sponge cake and champagne, but she notched up an impressive array of routes which included several first ascents.

Until 1865 climbing as a sport remained the preserve of the climbers, with the general public having very little awareness and less understanding of what was being done. The Matterhorn was to change all that. Its shapely elegance, its steepness and obvious difficulty made it a focus almost as strong as Mont Blanc had been at the end of the eighteenth century, or as the North Wall of the Eiger was to be in the following century.

The race for the first ascent of the Matterhorn revolves round two names, Jean-Antoine Carrel, a local chamois hunter and occasional guide from Valtournanche who in his heart of hearts wanted to climb the mountain for himself and the glory of Italy, and Edward Whymper, draughtsman and wood engraver, who arrived in the Alps for the first time in 1860 at the age of twenty-one, preparing alpine sketches for Longman's. Whymper finished up at Zermatt where he slipped easily into adventure which led equally naturally to alpinism as he found a new route back to town:

> It seemed that it would be easy enough to cross the glacier if the cliff could be descended though higher up, and lower down, the ice appeared, to my inexperienced eyes, to be impassable for a single person. The general contour of the cliff was nearly perpendicular, but it was a good deal broken up, and there was little difficulty in descending by zig-zagging from one mass to another. At length there was a long slab, nearly smooth, fixed at an angle of about forty degrees. Nothing, except the glacier, could be seen below. It was an awkward place, but being doubtful if return were possible, as I had been dropping from one ledge to another, I passed it at length by lying across the slab, putting the shoulders stiffly against one side, and the feet against the other and gradually wriggling down.

Whymper's courtship of Carrel as the best guide for a first ascent of the Matterhorn began the following year. But Carrel was a hard man to pin down and Whymper, impatient to try the South-West (Italian) Ridge set off with somebody else. All went well until they reached the feature known as the Chimney:

> With some little trouble I got up unassisted, and then my guide tied himself on to the end of our rope, and I endeavoured to pull him up. But he was so awkward that he did little for himself, and so heavy that he proved too much for me, and after several attempts he untied himself and quietly observed that he should go down. I told him he was a coward, and he mentioned his opinion of me. I requested him to go to Breuil, and to say that he had left his monsieur on the mountain, and he turned to go; whereupon I had to eat humble pie and ask him to come back; for, although it was not very difficult to go up, and not at all dangerous with a man standing below, it was quite another thing to come down, as the lower edge overhung in a provoking manner.

It was going to be worth persisting with Carrel. So Whymper wooed 'the cock of the Val Tournanche' from season to season, holding his breath while others made and failed in their bids for the summit, and honing his skills elsewhere in the Alps.

Whymper took a very modern interest in the equipment that was only gradually being devised for climbing. He himself developed what was to be the prototype of the modern mountain tent, used with very few modifications on the 1920s Everest expeditions. I even had a Whymper tent, manufactured by Edgington's, on my first Himalayan expedition in 1960. He also designed some fascinating climbing hardwear: a small grappling hook, very similar to the modern sky hook, for pulling up on or lowering down from rocky projections; and an ingenious ring device to attach to the end of the climbing rope, so that it could be looped over a rocky spike. Attached to the ring was a light string, which could be pulled to open the noose, enabling the climber to flick the rope off the spike, once he had safely

Left, equipment used by Whymper in 1865. This was not too different from that still used in the 'thirties. Then ice axes had got shorter, the boots were better nailed and the crampons a little lighter. Above, Edward Whymper, the draughtsman and wood engraver who made the first ascent of the Matterhorn in July 1865, but at a terrible price. Below, Jean-Antoine Carrel, 'the cock of the Val Tournanche' and Whymper's rival in the race for the Matterhorn.

lowered himself. No doubt both these ideas had been sparked by his first experience on the Matterhorn.

Waiting for Carrel to stop making excuses, Whymper spent a night out alone in his new tent on the lower slopes of the mountain:

> The sun was setting, and its rosy rays, blending with the snowy blue, had thrown a pale, pure violet far as the eye could see; the valleys were drowned in purple gloom, whilst the summits shone with unnatural brightness: and as I sat in the door of the tent, and watched the twilight change to darkness, the earth seemed to become less earthy and almost sublime; the world seemed dead, and judicious repression of detail rendered the view yet more magnificent. Something in the south hung like a great glow-worm in the air; it was too large for a star, and too steady for a meteor; and it was long before I could realize the scarcely credible fact that it was the moonlight glittering on the great snow-slope on the north side of Monte Viso, at a distance, as the crow flies, of 98 miles. Shivering, at last I entered the tent and made my coffee. The night was passed comfortably, and the next morning, tempted by the brilliancy of the weather, I proceeded yet higher in search of another place for a platform.

In search of a platform, or in the back of his mind, hardly admitted, the dream of finding a way to the summit, he scrambled up towards the Great Tower.

> I have a vivid recollection of a gully of more than usual perplexity at the side of the Great Tower, with minute ledges and steep walls; of the ledges dwindling away, and at last ceasing; of finding myself with arms and legs divergent, fixed as if crucified, pressing against the rock, and feeling each rise and fall of my chest as I breathed; of screwing my head round to look for a hold, and not seeing any, and of jumping sideways on to the other side. 'Tis vain to attempt to describe such places. Whether they are sketched with a light hand, or wrought out in laborious detail, one stands an equal chance of being misunderstood. Their enchantment to the climber arises from their calls on his faculties, in their demands on his strength, and on overcoming the impediments which they oppose to his skill.

This could have been written by Bonatti or Messner in the present century.

In 1863 he managed to capture Carrel to make his sixth attempt on the mountain, but they were to be turned back by a violent thunderstorm, not before Whymper made some pertinent notes on rope management:

> We had abundant illustrations during the next two hours of the value of a rope to climbers. We were tied up rather widely apart, and advanced generally in pairs. Carrel, who led, was followed closely by another man, who lent him a shoulder or placed an axe-head under his feet, when there was need; and when this couple were well placed the second pair advanced, in similar fashion, the rope being drawn in by those above, and paid out gradually by those below. The leading men advanced, or the third pair, and so on. This manner of progression was slow but sure.

He left the Matterhorn alone in 1864 but was back on the attack early the next year with three experienced guides, Christian Almer and Franz Biener from the Valais, and Michel-Auguste Croz from Chamonix. Whymper had become convinced that the East Face offered the clue to success. His plan was to start on the Italian side, climb an obvious gully leading up to the crest of the South-East Ridge and then traverse onto the East Face where it became a relatively easy-angled snow slope. A good deal of his knowlege had been provided by Adams-Reilly, a mountain cartographer with whom Whymper had worked and climbed the previous year around Mont Blanc.

On this attempt the two Swiss were half-hearted from the beginning, their fears confirmed when a fusillade of stones ricocheted down the gully. Whymper tried to lead by example, climbing the rocks to the side, followed by Croz and his tent carrier, Meynet, but he was eventually forced to retreat. Beiner and Almer had had enough and stated firmly that they were not prepared to make another attempt. Croz had to meet another client, so Whymper temporarily abandoned the campaign, travelled to Courmayeur and made a further series of impressive first ascents – the lower summit of the Grandes Jorasses, now known as the Pointe Whymper, the Aiguille Verte and the Ruinette, with a couple of bold col crossings thrown in for good measure.

But it all led back to the Matterhorn. Whymper saw Carrel as his sole hope, since he was the only guide who was both committed to the mountain and convinced that it could be climbed. He went to see him in Valtournanche on 7th July, proposing that they attempt the East Face. Carrel temporised, saying that he still thought the South-West Ridge was feasible, but he eventually agreed to join Whymper once the weather had settled.

Whymper spent the following day getting ready for the climb, purchasing food and sorting out all the gear. Then when on his way down to Breuil to bring succour to a sick Englishman he had heard needed help, to his surprise he came across Carrel and his kinsman, Cæsar, escorting a mule and some porters laden with baggage. They assured him they were just helping out a foreigner for the day, but warned him that they would not be available after all for the attempt on the Matterhorn, since they had a prior engagement to accompany some travellers in the valley of Aosta.

Whymper was quite philosophical about it. He even spent the evening drinking and reminiscing with Carrel, but two days later he was horrified to learn that climbers had been sighted on the South-West Ridge. It wasn't long before the truth came out. Carrel had 'bamboozled and humbugged' him from the start. He had never had any intention of climbing with Whymper, but had already been commissioned to mount an attempt on the South-West Ridge by Felice Giordano, a geologist who was planning to climb the Matterhorn with Quintino Sella, the Finance Minister of the Kingdom of Italy. When Carrel had met Whymper two days earlier he had been carrying gear into position for this ascent.

Not unnaturally, Whymper was furious, but he was also impotent to do much about it. He could not even find any porters to carry his baggage over the pass to Zermatt, where he hoped to engage some guides and attempt the East Ridge. Then a series of coincidences occurred that gave him his chance to return to the race, but which were to contribute to the imbalance of the team, and, in turn, change triumph to tragedy. Whymper, partly because of his own background, and partly from temperament, seems to have been outside the close Alpine Club circle. His single-minded competitiveness and drive, whilst being very understandable to later generations, was suspect not only to Victorian mountaineers, but to the majority of the British climbing establishment until very recent times.

The sequence of events began with the arrival in Breuil of another young English climber, Lord Francis Douglas, with the younger Peter Taugwalder as his guide. They had seen each other's names in hotel log books, notching up impressive first ascents in parallel. Whymper's plea for help in getting over the Théodule Pass quickly developed into their deciding to join forces and make an attempt together. Peter Taugwalder encouraged them further by telling them that his father, old Peter, had been a long way up the Hörnli Ridge and was convinced the upper part was climbable.

And so they crossed the Théodule Pass and dropped down into Zermatt, carrying with them altogether 600ft of rope – enough for a small Himalayan expedition! In Zermatt, Whymper was delighted to see Michel Croz, the boldest and best of the guides he had climbed with in the past two seasons. He was employed by the Rev. Charles Hudson, one of the most experienced alpinists of that period and a prodigious walker, who thought nothing of covering fifty miles a day. He also was planning to climb the Matterhorn and so they agreed to combine their parties, though this meant taking with them D.H. Hadow, Hudson's climbing partner. Hudson assured Whymper that Hadow 'had done Mont Blanc in less time than most men', but he was less experienced than the others.

The team was to number six: the four 'tourists', with the two guides, old Peter Taugwalder and Michel Croz, and three porters, one of whom was young Peter who, in the event, went with them all the way. They set out from Zermatt on 13th July, walking up past the chapel at the Schwarzsee, and were pleasantly surprised, as they started up the East Face, at how easy it was. They stopped at noon, erected Whymper's tent and lazed for the rest of the day, enjoying the magnificent situation.

Setting out at dawn, the going became steeper, but it was at an altogether lesser scale than had been the face of the Ecrins, the previous year. Hadow, however, was beginning to experience difficulty, needing a helping hand from old Peter Taugwalder. It was becoming obvious that he had never been on ground this steep before. Nonetheless they breasted the steep section and the angle relented, giving way to an easy snow slope leading to the top. Whymper was on tenterhooks as to whether Carrel had beaten him to the summit, but no footprints were visible and when he looked over the edge on the Italian side, he could see the rival team far below. His delight can be understood.

> Up went my arms and my hat. 'Croz! Croz!! come here!'
> 'Where are they, Monsieur?'
> 'There, don't you see them, down there?'
> 'Ah! the coquins, they are low down.'
> 'Croz, we must make those fellows hear us.' We yelled until we were hoarse. The Italians seemed to regard us – we could not be certain. 'Croz, we must make them hear us; they shall hear us!'
> I seized a block of rock and hurled it down, and called upon my companion, in the name of friendship, to do the same. We drove our sticks in, and prized away the crags, and soon a torrent of stones poured down the cliffs. There was no mistake about it this time. The Italians turned and fled.

Competitive euphoria – something most of us would feel, particularly after the deception that Carrel had practised on Whymper. I can vividly remember reaching the top of the Torre Paine in Patagonia with Don Whillans in 1963, also after a race with some Italians, in circumstances in which we felt every bit as self-righteous as Whymper did on the Matterhorn and every bit as pleased to beat our competitors whom we passed, still on their way up, as we descended the following day. We had become so paranoid on our ascent, we had even pulled up the fixed ropes we had left to safeguard our retreat, so that the Italians would not be able to use them, even though this could have put us at risk on our way down.

Whymper's group reached the top without any further difficulty. It was a perfect, cloudless day. Croz tied his shirt on to the tent pole and used it as a flag to show the world they had reached the summit. It was seen from all sides, the people of Valtournanche and Breuil thinking it was their men who had succeeded, while the people of Zermatt assumed it was Whymper and his party.

It was then time to descend. While Whymper, with the young Taugwalder, remained on the summit to complete his sketches, the others roped up, Michel Croz going first, followed by Hadow, then Hudson, with the older Taugwalder bringing up the rear. Whymper caught them up as they reached a slabby section, moving slowly, one at a time. The elder Taugwalder asked Whymper to tie on to him to act as an extra anchor as they laboriously clambered down the smooth, slabby rocks that form the most awkward part of the Hörnli Ridge. Croz seemed to be helping Hadow find his footholds, when Hadow slipped, knocked Croz over and pulled first Hudson and then Douglas down after him. Taugwalder and Whymper braced themselves to hold the fall, but as the rope came taut, it parted, and the four went hurtling to their deaths.

This was by no means the first fatality in the history of climbing but it was by far the most spectacular and caught the attention of the world in the way that, years later, was to happen with the disasters on the North Wall of the Eiger and the Central Pillar of Frêney and, in more recent times, the sequence of accidents on K2 in 1986.

It is barely relevant whose fault the accident was or who was responsible for checking the rope. They had had three, two of which were strong manila, but the third was a light line, probably ordinary sash line, which would have held little more than the weight of a single person. It was this which failed. There was also the question whether Hadow was too inexperienced, or whether Croz should have brought up the rear, rather than being out in front, finding the way down. The diverse nature of the team and the fact that they had not climbed together before all contributed to the accident but, like so many incidents in the mountains, the divide between glorious success and stark tragedy is a very fine one. In many successful ascents can be discovered the seeds of potential disaster, which because of good fortune, never come to fruition.

Whymper did not make any further first ascents in the Alps. At the age of twenty-five, after a meteoric career, reflected in his book, *Scrambles Amongst the Alps*, he no longer had the heart to play the climbing game. He continued to travel, however, going to Greenland and Ecuador, but with firmly scientific objectives. *Scrambles Amongst the Alps* remains one of the most inspiring of all climbing books, with a sense of fresh adventure and a deep appreciation for the beauty of the mountains that is easily understood by the climber of the 1990s. In its day it was regarded with reservation, not only by many of his peers, but also by the climbing historians and commentators of the period between the wars, when the drive and competitiveness of the new wave of European climbers seemed to attack the values established by the British founders of the sport.

CHAPTER FOUR

A NEW BREED

Alpine climbing up to the First World War

•

O n the same day that Whymper climbed the Matterhorn, another great route was pioneered on Mont Blanc, when G.S. Mathews, F. and H. Walker and A.W. Moore, with Melchior and Jakob Anderegg, climbed the huge Brenva Face, a complex route, picking a way up steep snow slopes and sérac walls to the top of the mountain. Although most of the major mountains above 4000m had been climbed, there was still a wealth of difficult peaks awaiting ascents, as well as countless unclimbed ridges and faces and different challenges on once climbed mountains.

The Matterhorn was to have its second route only a few days after Whymper's triumph. Carrel and the guides had returned to Valtournanche tired and dispirited after having stones rained down on them by the victorious Whymper when they had already abandoned any hope of forcing their route. It was Abbé Gorret, a local lad who had just returned from the seminary in Turin, who rallied the team for another attempt next day for the glory of Italy. They made good progress this time to Pic Tyndall, and onto the unclimbed section, across the upper part of the Zmutt Face, to a gap in the ridge, where Gorret volunteered to stay behind so that he could lower Carrel and Bich who went on to complete the climb of the Italian Ridge safely just three days after the first fateful ascent.

The last 4000m peak to be climbed was the Meije, in the Dauphiné, massive, complex and more formidable than the Matterhorn; its Pic Centrale was climbed in 1870 by Miss Brevoort and W.A.B. Coolidge, but the higher West or Grand Peak held out against many attempts until 1877, when at last it was climbed by the Frenchman, Boileau de Castelnau, with two guides, the Gaspards, father and son. They were caught by a blizzard on the way down and were lucky to survive the bivouac. Coolidge made the second ascent the following year, with his regular guides, Christian Almer and his son, also bivouacking after an eighteen-hour day.

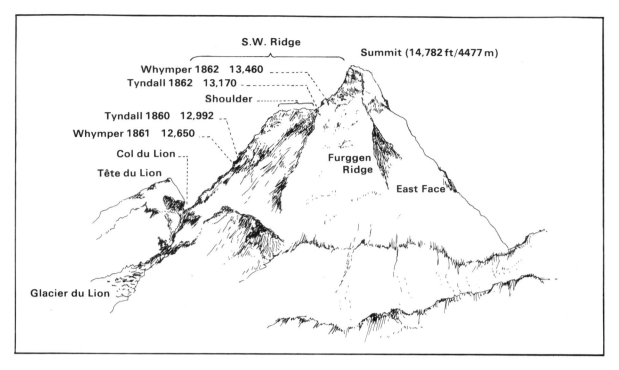

S.W. Ridge

Summit (14,782 ft/4477 m)

Whymper 1862   13,460

Tyndall 1862   13,170

Shoulder

Tyndall 1860   12,992

Whymper 1861   12,650

Col du Lion

Tête du Lion

Furggen Ridge

East Face

Glacier du Lion

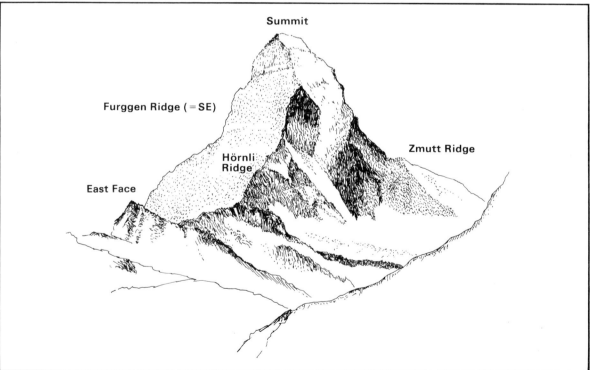

Summit

Furggen Ridge (= SE)

Zmutt Ridge

Hörnli Ridge

East Face

The Matterhorn: top, the Italian (South-West) Ridge by which the mountain was attempted through the early 1860s and, above, the three major ridges. The Matterhorn was eventually climbed by the Hörnli Ridge in 1865.

A new breed of climber was emerging, challenged by technical difficulty as much as by conquest of height. C.T. Dent, a distinguished surgeon, took a leading part in this phase of alpine development. With J.M. Hartley, he laid siege to the Aiguille du Dru, the most dramatically impressive of all the peaks that dominate the Chamonix skyline. It also developed into a great partnership with his guide, Alexander Burgener, who was to go on to do so much with Mummery. In the *Alpine Journal* he records that gradual dawning of possibility which every climber can recognise today:

> Up to that moment I had only felt doubts as to the inaccessibility of the mountain. Now a certain feeling of confident elation began to creep over me . . . Here and there we fancied we could trace short bits of practicable rock. Gradually, uniting and communicating passages developed themselves. At last we turned and looked at each other; the same train of ideas had been coursing through our minds. Burgener's face flushed, and we rose almost together, exclaiming '*Es muss möglich sein.*' (It must be possible).

Sitting out the bad weather is another familiar experience. When I was laying siege to the South-West Pillar of the Dru our accommodation was a leaky tent on the campsite behind the Biollay, our recreation table football in the Bar National. Dent's activities were slightly more patrician: 'Lawn tennis with parti-coloured balls and wooden bats, in front of Couttet's for a while. Then we went a cray fishing, Maund driving us to Chatelard in Couttet's basket carriage.'

Dent's first effort was in 1873 and after eighteen attempts he at last achieved the summit in 1879. It was an exacting climb in which Burgener displayed his determination, outstanding strength and ability. It led Dent to write: 'I knew that any guide was immeasurably superior to an amateur in the knack of finding the way. I was aware that in quickness on rocks the two could hardly be compared. But I had always thought that the amateur excelled in one great requisite – pluck. This record will show that in one instance at least this was an error.'

This ascent represented the height of Dent's climbing career and it was to be Mummery in the next ten years who was to dominate British climbing, initially in partnership with Burgener. His ascent of the Grépon was just one of many impressive innovative ascents. He was not a natural athlete. As a child he had developed a weakness in his spine that meant he could never carry heavy loads. He was tall, gangling, and so short-sighted that without glasses he frequently tripped on mountain paths. But he had the long arms and a huge pair of hands typical of many of today's hard climbers, and puts me in mind of someone like Martin Boysen, one of Britain's most outstanding rock climbers. Mummery's passion for mountains was kindled by his first schoolboy visit to the Alps, when he gazed on the Matterhorn by moonlight 'still shrouded with a halo of but half-banished inaccessibility'. He was only nineteen when he repeated Whymper's route on the Hörnli Ridge. Five years later in 1879 he had completed his apprenticeship and now spied out a line on the superb unclimbed West or Zmutt Ridge of the Matterhorn. He came to Zermatt to find the right guide to go with him.

Very much the outsider, unproven and without any contacts in the Olympian inner circle of the Alpine Club, he was lucky to come across Alois Burgener, with whom he had climbed in the past. Alois told him that his brother Alexander, already reputed to be one of the best guides in the Alps, was free. Mummery went to see him and described his plan for the Matterhorn, but Burgener 'bluntly expressed his opinion that to go on such an expedition with a *Herren* of whom he knew nothing would be a *verfluchte Dummheit'*.

Mummery was not taken aback and respected Burgener's distrust of an untried climber. They agreed to complete some training climbs, in six days crossing four passes and completing two new routes, one of them on an unclimbed peak, the Sonnighorn. Mummery had certainly demonstrated his stamina and they built up the trust and mutual respect needed for a climb as challenging as the Zmutt Ridge. They even allowed themselves a rest day, but that evening they learnt that they had competition. Penhall, another talented young climber, with two experienced guides, Ferdinand Imseng and L. Zurbriggen, were reported to have set out for the ridge.

Mummery was quite relaxed about it, resolving to cross the Col Durand, watch their progress and, should they succeed, go for the East Ridge or North-East Face of the Dent Blanche. In 1879 there was no shortage of worthy unclimbed objectives and so the following morning they set out, even though the weather was unsettled, with clouds scudding across the tops. Mummery commented: 'I was, however, much too young and too eager to dream of returning and, being wholly ignorant of all meteorological lore, I was able to prophesy fair things with such an appearance of well-founded knowledge that Burgener was half convinced.'

Dent's comment about amateur pluck could be unkindly translated as naïve enthusiasm, particularly when the weather is in question. Most climbers have experienced this special brand of wishful thinking. When I completed the Walker Spur on the Grandes Jorrasses with Ian Clough in

Alfred Mummery, left, whose purposefulness and success rate make him a recognisable figure today but ruffled Alpine Club feathers in the 1880s. Right, Alexander Burgener from the Saas valley was the most outstanding guide of the 1870s and 1880s, climbing first with Dent and then with Mummery.

1962, a scum of high threatening cloud drove off all the other teams that were attempting it, while we pressed on. We happened to be right and the weather stayed fine, and I've remembered this incident ever since, conveniently forgetting all the times I have been wrong.

Mummery and Burgener met Penhall retreating to Zermatt in the face of the bad weather as they set out, and the following morning they were rewarded by a perfect dawn. Mummery's stock with Burgener was in the ascendant. The team had now swelled to four with the addition of Gentinetta, acting as porter, and the reinforcement of Petrus, another very experienced guide. They bivouacked on some rocks at the foot of the ridge, demolishing the provisions, mostly alcoholic, a mixture of red wine, marsala, bottled beer and cognac that Gentinetta had been sent down that day to collect, and then shivered under the sparse covering of blankets. In the days before down jackets or sleeping bags climbers had to be hardy.

Setting out in the chill gloom of the pre-dawn, they picked their way up the ridge. It is fairly straightforward at first, a graceful crest of snow leading up to a forbidding rocky buttress that guards the summit. They paused, appalled by just how steep and loose it all seemed. Burgener and Petrus went ahead in an effort to find a way, but came back, discouraged. It was at this point that they noticed figures on the rocks far below them, and deduced this must be Penhall and his team returning to the mountain, but on a different line, taking the West Face itself. They watched until the figures disappeared behind a corner. Maybe it was because of this renewed challenge, combined with the reassurance that they were no longer alone on the mountain, that they returned to the fray.

On this occasion it was Petrus who took the initiative, starting to cross the broken slabby rocks, then Burgener led up a formidable ice slope. Though by no means a big man in the valley, on an ice-glazed slope, he appeared to dilate visibly, looking like a veritable giant when wielding his mighty axe. They picked their way up the upper part of the West Face to reach Carrel's corridor from the first ascent of the South-West Ridge, and then went on to the summit. They traversed the mountain, descending the easier and now chain-clad Hörnli Ridge, pausing on the shoulder to watch Penhall's party reach the crest of the Zmutt Ridge. Two new routes, each of them much harder than anything previously climbed on the Matterhorn, had been completed that day. Mummery's route was to become a classic, while Penhall's route, which was probably technically harder and certainly very much more dangerous, is rarely climbed.

The climb marked Mummery's sudden arrival as one of Britain's most outstanding pioneers and it is not surprising that he was invited to join the Alpine Club. He could not have had a better proposer and seconder than C.T. Dent and D.W. Freshfield, two of the finest and most adventurous climbers of their day. His election should have been a foregone conclusion. It was passed by the committee, but when it came to the club ballot he was black-balled in that discreetly obscure club-land manner where a choice of small black or white balls is dropped into the box. The rules stated that 'one black ball in five' shall exclude, so it only needed a small caucus to oppose Mummery's election.

It is still difficult to conceive how anyone could have objected to Mummery. He was personable and friendly with a good sense of humour. In an age when such things mattered, it was rumoured he was in trade and kept a shoe shop, but in fact he came from a prosperous tannery-owning background, with a father who had been mayor of Dover. It was suggested he had stolen Penhall's route on the Matterhorn, but not by Penhall since he and Mummery joined forces for the first ascent of the Dürrenhorn, immediately after their so-called race. The real cause of his unpopularity seems to have been the very speed of Mummery's rise and the feeling of a significant group that he was a dangerous newcomer, foreign to the tenets held dear by the Alpine Club. To a degree they were right. Mummery had the spirit of a modern climber, so much so that Ronald Clark, in his excellent history, *The Victorian Mountaineers*, left him out altogether. And yet his background and certainly his start were completely traditional, not only in the way he climbed with guides but also in the relationship he formed with them. His approach, and for that matter the style of his writing, was not dissimilar to that of E.S. Kennedy on Disgrazia. The difference was one of degree. Mummery had a greater drive and natural ability.

Although he never wrote or talked about his rejection, he must have been bitterly hurt by it, and this is hinted at in one of his letters to Coolidge, who as editor of the *Alpine Journal* was seeking information about his climbs. Mummery replied: 'I am much too fond of climbing to think it any trouble to write about my scrambles. My only regret is that the peculiar position in which I am placed prevents my fully satisfying your wishes.' Nonetheless he went on to give Coolidge a very full account of his climbs of the summer of 1880 – they made an impressive list, starting with the first traverse of the Col du Lion.

Mummery was climbing with Burgener once again. The way to the col was dark, enclosed, icy and forbidding, comparable in steepness to a modern Scottish gully climb. Because of its length and the need for speed, they were sharing the lead like a pair of modern climbing partners. The angle was getting progressively steeper. Burgener was out in front when the shaft of his axe broke. They now had only one axe between them and Mummery tied his own to the end of their rope so that Burgener could haul it up. But when the guide came to throw the rope back down to his client, it caught on some rocks. Mummery had no choice but to climb the precarious steps cut in the ice without the security of rope or axe.

The difficulties were by no means over and the climbing sounds as hard as the top grades today. 'The ice was too thin to allow steps of such depth to be cut as would enable us to change our feet in them. Burgener therefore adopted the expedient of cutting a continuous ledge along which by the aid of handholds cut in the ice above, one could just manage to shuffle. This involved an extraordinary amount of labour. One hand had always to be clinging to the hold above, whilst the other wielded the axe.'

And it wasn't the modern short axe, but the long and cumbersome alpenstock. It must have been this climb that really moulded the partnership between Mummery and Burgener. There is something especially committing about a deep-cut gully and they were both totally dependent on each other's skill and nerve to come out alive onto the Col du Lion.

The gully on the Italian side was filled with mist but it was also filled with snow, and so, breaking one of the cardinal rules of safe climbing – never glissade down a slope that you can't see the bottom of – they plunged down it in a standing glissade. Mummery, who was out in front, fortunately glimpsed a huge gaping bergschrund at the bottom, yelled to Burgener to stop and they managed to halt themselves on the very brink. Traversing they found a snow bridge over the chasm but, because it was too rotten to crawl over, they shot across in a sitting glissade and then ran and glissaded round crevasses and ice walls to where the glacier flattened out. There is an exuberance in Mummery's description of this descent, the elation of having made a desperately hard, potentially dangerous climb, of shared experience and the joy of being alive.

They reached the little hamlet of Breuil just an hour and three-quarters after leaving the col, and went to the inn to find Venetz, the second guide who had been sent across by the Théodule Pass, carrying all their heavy baggage, with instructions to buy some fowl and wring their necks for supper that night. This is the first time the the name of Venetz appears in Mummery's account. He fills an intriguing role, part fool or court jester, yet it was he who was always thrust out in front, as soon as the going on rock became hard. He drifts into the story with hardly an introduction and vanishes without a trace. There are, as far as I can discover, no photographs of him, no record of his former or later life, and yet he was the most brilliant rock climber of his time.

They found the inn locked and shuttered, but they knew their Venetz, and kept hammering until eventually a sleepy Venetz peered out: 'He excused his failure to wring the necks of the fowls on the ground that he fully expected the mountain would have broken ours. He had also considered it a wise precaution, with the fatigues of a "search party" before his eyes, to put in a good sleep as a preliminary.'

The threesome went on to Courmayeur, made a crossing of the Col du Géant, dropped down to Chamonix and from there made the first ascent of the Grands Charmoz. In doing so they effectively reconnoitred the route from the Col des Charmoz towards the summit of its neighbour, the Grépon. It was a hard and challenging climb up an icy couloir, where Venetz was thrust out in front to surmount a bulge of hard green ice. They climbed the Grands Charmoz, from Chamonix, to the summit and back to Chamonix in a gruelling fourteen-hour day. Most climbers, then or now, would have taken a rest the following day, but Mummery had the unclimbed Furggen Ridge of the Matterhorn next on his itinerary and he and Burgener literally ran part of the way to the railway station to catch the mid-day train, Burgener picking up a great stone jar of beer to refresh them en route. Two days later they nearly climbed the Furggen Ridge, traversing across the East Face to finish by the Hörnli Ridge.

In 1883 Mummery married. His wife, Mary, sometimes joined the rope, writing with evident satisfaction of Burgener that he held 'many strange opinions; he believes in ghosts, he believes also that women can climb.'

In 1888 Mummery looked further afield, setting out for the Caucasus with the Mehringen guide, Heinrich Zurfluh. As early as 1868, Freshfield, Moore and Tucker had climbed the lower east summit of Mount Elbruz, the highest mountain in Europe at 18,480ft/5632m. Then there was a pause during the Russian-Turkish wars, but in the late 'eighties the Caucasus became the principal arena for the adventurous mountaineer; it was wilder and more inaccessible than the Himalaya is today. To get there took an eight-day journey by train across Europe with plenty of bloody-minded customs stops, followed by two and a half days on a Tartar pony to Bezingi, in the heart of the Caucasus, site of a modern climbing camp. Maps were inaccurate, only a few peaks had been climbed and there were practically no roads, even in the main valleys. For Mummery the sense of adventure must have been heightened by the fact there were just the two of them. They had to be completely self-sufficient and even a minor injury on the mountain would have been very serious. Their self-sufficiency was high-lighted by the equipment brought out by Zurfluh, 'a pot of most evil-smelling boot grease – brought all the way from Mehringen – a large hammer, an excellent stock of hobnails and a sort of anvil to assist in their insertion'.

They explored the area, crossed several passes and looked at other mountains, but Mummery's prime objective was the magnificent Dych Tau (17,074ft/5180m), the highest unclimbed peak in the range. It was much steeper and more rugged than Elbruz, whose higher west and east summits were little more than gigantic snow domes. The scale and terrain were almost Himalayan, with an approach up a long valley, guided by a local hunter, getting lost on a glacier in thick mist and having a high camp by the summer grazing of a flock of sheep, which provided them with a staple diet of freshly killed mutton, cooked over a wood fire.

The mountain had been attempted before by Dent and Donkin, but Mummery and Zerfluh quickly passed a cairn of red rocks that marked the previous high point. Dych Tau presented a complex array of crumbling ridges riven by couloirs filled with part-melted snow. Zerfluh dislodged a huge lump that landed on Mummery's head, momentarily stunning him. But they kept going, steadily gaining height, weaving their way from one side of the ridge to the other, until, near the top, at a particularly steep wall which Zerfluh had just climbed, Mummery decided it really was time to put on the rope, commenting with characteristic humour:

> that it was 'born upon me' – as the Plymouth Brethren say – that the second peak in the Caucasus ought not to be climbed by an unroped party. Would it not be contrary to all the canons laid down for the guidance of youth and innocence in the Badminton and All England series ? Might it not even be regarded as savouring of insult to our peak? I mildly suggested these facts to Zurfluh.
>
> He asked me whether I would come up for the rope or whether he should send the rope down to me.

Mummery elected to have the rope sent down, and was much relieved, as I have frequently been, to discover how an angle, that had seemed near vertical before, became a reasonable sixty degrees once he had the rope round his waist. A final wriggle through a hole in the ridge and they were on top with the magnificent vista of unclimbed peaks arrayed beneath them. On getting back to their base, Mummery, ever insatiable, would have liked to tackle some more virgin summits, but Zurfluh had had enough and insisted on returning home.

It had been a good season and one for which Mummery at last received recognition. He was invited to talk to the Royal Geographical Society and was elected to membership of the Alpine Club. This time there were no black balls. It was around this time that Mummery started a fresh phase in his climbing career, for he began questioning the use of guides. He was not the first to do so. The Parker brothers had made their guideless attempts on the Matterhorn in 1860 – and the mountain had its first guideless ascent by Cust, Colgrove and Cawood in 1876. The Pilkington brothers and Gardiner climbed the Meije without guides in 1879.

Mummery captured the reason for climbing without guides, writing of his return to the Charmoz with a group of friends:

> This time we were without guides, for we had learnt the great truth that those who wish to really enjoy the pleasures of mountaineering must roam the upper snows trusting exclusively to their own skill and knowledge. The necessity for this arises from many causes, and is to no small extent due to the marked change that has come over the professional mountaineer. The guide of the *Peaks, Passes and Glaciers* age was a friend and adviser; he led the party and entered fully into all the fun and jollity of

the expedition; on the return to the little mountain inn, he was still, more or less, one of the party, and the evening pipe could only be enjoyed in his company. Happy amongst his own mountains and skilled in ferreting out all the slender resources of the village, he was an invaluable and most pleasant companion.

He went on to regret the way in which increasing pressures of tourism had reduced the relationship of guide and client to a contract for the one to take the other up a specific route which the guide had already climbed on innumerable occasions. He also lamented the crowds:

> I once met a man who told me, at 11 a.m., that he had just been up the Charmoz. He seemed mightily proud of his performance, and undoubtedly had gone with extraordinary speed.
>
> But why, I asked myself, has he done it? Can anyone with eyes in his head, and an immortal soul in his body, care to leave the rugged beauty of the Charmoz Ridge in order to race back to the troops of personally-conducted tourists who pervade and make unendurable the afternoon at the Montenvers?

With a small group of friends Mummery now repeated some of the best routes he had pioneered with guides, traversing both the Charmoz and the Grépon, and climbing the Zmutt Ridge. They also went for new routes, attempting the North Face of the Plan and the Hirondelles Ridge of the Grandes Jorasses, either of which would have been a route well ahead of its time. They were successful on the Dent du Requin, a tough rock route, the big rambling West Face of the Plan, and made the first guideless ascent of the Brenva Face of Mont Blanc, carrying with them a lightweight silk bivouac tent.

He not only introduced his wife to climbing, but also her closest friend, Lily Bristow, whom he took on the Charmoz, Grépon and the Petit Dru. When he led Miss Bristow up the Mummery Crack on the Grépon, it was plastered with snow. It was on this ascent that she took the only surviving photograph of Mummery in action.

His other climbing partners were among the outstanding British mountaineers of the end of the century – Carr, Slingsby, Solly, Collie, Hastings and Conway, men who were to make their mark on British rock, in the Alps, and on mountains further afield. Slingsby was to become known as the father of Norwegian mountaineering as a result of his pioneering work through the length of that ruggedly mountainous country. Martin Conway, later Lord Conway of Allington, completed the first ever climbing guide book, to the Zermatt valley, and was to traverse the Karakoram, up the Hispar Glacier, down the Biafo and then up the Baltoro, opening up some of the greatest mountains in the world. He had intended to take Mummery with him on this expedition, but when they climbed together in the Graian Alps they quickly discovered how different was their approach to the mountains and amicably parted. Mummery was very much the modern climber, eager to seek out technical difficulty and new ways up mountains; Conway was the traveller, meticulous in his planning, more interested in exploration and survey than hard climbing.

Mummery seems to have climbed comparatively little in Britain, perhaps because he lived in the south of England, from where it was almost as easy for him to cross the Channel and catch the train to the Alps as go north, where his only recorded ascent was the second ascent of Great Gully on the Wastwater Screes in the Lake District. At this stage rock climbing in Britain was just developing as a sport in its own right. Climbers had started by exploring the deep-cut, mossy gullies and were beginning to venture onto the open buttresses and faces. Napes Needle, that magnificent pinnacle on Great Gable was first climbed in 1886 by Haskett Smith, one of the first brilliant 'rock gymnasts'.

Mummery completed *My Climbs in the Alps and Caucasus* just before setting out on his expedition to Nanga Parbat in 1895, an objective that he saw as a logical evolution from his adventures in the Caucasus. In the concluding chapter, he registered his awareness and acceptance of the element of risk.

> The memory of two rollicking parties, comprising seven men, passes with ghost-like admonition before my mind and bids me remember that of these seven, Mr Penhall was killed on the Wetterhorn, Ferdinand Imseng on the Macugnaga Monte Rosa, and Johann Petrus on the Fresnay Mont Blanc. To say that any single one of these men was less careful and competent, or had less knowlege of all that pertains to the climber's craft, than we who yet survive, is obviously and patently absurd.

The same proportions would hold good today. Looking at most of my major expeditions, around half of the principal climbers have subsequently died in mountain accidents. And yet there was no death wish in Mummery and his contemporaries, or in mine. There was a desire to pioneer, to push the limits but in a way that was essentially joyous. Once again in Mummery's words:

> The true mountaineer is a wanderer ... a man who loves to be where no human being has been before, who delights in gripping rocks that have previously never felt the touch of human fingers ... Equally, whether he succeeds or fails, he delights in the fun and jollity of the struggle. The gaunt bare slabs, the square precipitous steps and the black bulging ice of the gully, are the very breath of life to his being.

CHAPTER FIVE

FIRST STEPS IN THE HIMALAYA

Himalayan forays up to the First World War

●

Mummery set out for the Himalaya in June 1895 with just two companions, his tried alpine partners, Norman Collie and Geoffrey Hastings. Like any modern mountaineer, he wanted to make a challenging route up a high mountain with a small team. There is a glorious innocence in the simplicity of his objective – no thought of oxygen, teams of Sherpas, fixed rope and camps. It is difficult today to perceive just how far ahead of his time Mummery was. The mountain he chose, Nanga Parbat, had the attraction of great height (8125m/26,660ft), and accessibility, being within striking distance of Rawalpindi, and it looked steep and impressive. With the limited knowlege available at that time of the effects of altitude, it seemed another Dych Tau, but on a grander scale and certainly within their reach. He wrote home, 'There will be no need for anxiety; the expedition is much less formidable than the first Caucasian.' Maybe he wanted to reassure his wife, but I suspect this is what he really believed.

Although Mummery was not the first climber to venture into the Himalaya, he had the clearest and boldest set of objectives. His principal predecessor was W. W. Graham who visited India in 1883 with two Swiss guides and the object of climbing mountains 'more for sport and adventures than for the advancement of scientific knowledge', as he admitted afterwards to the Royal Geographical Society. His party visited the Garhwal, made a determined effort to penetrate the Rishi Gorge to reach Nanda Devi, attempted Dunagiri and claimed to have reached the summit of Changabang, the peak Martin Boysen, Dougal Haston, Balwant Sandhu, Doug Scott, Sherpa Tashi and I finally climbed with some difficulty in 1974. It seems very unlikely Graham's team were on Changabang and it is generally accepted they reached the top of a minor peak near Dunagiri. He went on to claim the first ascent of Kabru (7340m/24,082ft) in Sikkim by its South-East Face, but this claim has also been challenged.

Conway's expedition to the Karakoram in 1892 was very different in concept from Mummery's. Conway primarily wanted to map the great glacier systems. He certainly achieved a great deal, showing himself to be a determined mountaineer and an outstanding mountain explorer, ascending the Hispar Glacier, then going down the Biafo and up the Baltoro, to penetrate the glaciers around K2, making an attempt on Baltoro Kangri and climbing Crystal Peak, (5913m/19,400ft). It was Conway who named the Ogre, the mountain on which I survived my closest brush with disaster. Doug Scott broke his legs and I my ribs on a desperate descent in a storm from the (7285m/23,900ft) summit. The peak on which he originally bestowed the name is, in fact, an outlying peak, which is now known as Conway's Ogre, while its larger and more formidable neighbour lurks in wait behind, at the head of the Baintha Brakk Glacier.

One of Conway's companions in 1892 had been Lt. C.G. Bruce, an enthusiastic climber who three years later helped Mummery complete his local arrangements and joined the Nanga Parbat expedition in India with a couple of Gurkha soldiers. (In 1922 Bruce, by then a Brigadier General, went on to lead the second expedition to Everest.) The shortest approach to the mountain is up the Rupal valley to the South Face and this is the route they chose. On attempting one of the neighbouring peaks to get a good viewpoint, they soon discovered the unpleasant symptoms of altitude sickness and, even at a modest 16,000ft (4877m) they could see the Rupal Face was not for them. In Collie's words, 'Everywhere one precipice rose above another, whilst hanging glaciers were placed in all the most inconvenient places.' This face only succumbed in 1970 to a massively organised eighteen-man Austro-German expedition, climaxing in the desperate summit dash of Reinhold Messner and his brother, Günther.

Discouraged by what they saw, Mummery and his team decided to have a look at the other side, crossing the Mazeno La, a regular route both for traders and marauders. But even this proved a challenge with an endless slope of rocky moraines. Collie was badly affected by the altitude and barely made it to the top of the 18,000ft pass. That night they had an uncomfortable camp at the side of the glacier, before dropping down to its snout, below which they found an encampment of shepherds who sold them dirty goat's milk and a sheep. They continued down to join the Diamir valley and followed this up towards the Diamir Face of Nanga Parbat.

I went there in the summer of 1990 with the veteran American climber, Charles Houston, and the German, Sigi Hupfauer. We were keen to trace

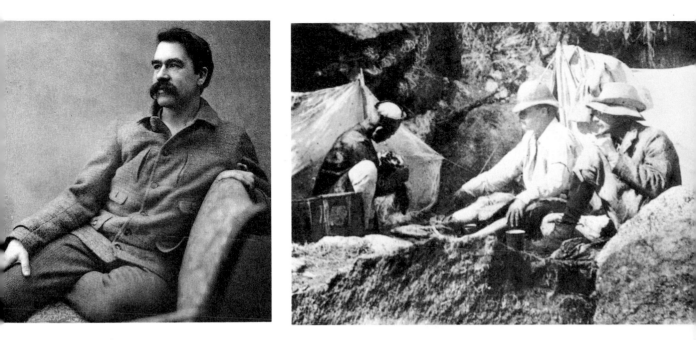

Left, W. M. Conway, explorer, cartographer and climber, who made the first systematic exploration of the Karakoram and went on to climb and explore in both Spitzbergen and the Andes. Right, Collie's photograph of Raghobir Thapa, C. G. Bruce and Mummery (wearing two hats with snow packed between to keep a cool head). Their 1895 pioneering expedition to Nanga Parbat underestimated the scale of the Himalaya and Mummery perished in an avalanche with Raghobir and another Gurkha on the upper Diamir Glacier.

at least part of Mummery's route, and in this magnificent environment reflect on the way Himalayan climbing had developed in the intervening years. At first glance, there did not seem to have been a great change. The Diamir valley is still part-clad in forest with the huge Diamir Face towering at its head. Mummery described it as 'uninhabited, but beautiful in the extreme; glorious trees (mostly birch and pine); thickets of wild roses; heaps of flowers and undergrowth'.

Today villages cling to every shelf which can be watered by irrigation channels carved out of the hillside. Terraced fields carry crops of maize. Mulberry and apricot trees give some shade and the flat-roofed, stone-walled houses nestle unobtrusively in small clusters. They have a beauty of their own, but there is also a price, for the forest is steadily being whittled away to feed cooking fires and build new houses, while ever-increasing herds of goats and sheep are devouring undergrowth, young saplings and the bark of mature trees.

Eleven expeditions had used the meadow at the side of the Diamir Glacier as a base camp that summer of 1990. From a distance, it was just another glacier meadow, with the Diamir Face drawing our eyes, as it had

Mummery's, to its complex structure of rock buttresses and ridges, sérac walls and snowfields. It was the way that the Messner brothers were to find their desperate way down in 1970.

But coming closer to the pasture, the debris of our packaged society became evident. An old base tent, which we learnt had been rented out by the village headman, stood in one corner of the field, filled with shattered glass ampules of coagulated blood, and other detritus of high-altitude research and then, as we ranged the field, we discovered that it was one huge refuse tip of plastic wrappings, containers and empty tins. It was difficult to believe that climbers could show such scant regard for the mountains they purport to love.

Mummery's first foray to this point had been a lightweight push. They were now nearly out of food, so decided to return to the Rupal valley, pick up the rest of their supplies and re-establish themselves below the Diamir Face. It was characteristic of Mummery that he chose to try a different way back and struck up a side valley on the south side of the Diamir Glacier which he hoped would lead over a pass into the Rupal valley.

They set out at midnight, but once again were caught out by the sheer scale of the area, Collie commenting in a paper he delivered to the Alpine Club, 'We did not seem to waste much time, but the Himalayas are constructed on a totally different scale either from the Alps or the Scottish mountains, and although no unnecessary halts were made we only reached the top of our pass at about 2.00 p.m.' They had some good rock climbing on a little ridge on the way up and magnificent views of the Diamir Face. But they found that their pass was not on the main ridge line of the Nanga Parbat range, but on a subsidiary spur leading from it. As a result, they were still on the Diamir side of the Mazeno La, so had to drop down to the glacier and walk through the night over the pass and back to camp on the Rupal Face. They were certainly getting in some good acclimatisation.

A week later they were back below the Diamir Face, this time with ample supplies, fully determined to start climbing. Mummery wrote to his wife: 'There is a nice little ridge of rock (broken) leading up between two glaciers. I think it is easy enough for Chilasi porters. If so I shall fix a camp at the very top, about 18,000 feet. From that point, with the two Gurkhas, one can push a camp to 22,000 feet, at the very foot of the final peak, which on this side is easy rock ... I think we are bound to have the summit, as it is merely a matter of steady training to get our wind in order.'

They slipped naturally into the procedure of any modern lightweight expedition, getting a toe-hold on the lower slopes of the mountain, and ferrying supplies up to a point from where they hoped to make a push for the summit. But for them every step was into the unknown. They knew nothing of the effects of extreme altitude, of the scale and extent of Himalayan avalanches, of the savagery of the jet stream winds. These were things that the climbers of the 'twenties and 'thirties were to discover painfully on Nanga Parbat, Everest, K2 and Kangchenjunga. Everything proved harder than it looked at first glance. In a later letter Mummery wrote:

> We find Nanga a tough nut to crack. The way up is easy enough, but it is very difficult to get our camps fixed and the air certainly does affect one.
>
> Unluckily the weather has gone all to pieces, and we shall have to wait for a week or so till it settles for the autumn ... We have got some of the luggage part of the way up Nanga (to 16,000 feet) but we find it no end of a job to get it higher, as the coolies won't go over 14,500 feet, where the upper glacier begins.

They perservered with Mummery and Collie carrying twelve pounds of chocolate, six tins of Huntley & Palmer's biscuits, Brand's soups and essence, first to 17,000ft and then, in a second push, to 19,000ft of which Collie wrote:

> Both the Chilasi Shikari and I had headaches at the top, but Mummery never felt the least fatigue. He led the whole way – sometimes in deep powder snow; sometimes he had to cut steps for nearly an hour at a time. The pace was quite as fast as he ever went in the Alps and we had climbed nearly 7,000 feet. Certainly that day the rarified air had not the slightest effect on him.

Mummery was obviously a natural performer at altitude. He'd outpaced Hastings and Collie, and moved up over some rock ribs, which now bear his name, to a high camp, with the Gurkha, Raghobir Thapa, as climbing partner. But at the high camp, Raghobir felt ill, presumably from altitude sickness, and Mummery had no choice but to lead him down. Had he been able to press on, in spite of his own fitness and good level of acclimatisation, it is most unlikely that he would have reached the summit of Nanga Parbat. He had a long way to go and the effects of altitude had barely started to bite.

Although repulsed on the Diamir Face, he didn't give up hope and they now resolved to move north to the Rakhiot valley to try to find an easier route. It was from this side Nanga Parbat was first climbed fifty-eight years later. To get there Mummery, with his unquenchable thirst for adventure, determined to ascend the Diamir Glacier and try to cross a high pass immediately below Nanga Parbat, to reach the upper reaches of the

Rakhiot Glacier. He set out with the Gurkhas, Raghobir Thapa and Goman Singh, on 24th August 1895 and they were never seen again.

It was in the dawn of 27th August 1990 that Sigi Hupfauer and I, on our last morning at the Diamir Base Camp, scrambled up the side of the ridge overlooking the glacier to reach a viewpoint on its crest, around 18,500ft (5638m), to gaze across at the face and the glacier up which the three of them had walked. It was a still clear morning. It all looked so innocent; the serried crevasses and blocks of the icefall, where the glacier swept round the buttressed prow of the West Spur of Nanga Parbat. This was the line of the Kinshofer route, which Sigi had climbed two years earlier. I could pick out the Mummery Ribs stretching up into the face and could follow the lines of descent of the Messner brothers. Reinhold had been ahead. Günther, just behind him, had taken a different line on the lower glacier and been engulfed in a huge avalanche. Could Mummery and his two companions have died in much the same place, or had they got further? They would have had to follow the Nanga Parbat side of the glacier, forced into it by the spread of crevasses and towers of the icefall. High to the left of the Kinshofer Spur, there was a huge ice cliff. Could that have spawned an avalanche, perhaps of powder snow or wind slab, that had fractured high above them?

A snow avalanche is such an ephemeral affair. It starts with a crack, an almost imperceptible movement of the slope, and breaks away over the first ice cliff in a great boiling cloud, that gives little hint of the colossal weight of the snow and the power of the vortices in the silent, plunging cloud. It lands on the glacier, the cloud spreads out, billowing like cumulus on a summer afternoon. The distant rumble of sound only reaches the onlooker as the cloud begins to clear. It leaves hardly a trace. The permanent avalanche cone will be a little bigger, but there is no way of measuring those thousands of tons of snow that fell through the still, silent air. Only a few minutes after the avalanche, the scene looks exactly as it did before. And yet someone perhaps is buried under that fresh mantle of snow.

With the death of Mummery and his companions the Himalaya had claimed its first climbing fatalities, among them the man who has more claim than any to be the founder of modern mountaineering. Mummery was very aware of the risks, commenting in the final lines of his book:

> High proficiency in the sport is only attainable when a natural aptitude is combined with long years of practice, and not without some, perhaps much, danger to life and limb. Happily the faithful climber usually acquires this skill at an age when the

1 (previous page): In the race for the Matterhorn through the 1860s, Whymper and Carrel emerged as the main contenders. But, as so often in the mountains, success was to be followed by tragedy.

2 (above): Not 250m lower than Everest, K2, seen here from Concordia, is far more difficult and committing. The first and the majority of later ascents have been by the Abruzzi Spur (South-East Ridge). 3 (left): House's Chimney at 6650m on the Abruzzi Spur was first climbed by House and Bates in 1938. Today its 45m is festooned with ropes and ladders from many expeditions. K2's fierce reputation was underlined in 1986 by a multiple tragedy above 8000m. 4 (facing): The Rakhiot Face of Nanga Parbat. The mountain took a terrible toll of German climbers in the 'thirties. Hermann Buhl made the first ascent by this route in 1953 and German expeditions went on to climb both the Diamir (1962) and Rupal (1970) Faces.

5 (overleaf): A distant prospect of Everest (left) across the Tibetan Plain from Tingri where the 1921 expedition placed its first camp. The local people would not be convinced that Everest was higher than Makalu.

6 (*previous page left*): *The Rishi Gorge affords the only break in the high cirque of the Nanda Devi Sanctuary. Investigated by Longstaff, it was first penetrated by Tilman and Shipton.* 7 (*previous page right*): *The South-West Pillar of the Dru soaring above the end of the Mer de Glace was a much sought prize after the Second World War. Walter Bonatti showed himself in a class of his own when he soloed the first ascent in 1955.*

8 (*above*): *The North Wall of the Grandes Jorasses and the Walker Spur, perhaps the most aesthetically pleasing of all the great north face routes in the Alps.* 9 (*left*): *John Harlin, 'the Blond God', watching for the right weather on the mountain where a broken rope was to plunge him to his death. The new Eiger Direct line was named after him. Had he lived, Harlin would have been in the forefront of the transference to the Himalaya of the American big wall skills introduced to the Alps in the 'sixties.*

responsibilities of life have not yet laid firm hold upon him, and when he may fairly claim some latitude in matters of this sort. On the other hand he gains a knowledge of himself, a love of all that is most beautiful in nature, and an outlet such as no other sport affords for the stirring energies of youth; gains for which no price is, perhaps, too high. It is true the great ridges sometimes demand their sacrifice, but the mountaineer would hardly forego his worship though he knew himself to be the destined victim.

The language is that of the late nineteenth century, but the feelings expressed are timeless; the acceptance of risk as an intrinsic part of the sport, as a price worth paying. There is also the element of self-delusion to which I'm sure most climbers are prone – the belief that the accident will not happen to them, that they're too careful, have survived the dangerous apprenticeship and have that precious sixth sense for danger.

Mummery had an essentially joyous approach to his climbing and to life. It was fun, something to be enjoyed to the full. He also had a real awareness of the beauty of the mountains, but he wasn't an explorer, or even particularly interested in studying the fauna or flora of the mountain ranges through which he passed. Like many modern climbers, he was primarily interested in the route to the top of a mountain, wanted a clear objective and went for it with great persistence.

Whilst Mummery's expedition had been close-knit, the next serious attempt on one of the Himalayan giants was the very opposite. Oscar Eckenstein set out to climb K2, at 8611m (28,253ft) the world's second highest summit, in 1902. He had been with Conway ten years earlier, but had gone home after they had traversed the Hispar and Biafo Glaciers, ostensibly because of a bad stomach, but it seems he had also fallen out with his fellow expedition members. Eckenstein's greatest contribution to mountaineering was the design of a new lightweight crampon and short ice axe, the direct ancestors of our modern ice tools, though they did not meet with approval by the more traditional members of the Alpine Club who regarded the use of crampons as cheating. Radical in his views, Eckenstein was always outside that establishment circle. It is not surprising that he didn't get on with Conway.

His team was compact and international. Aleister Crowley, G. Knowles and Eckenstein himself were from Britain, H. Pfannl and Dr V. Wesseley were reputed to be two of Austria's best climbers, and Dr J. Jacot-Guillarmod was Swiss. Mainly through his own self-publicity Crowley was later to gain an exaggerated notoriety for alleged satanic practices involving drugs and sex. Perhaps he was just ahead of his time and would have

Left, Oscar Eckenstein who designed a new short-handled ice axe and the first modern-style lightweight crampon and led an expedition to K2. Right, Aleister Crowley, self-proclaimed Great Beast 666, was also a capable mountaineer, if not the most sympathetic of expedition leaders. Never lacking in confidence, he attempted the world's second and third highest mountains, K2 and Kangchenjunga.

been very much at home in the British/American climbing scene of the 'seventies, reading Castenada and tripping on magic mushrooms.

As a climber Crowley was competent, if individualistic and, I suspect, totally self-centred. One can see plenty of parallels to him today. He voiced an antipathy for the establishment of the Alpine Club, which I imagine was heartily reciprocated, commenting in his *Confessions*. 'The policy of boycotting Eckenstein and his school, of deliberately ignoring the achievements of Continental climbers, to say nothing of my own expeditions, has preserved the privilege and prestige of the English Alpine Club. Ignorance and incompetence are unassailable. Ridicule does not reach the realms of secure snobbery.'

They established a base camp below the South Ridge of K2, but spent more time arguing than climbing. After taking a look at the South-East Ridge, which was to be the eventual way to the summit, they investigated the North-East Ridge, reaching a height of around 21,400ft (6525m). The weather that year was appalling, the team was riven by dissension and eventually they turned their backs on the mountain in a storm of acrimony, court-martialling Wesseley for helping himself to rations and expelling him from the expedition. Crowley is even reputed to have produced a loaded revolver at the height of one of the many expedition arguments. It is a sign perhaps of mutual antipathy that there is no mention of this expedition in the *Alpine Journal*, even though they did tread new ground and, in fact, achieved as much on K2 as Mummery had on Nanga Parbat. They were not, however, members of the Club, and were certainly not considered to be 'good chaps'.

Three years later, Crowley was off to the Himalaya again, this time to Kangchenjunga (8598m/28,208ft) to make the first attempt to climb the world's third highest mountain. He certainly believed in big challenges, but it was from a naïvety born, I suspect, from a combination of vanity and arrogance. Guillarmod, who had been with him on K2, had the temerity to join him again, with two other Swiss climbers and an Italian. He also has the distinction of composing the first expedition contract, which every member had to sign. It not only specified the financial arrangements but stated that Crowley was to be the 'only and supreme judge on all questions concerning Alpinism and the mountains'. He was to find, as many other leaders have since, that this kind of written authority has little relevance half-way up a Himalayan peak.

They chose the south-west aspect of the mountain, the direction from which the mountain was eventually to be climbed in 1955, followed the Yalung Glacier but got little further than its head. Their top camp was 20,000ft and their high point was around 21,350ft (6507m). The team was in a state of near mutiny and three of them, Guillarmod, Pache and de Righi, insisted on going back down one evening, despite Crowley's warning that the slopes below would be dangerous. He was proved right. One of their porters, who had not even been issued with climbing boots, slipped, pulled the rest off and they fell down the slope starting an avalanche. Pache and all three porters were buried and lost their lives. Crowley described his reaction:

> Less than half an hour later, Reymond and I heard frantic cries. No words could be distinguished, but the voices were those of Tartarin and Righi. Reymond proposed going to the rescue at once, but it was now nearly dark and there was nobody to send, owing to Righi's having stripped us of men. There was, furthermore, no indication as to why they were yelling. They had been yelling all day. Reymond had not yet taken his boots off. He said he would go and see if he could see what the matter was and call me if assistance were required. He went off and did not return or call. So I went to sleep and rose the next morning at earliest dawn and went to investigate.

It's not surprising that this was Crowley's last expedition.

Returning to the mainstream of Himalayan climbing, K2 was visited in 1909 by a large well organised expedition from Italy, led and financed by the Duke of the Abruzzi. On a climbing level they did no better than the previous party, abandoning an attempt on the South-East Ridge at

6250m (20,506ft) on the grounds that it was too steep for the porters to ferry supplies. But they carried out some invaluable topographic and photographic work on the surrounding glaciers, and it was the detailed map by Negrotto and Sella's superb panoramic photographs which clearly showed for future expeditions the way to the top of K2. They also made a serious attempt on Chogolisa but were turned back at around 7498m (24,600ft), which represented a height record that was to stand for thirteen years.

But the most successful of all pre-First World War expeditions were those of Dr Tom Longstaff. He first went to the Nanda Devi region in the Garhwal in 1905 with the guides, Alexis and Henri Brocherel of Courmayeur, exploring the south-eastern approaches to the mountain barriers that guard Nanda Devi (7816m/25,643ft), even reaching a col overlooking the Nanda Devi Sanctuary and making an attempt on the South-East Ridge of the East Peak, only turning back because they had run out of food. Once again this was alpine-style in the modern idiom. He continued his explorations, travelling into Tibet and making a determined attempt on Gurla Mandata (25,355ft/7728m), where they experienced problems. They were caught in an avalanche, described graphically by Longstaff:

> Just as I turned to take in the slack of Henri's rope I heard a sharp hissing sound above me: Henri, lying flat and trying to stop himself, came down on the top of me and swept me from my hold. As I shot past Alexis I felt his hand close on the back of my coat, and we went down together ... I could do nothing but try and keep on the surface of the avalanche. Then somehow I got turned round with my head downwards ... I seemed to rise on a wave of snow and dropped over a low cliff, with Henri mixed up in my part of the rope ... On we went with the rope round my neck this time; but it was easy to untwist it. Then came a longer drop, which I thought must be the last from my point of view. The next thing I remember was that suddenly, to my intense surprise, the rope tightened round my chest, stopping me with a jerk which squeezed all the breath out of my body.

They were lucky where Mummery and his two Gurkha companions had been less fortunate. They certainly didn't lack in determination, but bivouacked where they had stopped at around 23,000ft (7010m), the highest point at which anyone had slept up to that time, and the next day continued up the mountain, until at last exhaustion compelled retreat. They had probably reached a height of around 24,000ft (7315m). But they hadn't finished their explorations and, on returning to the Garhwal, approached the western side of the Nanda Devi Sanctuary, visiting Tapoban and reconnoitring an approach to Trisul (23,360ft/7120m).

Left, the Duke of the Abruzzi who led the Italian assault on K2, model for future siege-style expeditions. Right, Tom Longstaff whose alpine-style exploration round the Nanda Devi Sanctuary and in Tibet gives him a kinship with the late twentieth century.

When I compare this to how we all felt in 1974 after climbing Changabang, it makes me realise what perserverance those early climbers had. We had originally talked of walking out over Longstaff's Col – the spot he had reached that summer of 1905 – but after what we perceived to be the rigours of the climb, we had opted to return by our approach route and had then spent a week lazing by Tapoban, soaking ourselves in a little hot spring, waiting for our transport to arrive. Are we softer today, or is it that the intensity of the push to a summit gets us there, but then leaves us sated, and perhaps with a feeling that we have used up our reservoir of luck for that season?

Longstaff returned in 1907 to attempt Trisul with a larger team which included C.G. Bruce and the Brocherel brothers. Their original objective had been Everest, but they had been refused permission and so consoled themselves with Trisul and made a leisurely exploratory approach. They were stopped by high winds on their first attempt and when they returned to the fray Longstaff, the two Brocherels and the most experienced of Bruce's Gurkhas, Karbir, were the only ones still fit enough to make a push for the summit. They decided to make a quick dash from a low camp at only 17,450ft. This would eliminate having to camp in a position exposed to the high winds and would avoid much of the misery of high-altitude living. In many ways they were pursuing the same technique that Reinhold Messner was to perfect on higher peaks in the 'seventies and 'eighties. They had acclimatised thoroughly with their earlier exploration, were fit without being debilitated by excessive exposure to altitude, and so able to make fast progress on their summit bid entailing 6000ft of ascent in ten hours. The climbing on Trisul is not difficult – it is a straightforward snow peak. Nonetheless their success was a major achievement, not just because of its record height, but also the elegant way with which it was climbed, certainly a forerunner of modern alpine-style climbing.

It was characteristic of Longstaff that he was not content with just the one peak, but immediately set off to try an even higher one – Kamet (25,447ft/7756m) lying to the north near the Tibetan border. But they were running out of time. The monsoon rains engulfed them and they had no choice but to abandon any further climbing, though Longstaff pressed on to visit the valleys to the west of Trisul to complete the map he had been working on in the course of both his expeditions. Unlike Mummery, Longstaff was both an explorer and mountaineer, and indeed the exploratory side of his nature seemed to be gaining in strength, for in 1909 he visited the eastern Karakoram, exploring the Baltoro region without attempting any of the peaks.

No further major peaks were climbed before the start of the First World War, though Kamet became a focus of attention. C.F. Meade, with a guide and two Bhotia porters, established a camp at 23,000ft and A.M. Slingsby, one of the most talented of the young climbers who died in the First World War, reached 23,350ft. Another outstanding mountain explorer was Dr A.M. Kellas who made a series of journeys into Sikkim, most of them with Sherpas as his sole companions. He trained them in mountaineering techniques, teaching them to cut steps and manage the rope. Bearing this in mind, his ascents were particularly impressive, including Pauhunri (23,375ft/7125m), Chomiomo (22,408ft/6829m) and Kangchenjhau (22,605ft/6889m).

The numbers venturing into the Himalaya in this wonderful period of virgin exploration were still a trickle, largely because of the high cost in terms of time and money, particularly when it came to employing guides from the Alps as the backbone of the party. It is tantalising to wonder what Mummery might have done had he survived the Nanga Parbat climb. A superb performer at altitude, he had the single-minded focus of the modern climber which I am sure would have drawn him back to the high peaks with an increasing level of success. The First World War caused a break in all forms of mountaineering but, like the Second World War, it also brought about a climate of social and economic change that marked the next surge forward in climbing development.

CHAPTER SIX

PROFANED WITH SPIKES

Aid climbing and north faces between the wars

•

Even before Mummery vanished on Nanga Parbat, the impetus for new development in mountaineering was already passing to the European alpine clubs, especially those connected with the major universities of Vienna, Zurich, Berne and Munich. The Alpine Club, which had then been in existence for fifty years, was earning a reputation for being stuffy and a club of old men. It frowned particularly on guideless climbing and what it saw as an evolving cult of danger. Strict climbing qualifications and restrictive social attitudes resulted in far more energy being devoted towards keeping people out of the Club than in sowing the seed for future growth. Some individual members, it is true, like Captain Farrar and Geoffrey Winthrop Young, positively encouraged rising stars, but the Club itself held slim attraction for aspiring mountaineers, especially those of modest means.

By contrast, continental clubs required little of their members beyond enthusiasm. They distributed information, built huts, offered instruction and fostered talent. The daring young activists they bred fixed their sights mainly on rock challenges which were previously considered impossible. They were prepared to risk more than their elders, and their level of training and practice on enviably accessible mountains quickly imparted an assurance that guided vacation-climbers could take several seasons to acquire, if indeed they ever did. The best of these new amateurs were easily the equal of many guides.

Most brilliant of all was Paul Preuss. He was born in August 1886, the centenary month of the first ascent of Mont Blanc, just two months before George Leigh Mallory, who was to achieve such tragic fame on Everest. Mummery was at his peak, Zsigmondy had just lost his life on the Meije and Winkler, at the height of his meteoric solo climbing career, was soon to be lost in a lone bid on the Weisshorn. Preuss began climbing at the age

Paul Preuss, the outstanding rock climber of the new school in the Eastern Alps.

of eleven with an ascent of the Grosser Bischofsmütze. By the time he was sixteen he had been to the top of no less than 300 summits and laid down the self-confidence and experience on which he would draw for his later, greater climbs. By 1908, when he was a student at the University of Vienna, he was systematically seeking out increasingly difficult problems. He climbed for the sheer exuberance of it. Mountains were media through which to test and measure himself. He could no sooner stop climbing than breathing. His inspirations were Emil Zsigmondy and Georg Winkler, whose portraits graced his walls.

Preuss was a neat and elegant climber, and no less neat and stylish in his dress. He usually climbed hatless, wearing a silk cravat. The first of his climbs to attract wide attention was a solo ascent of the West Face of the Totenkirchl, made early in the summer of 1911 in less than three hours, and adopting a new route variation in its upper section. By this time Preuss's studies had taken him to Munich where he was working towards a Doctorate in Philosophy. There he took part in student 'night-climbing' and gave the first of his climbing lectures. These soon became very popular for he was a clear thinker and persuasive speaker, humorous and charming, addressing all aspects of alpinism, as well as ski-ing and the effects of tourism.

Preuss also saw the dangers posed to the sporting concept of mountaineering by the adoption of new techniques involving artificial aids. Pitons, he said, should only have emergency use, not form the basis of a system of mountaineering; the rope, though it may legitimately facilitate matters, should never be the direct means for making an expedition possible. Its constant use encouraged sloppy climbing and gave an inflated sense of moral support. The principles of safety were embodied not in the use of ropes and other artificial aids, but in one's own ability and fitness. Thorough reconnaissance, constant vigilance and sound judgement were, he considered, the keynotes to safety. Preuss's demand was for a purity of style. The climber should always limit his ambitions to his capacity.

In a few years Paul Preuss ran up an astonishing list of climbs, including a large number of new ascents in nearly all parts of the Eastern Alps. His boldest was on the Guglia di Brenta – an ascent of the East Summit Face and the first complete traverse of the mountain. 'A masterpiece of a route,' Reinhold Messner has described it, with its vertical rock, logical line and enormous exposure. Preuss climbed it free and without hesitation, stopping briefly only once in the middle of the face to leave a piece of paper with the date and his signature upon it. That was in July 1911. No other route, says Messner, exhibits his ability and dash as this. It was seventeen years before Hans Steger and Ernst Holzner made the first repeat ascent.

Preuss made first ascents of the Kleinste Zinne (Cima Piccolo), again solo, the North-East Face of the Crozzon di Brenta, and the South Wall of the Innerkoflerturm. His solitary traverse of the Langkofel, Fünffingerspitze and Grohmanspitze in a single day was an outstanding example of the sustained nerve and physical endurance by which he is remembered. But Preuss was not merely a rock gymnast. He paid his first visit to the Western Alps in 1908, to Zermatt, where he had undertaken to coach the son of an English baron in German and French. While he was there, he fitted in solo traverses of the Zinal Rothorn and, two days later, the Matterhorn by the Hörnli Ridge and Carrel route, going on to the Théodule Pass and up the Breithorn before returning to Zermatt that same evening.

One September evening in 1913, Preuss was enjoying the autumn sunshine with some friends outside a small gamekeeper's hut in mountains not far from his home when he suddenly exclaimed, 'Just look! That's the finest problem in the Gosaukamm!'

What had seized his attention was the formidably smooth North Face of the Mandlkogel, and with a spyglass he at once became engrossed in the study of its finer features. 'Over the Schrofensockel to the Plattenschuss, traverse up right to the ridge – there, where the North and West Faces join – follow that, I don't know, for about 600 feet, I should think ... Goodness, it's steep, maybe eighty degrees! Then, at the top, traverse left to that short crack which goes up between the two summit teeth. How about it? Shall we try it tomorrow?!'

There were no takers. Besides doubting the possibility of such a route, his companions could see no way of securing effective rope protection on the gaunt, exposed rock. Instead they climbed other routes, but Preuss did not abandon the idea. He returned alone two weeks later.

The last time anyone saw him alive was on 2nd October. Twelve days later his body was found under a foot and a half of new snow vertically below the ridge of his dreams. Friends surmised he had fallen from near the top of the thousand-foot face – 'a victim of his own theories', the Italian climber, Riccardo Cassin, suggested. More generously, Messner commented, 'What energy the man had, what enthusiasm!' Between 17th February and 6th March in 1912, he had climbed no less than sixteen summits in the Grossglockner area.

Legend likes to record that Preuss, with his insistence on clean climbing, was at loggerheads with other leading climbers of his day. This was the time when pitons and karabiners were making possible blank faces that had hitherto seemed destined to remain inviolate. The outstanding Dolomite guide, Angelo Dibona, and the daredevil, Giovanni Battista 'Tita' Piaz, are often portrayed as targets of Preuss's wrath, whereas, in fact, he very much admired both men, and the respect was mutual. Dibona, whose long career included some sixty new ascents, probably only hammered in some fifteen pegs in his whole life. Tita Piaz, too, had a great antipathy for artificial climbing, but he was considered by many British climbers to be something of a stuntman for lassoing an inaccessible pinnacle and traversing airily across to it by rope. Among his best remembered climbs were the first ascent (solo) of Punta Emma in 1900, the West Wall (Piaz route) on the Totenkirchl in 1908; and various lines on the Vajolet Towers, including the South-East Face of Torre Est and the South-West Ridge of the Torre Delago. He died at the age of sixty-nine when he crashed a bicycle with faulty brakes.

Once every summit in the Alps had been reached by the most accessible route, and then by its major ridges, mountaineers turned their attention to the harder unclimbed faces, tracing over them a network of often interconnecting lines. Free climbers, like Preuss, operating predominantly on the rock faces of the Eastern Alps, had raised standards so spectacularly that only a very small élite could hope to perpetuate progress along the same lines. Much the same could be said of the problems left unsolved in the Western Alps. Yet the number of young climbers was increasing all the time and they were not to be denied. They needed new achievable challenges. The last years running up to the First World War saw the appearance of 'artificial' devices and techniques which enabled the field of action to be extended once more. Older alpinists, already alarmed by an increased competitiveness and nationalism among European climbers, viewed the alien gadgetry and the new gymnastic approach it encouraged, with the gravest suspicion. The *Alpine Journal*, under the editorship of Colonel Strutt, found examples of 'steeplejack' antics to fulminate against in almost every issue. 'The construction of a *téléférique*,' Strutt would remark acidly when obliged to record new climbs employing modern methods, 'would provide a more practical solution.' Such routes he dismissed at best as 'foolish variations', more often as 'profanations and degradations'. The spirited sieges of the mid-thirties on the last great alpine North Faces were 'the most revolting and unsportsmanlike travesty of mountaineering yet reported'.

Also writing in the 'thirties, R.L.G. Irving drew attention to the fact that until comparatively recently no implements were used in climbing which could not have been found in similar, if more rudimentary, form hundreds of years ago, long before mountains were thought of in sporting terms at all. The rope, he reminded his readers, was in use in the sixteenth century; snowshoes for deep snow had been known to the Greeks; crampons made of circular pieces of hide and bearing spikes were employed in the Caucasus in the wars of Pompey against Mithridates; the first ice axes were a handy combination of alpenstock and the peasants' chopping axe. All were legitimate aids and did not affect the integrity of the sport. But pitons and karabiners – that was a different matter entirely! They were mechanical devices destined to alter the very essence of climbing. To Irving it was even significant that no word existed in English with which to describe a karabiner, and this he claimed was because of its decidedly un-English nature. It offended against all notions of fair play.

In the growing mistrust of the inter-war years it was a short step to lump hated climbing methods with ascendant political forces. Geography even lent itself to the theory, for Munich in the Bavarian Alps, was not only the cradle of National Socialism, but also the centre of this new mechanisation or, as Irving liked to describe it, 'the gospel of force', or even 'sporting-heroic-arithmetic' climbing. That was his dig at the new six-tier grading scale evolved by Dr Willo Welzenbach to measure more accurately the technical difficulty of a climb and, by the same token, of course, a climber's prowess. To conservatives this smacked of records, record-breaking, and personal vanity but it was employed throughout Europe for over twenty years until revised by international consent in 1947.

Welzenbach was perhaps the greatest climber of the inter-war period and the father of modern ice climbing. He was a Bavarian, born in Munich in 1900 and he died on Nanga Parbat before reaching his thirty-fourth birthday, yet in an all too short career he accomplished almost a thousand alpine expeditions, among which were forty-three formidable first ascents.

Like Preuss, Welzenbach had no aversion to pitons and rope manœuvres if they were employed sparingly and to extend range, not merely as a cover-up for inept technique, and he saw no reason why similar modern methods should not be applied to the more complex problems of mixed routes and ice climbs. In this, he found his thoughts concurred with those of the veteran mountaineer, Fritz Rigele. Their climb of the North-West Face of the Grosses Wiesbachhorn in 1924 was the first on which ice pitons were used, and the following year Welzenbach crowned a full season in the Western Alps with a magnificent direct ascent, with Eugen Allwein, of the Dent d'Herens North Face, which included a tensioned rope traverse.

Welzenbach always maintained that it was better to climb without elaborate bivouac equipment. To have it was to use it, he said, when the real principle of survival lay in expeditious movement, especially in winter climbing. However, in 1931 he demonstrated phenomenal powers of endurance when, with Willy Merkl, he was forced to sit out four days of continuous storm on the North Face of the Grands Charmoz, sixty hours of which were spent trapped on a tiny ledge.

The face had attracted Welzenbach for several years. He and Merkl set out early on 30th June and from the Thendia Glacier climbed the difficult lower rock ramparts to establish a bivouac at mid-height on the face. Next day they attacked the icefield directly below the steep and slabby summit rocks, but found themselves forced to deviate to the left, so that they gained the North-West Ridge some 120m below the summit. Bad weather prevented them going higher. With a further bivouac on the descent, they returned to Montenvers, disappointed not to have completed the climb as they envisaged it. A couple of days later, with the weather still bad, they came across Anderl Heckmair and Gustl Kroner in the Leschaux Hut. This pair had plans of their own for the Grands Charmoz. It was enough to send Welzenbach and Merkl scurrying back up the mountain. On 5th July they climbed the North-West Ridge once more and next day traversed out onto the face to regain their high point at the top of the central ice slope. Avoiding the dangerous ice gully that led straight to the summit notch, they clambered up steep rocks to the left-hand side where, in the middle of the afternoon, they were forced to take shelter in a minute recess when a sudden storm swept in. They were 92m short of the summit and the storm kept up all night and throughout the next day, the 7th, and the day after that, the 8th. Continuous snowfall forbade any movement up or down. Welzenbach wrote of the experience:

> An interminable fourth night began. Sitting it out on such a constricted spot had become almost unbearable torture. For days we had been unable to move our limbs at all and every muscle ached from being cramped so long on this tiny spot. Towards midnight the snowfall eased, the wind died down and it grew considerably colder. We froze terribly, but treated the sudden drop in temperature as a portent of better weather and awaited daybreak with renewed optimism.

Once it was light, it became clear this would be only a temporary reprieve. Another storm could be expected in a few hours, yet there was no option but to move while they still could, and no question of going down the snow-heavy, avalanching face. They must continue upwards. The final rocks, on which all holds had to be excavated from under fresh snow, were the hardest work of the whole climb, but the pair were spurred on by the knowledge that their lives depended on the effort they made now. They breasted the summit ridge as the storm hit them, but there was still a final wall to the highest point of the mountain. From somewhere they summoned the willpower to surmount this and they reached the top at three o'clock that afternoon. It was then essential for them to descend as fast as possible. This time they used the Charmoz-Grépon couloir which was in an extremely dangerous condition. At 10.30 p.m. they staggered back into Montenvers.

Welzenbach's celebrated north wall climbs, which include also the Nesthorn, the Grosshorn, the Lauterbrunnen Breithorn, the Gletscherhorn and the Gspaltenhorn, have lost none of their reputation. They are still

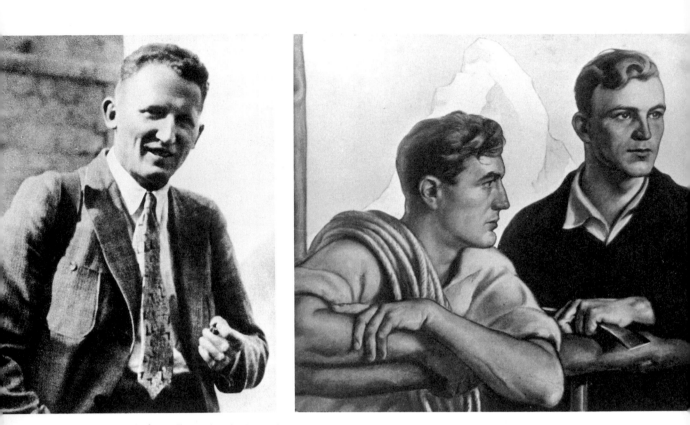

Left, Willo Welzenbach, the father of modern ice climbing, based in Munich, cradle too of National Socialism. Right, Toni and Franz Schmid who made the first north face ascent, climbing the Matterhorn in 1931 and receiving Olympic Gold Medals from Hitler.

regarded as among the most testing and worthwhile in the Alps. Little escaped him. It was his habit to concentrate on one area at a time and work methodically through its many possibilities. He brought every sense to bear on the problems, designing new equipment where necessary and having this manufactured under his name. Welzenbach was encouraging to others, loyal to his friends and, as was to be demonstrated in his last trip to Nanga Parbat as a member of Willy Merkl's 1934 expedition, selfless unto death.

The Matterhorn had been the first north face to fall, in 1931, to the student brothers, Toni and Franz Schmid. Strutt reported the climb with uncharacteristic reticence in the *Alpine Journal*, but elsewhere in the same issue he deplored the wave of recklessness and folly he fancied spreading throughout the Alps. 'With the forcing of the N. face of the Matterhorn, with the Mont Mallet Glacier face of the Grandes Jorasses profaned with spikes but still unconquered, infinite possibilities of notoriety or disaster lie open.'

These were years of depression and mass unemployment, but for two young men from Munich with the will and a bicycle apiece, the Alps were

When picked out again on the Monday, they were at the upper edge of the Second Icefield, disappointingly lower than expected and moving extremely slowly. They had not yet reached Death Bivouac, the previous year's high point. Soon the figures were seen to be retreating. This time there was no mistaking that one of the party was being assisted by the others. Painstakingly the four inched down the great Second Icefield and abseiled over the rocks separating it from the First. Their third night out was spent at, or near, what is now known as the Swallow's Nest. The weather was grim and worsening.

Coming at length to the bleak slabs of his traverse, Hinterstoisser tried in vain to recross them. Exhausted and without a rope in place, it was impossible to make any progress across the smooth glazed rock. There was no alternative but to rope straight down the overhanging cliffs below them. Don Whillans and I were in a similar position twenty-six years later, when we helped a British climber, Brian Nally, back across the Second Icefield, after his partner had been killed by stonefall. Don demonstrated his uncanny route-finding ability when he traversed above the line of the Hinterstoisser Traverse so that we could make a diagonal abseil to the top of the Difficult Crack. If only Hinterstoisser had found the same spot, the outcome would have been different. For when they started abseiling straight down the overhanging wall of the First Band, things quickly began to go very badly wrong.

Around mid-day a railway worker had made shouted contact with the party through the gallery window that gives onto that section of the face below the Rote Fluh. The climbers were then only a few rope-lengths above him, and seemed in good spirits. It surely couldn't be long before they made it down to his level and, to help them identify the spot, he shovelled out a platform and left the spade sticking in the snow as a marker. Then he disappeared inside to get a brew going.

When they failed to arrive, he went to take another look. This time desperate cries were coming from above and immediately he ran inside to raise the alarm over the railway telephone. Officially at this time there was a state ban on climbing the North Face of the Eiger, and Swiss guides were not obliged to go to the aid of anyone in difficulty. Nonetheless, three guides sitting out the storm at the nearby Eigergletscher station immediately came up by special train and traversed out onto the face from the gallery window to a position some 90m below where Toni Kurz could be seen hanging in a rope sling. He begged piteously for help. His companions were all dead. Hinterstoisser had plunged to the foot of the face that afternoon; Angerer had been strangled in the rope, probably as Hinterstoisser fell, and Rainer had frozen to death. The two Austrians were still tied in to the rope with Kurz. Stones and sluicing water poured over him but there was nothing that could be done that evening as it was already getting dark. The guides stayed in the railway tunnel all night and first thing next morning walked out onto the face once more. Remarkably, Toni Kurz was still alive, still shouting for help. The nearest they could get to him was a band of snow beneath the overhang from which he hung suspended, 37m above their heads, hidden from view by the curve of the rock.

'We'll help you, don't worry,' they shouted up to him. 'First, can you lower a line so that we can send up a rope and pegs for you to set up an abseil?'

Poor Kurz clambered between the two corpses cutting free what rope he could. It was nowhere near enough. The only way to get a longer length was to unravel the threads. By this time his left arm was completely useless from frostbite, but between his good hand and his teeth he somehow managed to cobble together a 45m length which he lowered to the waiting guides. They did not realise until too late that the rope they sent up to him was not sufficiently long to bring Kurz all the way down to where they stood. Quickly another length was knotted to it. The guides were careful to keep hold of their end so as to be able to guide him to the ledge.

At last the abseil was set up and Kurz began his interminable descent. He crooked his useless arm around the rope for balance, using the other to guide and steady his progress. When finally he appeared over the lip of the overhang, the guides could see he was in very poor shape indeed. When he came to the knot in the rope, it would not pass through the karabiner. Kurz no longer had the strength to free the jam, and the guides were powerless to help him as he was still beyond their reach. Hoping to take advantage of any elasticity in the rope, Arnold Glatthard, who was holding the end, tried desperately to pull Kurz towards them. It almost worked: they could just touch the tip of his boots, but could gain no grip. In the end Glatthard was forced to let him go and Kurz bounced wildly back and forth, as if on a rubber band.

The guides tried encouragement. 'Come on,' they urged. 'You're nearly here, we've got you safe. Try one more time!'

Again, Kurz struggled to force the knot through his snap link. His face was red and swollen, his expression blank. They knew they were losing him. Glatthard tried to persuade him to cut the rope; he would not fall far. But it was all too much.

'No more, no more . . .' Kurz moaned and tipped over. Within minutes he was dead, swinging on the line like a useless bundle of rags.

Agonisingly near helping hands, Toni Kurz (and inset) died on a rope which was just not long enough for him to abseil to safety.

The following year brought more attempts – and another death.

In 1938 Ludwig Vörg, who the year before had got just above Death Bivouac, was back, this time with Anderl Heckmair. They had come as well prepared for ice climbing as for rock. They had twenty ice pegs in assorted strengths and sizes, also the new twelve-point crampons.

In the Flat Iron section above the Second Icefield they caught up with Austrians Heinrich Harrer and Fritz Kasparek who had set off a day ahead of them. Both pairs agreed to continue as a single team. Heckmair took the lead, as he would throughout the climb. Entering the Ramp they were on unknown ground. They squatted out their first night together towards its top, Heckmair suffering an upset stomach from gobbling down a whole tin of sardines by way of an evening meal, and Harrer being startled awake to find he had slipped off his perch and was dangling from one thin piton over the void. The next day was one of difficult climbing in deteriorating weather as they surmounted ice-choked chimneys and bulging overhangs, striving to gain the rocky band, named the Traverse of the Gods, that would lead them into the White Spider. This is the conspicuous steep funnel-shaped snowfield in the upper heart of the face that acts as a crucible for storms and a natural chute for all avalanches and stonefall.

Harrer, as last man, had the job of removing all the pitons and ice pegs as he passed. In the middle of the afternoon on the last patch of bare ice leading to the Spider, Heckmair found he was out of ice pegs; poor Harrer was struggling up behind under the weight of them all. A thunderstorm was brewing and several stones went whistling past. Suddenly it did not seem worth waiting for Harrer and Kasparek, who were climbing separately, to reach them. Heckmair and Vörg headed out onto the Spider belaying each other with their ice axes. Near the top they settled themselves onto a rocky pulpit to await their friends. By this time, it had gone very dim and lightning and thunder heralded great squalls of sleet and hail. The two Austrians were caught mid-Spider, bombarded with granular ice and a steady stream of small avalanches. When things eased Heckmair and Vörg were both surprised and delighted to see their companions were still there. They clipped in to a belay on the rock wall above and sent a rope down to them. After that, all four stayed on a single rope for the rest of the climb.

Late that evening they were obliged to settle for two exposed outward-sloping ledges as bivouac sites. A line was fixed between them, along which could be passed a billycan on a string. The two Austrians could not even sit down. Next morning they jettisoned all their spare rope and gear in order to be able to move quickly up the final pitches. There was one very tricky moment when Heckmair fell in the Exit Cracks, his crampons penetrating right through Vörg's hand, but by a nimble somersault he regained his footing and caught hold of Vörg, who had been knocked off his stance. The offending passage yielded at the second attempt, and after that, although the weather worsened, the climbing was easier.

They mounted the final metres to the summit in a full-blown blizzard. The visibility was so bad that when Heckmair reached the summit cornice, he put his foot clean through it, commenting afterwards, 'What a terrible thing to have climbed all the way up the North Face only to shoot straight down the other side!'

Then the race was on to get off the mountain by dark. They were tiring fast, Heckmair, now his mammoth task of route-finding was over, frequently flopping in the snow and letting the others haul him down the West Flank. Once they could make out the buildings of Kleine Scheidegg, they were amazed at the seething mass of people awaiting them. They had no idea their climb had been the focus of so much attention, and could never have foreseen how they would be immediately swept up as heroes of the Third Reich and paraded as fine examples of Austro-German co-operation and triumphing will.

The *Alpine Journal* saw no reason to amend its earlier held view that desire to scale the Eigerwand was 'an obsession for the mentally deranged'.

'An obsession for the mentally deranged' according to the 'Alpine Journal'. The successful 1938 Eiger Nordwand team, l to r: Harrer, Kasparek, Heckmair, Vörg.

The Eigerwand showing the routes of the 'thirties:
– – – – Sedlmayer and Mehringer, 1935
——— Austro-German first ascent, 1939

You certainly gain the impression that in those inter-war years all the alpine countries' most thrusting new extreme climbers were dashing about, one behind the other, from one 'last great problem' to another. The Italian star, Riccardo Cassin, had arrived at the foot of the Eiger with two companions to find the Heckmair party already well up the face. When they succeeded, Cassin wasted little time in redirecting his attention to the Walker Spur on the Grandes Jorasses, which had thus been elevated into the latest 'last great problem'. The Italian party successfully made its first ascent over eighty-two hours in the first week of August, a superb climb on sound, but difficult rock, which required fifty pitons, half of which were left in the face. It seems a lot of hardware and received the predictable lambasts from the traditionalists, but fifty pitons in a thousand metres is not that many, and the route itself has stood the test of time. It is the most popular, and certainly the most aesthetically pleasing way up, not only the North Face of the Grandes Jorasses, but of all the great north faces of the Alps.

Riccardo Cassin (left), with his companions, Esposito and Tizzoni, after the first ascent of the Walker Spur of the Grandes Jorasses, perhaps the most aesthetically satisfying of all the great alpine north faces.

But what of the British? They took no part in the onslaught on the big walls of the Western Alps or the high standard technical climbs being developed in the Dolomites and Austria. Although they were not completely inactive, they tended to maintain the guided tradition of the Golden Age. Geoffrey Winthrop Young completed a series of great climbs, climaxing with the Mer de Glace Face of the Grépon in 1911, but it was his guide Knubel who did most of the leading. Ryan produced a similarly rich crop of routes with Lochmatter as his guide. Immediately after the First World War Courtauld and Oliver made the first ascent of the Innominata Ridge, but once again with guides. The most outstanding British route, between the wars, was the first ascent of the Route Major on the Brenva Face of Mont Blanc by Graham Brown and the young Frank Smythe. Graham Brown, usually guided, went on to explore this huge and complex snow face in detail. But to venture on the big rock walls, steep ice faces or difficult mixed ground, not only were pitons needed but also a different concept from that held dear by the majority of British climbers.

The development of British rock climbing contributed to this attitude. It had evolved as an activity in its own right rather than being regarded as training for the bigger mountains. Renouncing the use of pitons or other artificial aids was appropriate to our small crags, since their indiscriminate use would have diminished the scale of adventure to be discovered on them. Techniques did not advance much at all in the first half of the twentieth century. The climber had his hemp rope, a pair of nailed boots for most climbs and tennis shoes, which Mummery had used on the Grépon in 1881, for steeper rock. The steepness and difficulty of climbs tackled were inevitably affected by the equipment and techniques available, but some of the routes achieved were remarkable. Siegfried Herford's ascent in 1914 of the Central Buttress on Scafell in the Lake District, up an alarming impending flake, using what must have been frighteningly precarious combined tactics, gave access to an upper rock wall. It was a climb years ahead of its time. Herford was to be one of many who lost their lives in the First World War, thus leaving something of a vacuum in its immediate aftermath.

Rock climbing, especially in the north country, was beginning to spread to a wider social class than before, with young working-class lads getting out onto the gritstone crags of the Peak. Two distinct schools emerged; the northern-based climbers, few of whom could afford the time or money to reach the Alps, and the Oxbridge set, who had traditionally supplied the Alpine Club with recruits. The latter were particularly inspired by Geoffrey Winthrop Young, who, although he had lost a leg during the war, had maintained the tradition of weekend climbing meets, rather like the country house party, at Pen y Pass below Snowdon in North Wales.

The development of Clogwyn Du'r Arddu, arguably the finest crag in Britain south of the Scottish border, saw hot competition that merged into co-operation between these two groups. First blood went to the northerners, Fred Piggott, Morley Wood, L. Henshawe and J.F. Burton, a Leeds-based team and members of the Rucksack Club, one of the locally based clubs that proliferated in this period. They tackled the steep angular East Buttress in 1926 and achieved success the following year, showing considerable ingenuity within the acceptable ethics of the time, jamming chockstones into the crack and then heaving up on them.

The following year, two of Winthrop Young's most talented protégés, Jack Longland and Frank Smythe, both destined for bigger mountains, attempted the first ascent of the huge slabby West Buttress. Both they and the Leeds team made attempts in 1927 and finally joined forces for an onslaught at Whitsun 1928. Once again inserted chockstones were used and it was Jack Longland who led the crux pitch up an overhanging wall near

At the foot of the West Buttress of Clogwyn Du'r Arddu, l to r, T. Graham Brown, Ivan Waller, Frank Smythe and Jack Longland.

the top on the route that was to bear his name. It is an impressive piece of rock, and for the time, was a remarkable feat of climbing. Longland went on to lead a pitch, the Javelin Blade, on Holly Tree Wall above the Idwal Slabs in Cwm Idwal, which was perhaps the hardest to be completed before the Second World War. Of the ascent he commented: 'Quite frankly, I'd lost the way. I'd come to the famous thread belay at the end of the first pitch of the normal route, and I didn't know that the route ought to go to the right. I was, at that time, a pole vaulter, which I think gives you pretty strong fingers, and I remember that the pull-out on to the actual blade of the Javelin was very strenuous, though not dangerous – I had a belay about forty feet below me.' A masterpiece of understatement!

Another important name in the development of British climbing in the 'thirties was Colin Kirkus. A brilliant rock climber with a superb eye for a good line up a crag, he cleaned up some of the best of the remaining obvious lines on Cloggy, explored further afield and even visited the Gangotri, in the Garhwal Himalaya in 1933. Had he survived the war, he would have been a strong contender for the post-war Everest expeditions. Very different to Kirkus was Menlove Edwards. Squat and immensely strong, he had a tortured genius in which testing himself to the limit, rather than the fun of climbing, was the dominant motive. A conscientious objector during the war, he bridged the pre-war and immediate post-war period, pioneering a series of routes on the steep crags of the Llanberis Pass and around the Ogwen valley, specialising in fierce, if short, problems that were an indication of future trends.

The British were not the only climbers with a strongly held rock ethic. Some thousand miles to the east, in Saxony, above the banks of the Danube, is an array of sandstone towers where climbing ethics were as strict and standards perhaps even higher than those being practised in Britain. Pitons were forbidden and the only protection allowed was from knotted ropes jammed in the soft sandstone cracks. A young German climber called Fritz Wiessner was one of the climbing stars in the 1920s, cutting his teeth on Saxon sandstone and then going on to the bigger limestone walls of the Kaisergebirge to make a series of bold new routes. Like Smythe and Longland, he was to progress to the greater ranges.

The approach climbers from Europe and America used in the Himalaya, the ways their expeditions were structured and how they related to each other, were all deeply affected by these foundations on their local crags and the bigger peaks of the Alps.

CHAPTER SEVEN

EVEREST, A BRITISH PRESERVE

The earliest expeditions of the 1920s

•

With darkest Africa explored and the Poles reached, Everest, the 'Third Pole', had a very special allure and it was soon after the end of the First World War that British climbers began looking to the Himalaya once again in what became the start of a series of expeditions with national overtones. The British post-war efforts were triggered at a meeting of the Royal Geographical Society in 1919, when Captain John Noel read a paper on a journey he had made into Tibet in 1913 to reconnoitre the approaches to Everest. He had disguised himself as 'a Mohammedan from India', darkening his skin and hair and, travelling by pony with a Garhwali, a Nepalese Sherpa and a Bhotia, had slipped into Tibet without permission, avoided villages, and got within forty miles of the mountain before being turned back by Tibetan troops. He had succeeded where Freshfield, Bruce, Mumm and Longstaff had failed when they attempted to go via official channels.

Noel was a good photographer and a brilliant lecturer and after he had delivered his paper Kellas and Freshfield spoke enthusiastically of exploring and mapping the region, while Captain J.P. Farrar, President of the Alpine Club, enthused about sending two or three of the talented younger members to ensure that the mountain was climbed. The President of the RGS, Sir Francis Younghusband, who had done so much to start the exploration of the Himalaya and who had led the British army to Lhasa in their punitive expedition of 1903, sounded a jingoistic note, expressing the ambition that it should be an Englishman who first stood on the summit of Mount Everest.

A few days after this momentous meeting, Younghusband happened to have lunch with Colonel Charles Howard-Bury, a wealthy Anglo-Irish landowner who, though he had no mountaineering experience, had hunted game in the Alps and Himalaya and was happy to pay his own fare out to India, where with the backing of the RGS and the Alpine Club, he won

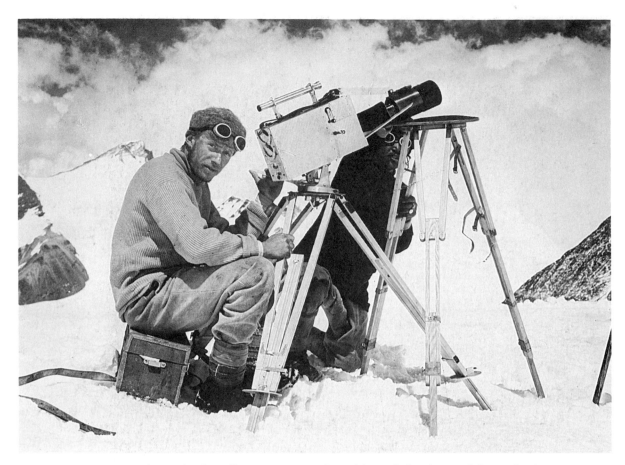

Captain John Noel, whose illicit journey into Tibet and lecture before the Royal Geographical Society inspired the quest for Everest. He accompanied both the 1922 and 1924 expeditions.

the approval of the government in India who, in turn, gained permission from the Dalai Lama for an expedition to go through Tibet to reach Everest. An approach through Nepal had been considered but the Nepalese had a firm policy against allowing foreigners into their country and it seemed a waste of time even to apply.

An Everest Committee comprising members of the RGS and the Alpine Club was immediately formed and was to control all Everest expeditions until the mountain was eventually climbed. Its most influential member was to be its Secretary, A.R. Hinks, who was also the Secretary of the RGS. He was to remain in this position for all the inter-war expeditions. This level of continuity, and the fact that he was the only 'professional' on the Committee, gave him all the power of the manipulative civil servant, a power which he used to the full.

With the gap created by the war and the loss of so many of the younger generation, there was a shortage of climbers to choose from. The number

A. R. Hinks, Everest Committee eminence grise through the 'twenties and 'thirties.

of dedicated climbers was small anyway, coming from the fairly narrow social base of those who could afford the time and expense of going to the mountains. In addition, the establishment, represented by the upper echelons of the RGS and Alpine Club, was still attached to the perceived amateur virtues of the Golden Age of alpinism that were to limit what British climbers were able to achieve in the Alps between the wars and were also to affect their approach to the Himalaya.

C.G. Bruce, the obvious choice for leader, was unavailable so the post went to Howard-Bury. This was, after all, a reconnaissance, though, as Younghusband made clear in his introduction to the official account: 'From the very first we decided that the main object of the expedition was to be the ascent of the mountain and that all other activities were to be made subordinate to the supreme object of reaching the summit.' But the climbers knew all too little of the problems and it was Longstaff who sounded a cautionary note about their chances of climbing the mountain first time.

Two of the good young climbers Farrar had in mind were Mallory and Finch. They couldn't have been more different. Mallory was accepted from the beginning by the climbing establishment, and very quickly by the general public, as the star of any attempt on Everest. Finch, on the other hand, was always an outsider. Mallory, the son of a parson, educated at Winchester and Cambridge, had become a teacher. He fitted very easily into the stereotype of the typical Alpine Club member. Good looking, athletic and personable, with a literary bent and an ambition to write, he had been taken to the Alps in his last year at school by one of his teachers, R.L.G. Irving, author of *The Romance of Mountaineering*. He continued climbing at university and as a schoolmaster at Charterhouse became a close friend of Geoffrey Winthrop Young.

Mallory had the ability but, unlike Whymper or Mummery, he had never translated this into major innovative climbing. In 1921 he was at a crossroads, thirty-five years old, discontented with teaching, and considering attempting to make a living as a writer. But with a wife and three children to support, this must have been a daunting prospect. He even agonised over whether or not he should accept the invitation to Everest and it was Winthrop Young who urged him to go.

George Finch's background was much more Bohemian. His father was Chairman of the Land Court of New South Wales, but when the family visited Europe in 1902, when George was fourteen, his parents decided the children should be educated there and that their mother should stay with them. This, in effect, was the end of the marriage. Charles Finch returned home and Laura settled in Paris, where the children were educated by tutors. George was very bright, initially studying medicine, then opting for physical chemistry which he studied in Zurich and Geneva. It was at this stage that he started climbing, showing considerable talent and becoming President of the Zurich Academic Alpine Club. Whilst Mallory was not practical, with a reputation, indeed, for being clumsy, Finch was full of original ideas for oxygen equipment and clothing, designing the first ever down suit and lightweight down sleeping bag, using the newly developed balloon fabric.

Although referred to as the young climbers, they were both in their mid-thirties, arguably the prime age for the Himalaya. If so, the other two members of the climbing team were on the old side. Raeburn, the climbing leader, was fifty-six, and beginning to show his age. He was opinionated, irritable and generally bloody-minded, though his credentials were strong. He had pioneered a whole series of routes in Scotland, climbed without

10 (left): Veteran of two earlier attempts on the South-West Face of Everest, Doug Scott reached the summit with Dougal Haston in 1975. He has gone on to take part in numerous imaginative alpine-style expeditions to challenging peaks on three continents. 11 (below): Traditional tents would have been impossible to anchor on the steep Himalayan faces being pioneered in the 'seventies. The problem was solved by Don Whillans who devised the aluminium framed Whillans box, seen here at Camp 4 on the 1972 European expedition to the South-West Face of Everest. L to r Scott, Whillans and Hamish MacInnes.

12 (overleaf): Climbers in the Western Cwm, on the way to the original South Col route up Everest. This southern approach was dictated by politics when the Chinese closed Tibet and the Nepalese frontier opened in 1950. Houston made the first reconnaissance and in 1951 Shipton's party found a way up to the Cwm through the formidable barrier of the Khumbu Icefall.

13 (previous page): The Biafo Glacier with the triple-headed Ogre the highest summit (left of centre) and the sharper Latok peaks right. In 1892 Conway camped at the point where the Uzum Brakk Glacier (centre) joins the Biafo.

14 (above): Joe Tasker at Camp 2 on the sheer granite West Wall of Changabang climbed in 1976 with Peter Boardman. The Boardman/Tasker partnership continued with, 15 (facing above), a semi-alpine-style ascent of Kangchenjunga North Ridge, attempted by Dyhrenfurth in 1930. 16 (facing below): Doug Scott follows Georges Bettembourg up to Kangchenjunga's North Col.

17 (top): *Manaslu South Face. Messner was the only one of his party to reach the summit in 1972.*
18 (above): *Gasherbrum I (Hidden Peak), the first 8000m summit to be climbed alpine-style, by Messner and Habeler, 1975.*

guides in the Alps and made some bold solo ascents at a time when such an approach was a rarity. Kellas was fifty-three, and his qualifications for leadership of the climbing team were better than Raeburn's. Quite apart from his pre-war climbs, he had made a determined attempt on Kamet the previous year and had pioneered the use of Sherpas as high-altitude porters. He was a warm-hearted, likable man, a lecturer in chemistry at the Middlesex Hospital, with a strong interest in high-altitude physiology. The team was completed by the expedition doctor, A.F.R. Wollaston, and two surveyors from the Survey of India, Morshead and Wheeler, both of whom had mountaineering experience. Morshead had been with Kellas on Kamet.

Although it was called a reconnaissance expedition, they dreamt of reaching the summit and Mallory in particular complained of the weakness of the team from a climbing point of view. Then, just six weeks before departure, a major crisis occurred. It had been decided that everyone should have a medical examination. Mallory passed with flying colours but Finch failed. He had had a severe attack of malaria during the war, was described as slightly anaemic, sallow, flabby, losing weight and very deficient in teeth. Finch would not be the last brilliant high-altitude performer to fail a medical. Don Whillans, one of the strongest climbers I have known, failed his National Service medical in the early 'fifties and John Hunt was rejected for the 1936 Everest expedition after a medical examination. One cannot help wondering, if it had been Mallory who had failed, whether the results might have been ignored, but Finch, although strongly supported by Farrar, was not popular with the Committee, so they decided to uphold the opinion of the doctors. Finch was bitterly hurt, feeling that he was only temporarily out of sorts, a view confirmed by a medical examination held a few days later in a decompression chamber at Oxford in preparation for some altitude experiments. He was passed not only as fit, but comment was made on how well he resisted the simulated effects of high altitude. As if to prove how wrong had been the Committee's rejection, he completed a series of long and exacting climbs in the Alps that summer. His place on the expedition was taken by G.H. Bullock, a contemporary of Mallory's at Winchester who was in the consular service but had climbed extensively in the Alps before the war. He was able to get on with anyone, important in a team of strong and, at times, cantankerous individualists.

Like many major expeditions that followed, this one was put together in a hurry; the organising Committee, mainly Hinks, often at odds with expedition members, particularly on the question of contracts, a recurrent source of friction up to the present day. There were problems in getting the gear together and the boat carrying out the supplies was delayed, but at last, in the middle of May, they were ready to leave Darjeeling.

In many ways this must have been one of the most fulfilling of all the Everest expeditions, certainly one that I would have loved to have been involved in. Although the mountain had been viewed from a distance, no-one had approached it closely. Tibet was still unknown and unspoilt. The approach from Darjeeling through the Himalayan divide led from monsoon-soaked forests, over the Jelep La to the Chumbi valley of Tibet where the rainfall is lower and the valley is clad with fir trees, great clusters of rhododendron, wild rose and clematis. Picturesque villages, prayer flags flying over flat roofs piled with firewood, nestled on the flanks of the hills, with Chomolhari, a magnificent snow peak, towering above. The villagers haven't changed much in the intervening years, with their ragged clothes, broad faces smudged with soot. Cheery, laughing and hospitable, the urchins mirror their parents, getting into everything, curious, light-fingered, as if it is all part of a game. Then the route lies over the Tang La, and onto the Tibetan Plateau itself, a high bleak desert of stone and gravel that stretches towards rolling hills of multi-coloured rock, with the occasional crest of snow. Clouds like mighty vessels sail across a sky of dark metallic blue. Yet, amazingly to me, Mallory didn't appreciate it, referring to Tibet as a 'hateful country inhabited by hateful people'.

His feelings were perhaps coloured, not only by doubts about his fellow team members, but also about himself. The death of Kellas didn't help. He had gone down with severe dysentery, kept struggling on and finally collapsed and died from heart failure while being carried over a pass on the way to Kampa Dzong. But the march went on as they swung well to the north of Everest, past Shekar Dzong (now Xegur), the district capital, with its magnificent monastery fortress that scales the peak above the town, to the village of Tingri, which lies in the middle of a broad plain with the peaks of Everest, Lhotse, Gyachung Kang and Cho Oyu providing a magnificent panorama some forty miles to the south. This was to be their base of operations, not just to find a way up Everest, but to explore the entire area.

The surveyors struck south towards the Khumbu La (now known as the Nangpa La), the pass leading into Nepal to the west of Cho Oyu, while Mallory and Bullock set out for Everest. It must have been a great feeling leaving Tingri with sixteen Sherpas, a few yak-herders and some yaks to

The Everest expedition of 1921. Standing l to r: Wollaston, Howard-Bury, Heron, Raeburn; seated: Mallory, Wheeler, Bullock, Morshead.

carry their gear. They could see the massed clouds of the monsoon filling the southern horizon and felt apprehensive about the immensity of the task in front of them. But a couple of days later they breasted a shoulder at the foot of the Rongbuk valley and there, at its end, was their objective. Mallory describes the moment in the expedition book. 'We asked no questions and made no comment, but simply looked ... There is no complication for the eye. The highest of the world's great mountains, it seems, has to make but a single gesture of magnificence to be lord of all, vast in unchallenged and isolated supremacy.'

They followed the valley, passing the Rongbuk monastery, the first Europeans ever to reach it, and camping at about 17,500ft near the snout of the Rongbuk Glacier. In the following days, between bouts of bad weather, they explored the Central and West Rongbuk Glaciers, peered round the corner of Everest to look into the Western Cwm and climbed one of the peaks to the west, which they named Kellas Peak. From its summit they noted that the spur leading up from the North Col towards the crest of the North-East Ridge seemed reasonable, but the approach to the Col from the south-west looked steep and dangerous. If they could reach it from the north, this could be the key to Everest. But they missed the most important feature of all, the East Rongbuk Glacier. They had noticed a stream flowing from a valley that curled round the eastern flank of Changtse, but it seemed of little volume and they assumed that this was just a small side valley and that the main glacier, leading from the other side of the North Col, must surely flow down to the east. Mallory has frequently been criticised for this mistake, but it is all too easy to suggest with hindsight that they should have nipped up the side valley just to make sure, and quite another matter to plod over endless rocky moraines on what might have seemed a wild goose chase.

By this time the rest of the team had almost completed the exploration of the western reaches of the massif and Howard-Bury was shifting the base to Kharta on the eastern side of the mountain. Bullock and Mallory now set out to find the way to the other side of the North Col and in the process explored both the Kangshung Glacier and the Kharta Glacier. Looking across to the upper reaches of the East Rongbuk Glacier they saw straight-forward snow slopes leading up to the North Col, and that the glacier itself had a ninety-degree bend, taking it down towards the Central Rongbuk Glacier and the valley they had dismissed as a cul de sac. This was something that Wheeler, working methodically as a surveyor, had already discovered.

But they had not really lost anything, for their chances of climbing the mountain were negligible, even though they still dreamt of having a try. Their attempt was impressive. They had been in the field a long time and were all getting tired, yet Mallory, Bullock and Wheeler set out to approach the North Col from Kharta, climbing to the head of the glacier, dropping all the way down into the head of the East Rongbuk Glacier and then reaching the North Col 22,900ft (6990m) in the teeth of a storm. It's not surprising that only Mallory managed to stagger a few hundred feet above the Col.

As a reconnaissance the expedition had been a real success. They had found a possible route to the summit, had mapped and explored the entire area to the north of Nepal all the way to Shisha Pangma, crossed the Fushi La, the route that I followed sixty-six years later on the way to Menlungtse, went down the Rongshar Gorge to identify Gauri Sankar and then crossed the mountains to the north-west to reach Nyalam, on what today is the main road from Kathmandu to Lhasa. It is remarkable how much they had achieved, though Mallory could not see it that way, writing to Geoffrey Winthrop Young on the way back:

> I think it was disappointment more than anything else that prevented me from writing before: the terrible difference between my visions of myself with a few determined spirits setting forth from our perched camp on that high pass, crawling up at least to a much higher point where the summit itself would seem almost within reach, and coming down tired but not dispirited, satisfied rather, just with the effort; all that, and on the other hand the reality as we found it – the blown snow endlessly swept over grey slopes, just the grim prospect, no respite, and no hope.

He saw very clearly that on the next attempt they had to start earlier to avoid the effects of the monsoon and they also needed a strong climbing team. He thought eight strong climbers would be about right, but finding them at short notice was not going to be easy, as Mallory commented when he wrote to his sister, Avie:

> They can't get eight, certainly not soon, perhaps not even the year after. Hinks (Hon. Sec.) already wants to know whether I'll go again. When they press for an answer, I shall tell them they can get the other seven first. How they'll pore over the A.C. list and write round for opinions about the various candidates! I wouldn't go again next year, as the saying is, for all the gold in Arabia.

But it is difficult to say no to an Everest expedition and, once home, he quickly accepted his invitation, even though the Committee had decided that six climbers would do for what would be an all-out attempt on the mountain. They had, perhaps tactlessly, invited General Bruce to be leader before Howard-Bury and his team had even left India. Bruce was now fifty-six and anything but fit, both from war wounds and slight arteriosclerosis, but he had the experience and a personality which was strong, rich, and full of humour. He seemed able to take firm control of an expedition without being authoritarian.

His deputy was to be Colonel Strutt, a rigid martinet, who was to rule the moral tone (in a climbing sense) of the Alpine Club with an iron hand throughout the inter-war period. Intensely conservative and snobbish, he detested Tibet and its grubby, happily dishonest population and yet there is something attractive about his loyalty to his mountaineering ethic and his fairness in dealings with others. He certainly didn't agree with many of George Finch's views, but on the expedition he was the only person to support him in his efforts to persuade the others to carry out training with the new-fangled and controversial oxygen system.

As for the rest of the team, there was no question of leaving Finch out this time and he was put in charge of oxygen. Dr A.W. Wakefield, from Kendal, was a good rock climber with a formidable record of long-distance fell walks. Howard Somervell, also from Kendal, was a surgeon by profession and a man of broad interests, considerable stamina, developed on Lakeland fells, and a good alpine record. Major E.F. Norton, grandson of Sir Alfred Wills, whose ascent of the Wetterhorn is used as a marker for the start of the sport of climbing, had done comparatively little mountaineering but was very good at pig-sticking, while Captain John Noel was going to act as official photographer and film-maker. Tom Longstaff, an even more distinguished mountaineer than Mallory, who had tried to reach Everest in 1907, was to be expedition doctor, commenting: 'General Bruce and I were too old for really high climbing.'

It is interesting that he perceived himself to be too old to go to altitude at the age of forty-seven, when today there are sixty-year-olds trying to climb 8000m peaks. Though I can vouch for the fact that as you creep into your fifties, your recovery rate slows down and carrying loads gets progressively harder.

Bruce strengthened the team further by bringing in two young officers from the Gurkhas, his nephew, Geoffrey Bruce and John Morris, also Colin Crawford from the Indian Civil Service, to act as transport officer, and Morshead, who had done such a good job of mapping the previous year and had supported Mallory's push over the Lhakpa La to the North Col. With these appointments Bruce had craftily brought the strength of the climbing team up to the eight that Mallory had originally recommended. Although several had little alpine experience, the Indian army officers were to prove invaluable, being adaptable, practical and fit.

Much had been learnt from the previous year. The food was to be greatly improved, with dainty morsels like quail in aspic to tempt jaded palates. Equipment, though, was still fairly basic with the standard alpine gear of tweed jackets and leather boots, nailed sparsely to reduce conductivity. They did have polar sledging gear of fine woven cotton anoraks and overtrousers, which are probably as windproof as anything available today, and big, but I suspect bulky, down double sleeping bags for the higher camps, once again developed from polar experience. George Finch had his own lightweight down clothing, but this seems to have been regarded with suspicion, even derision, by some of his peers.

Another controversial subject was oxygen. Finch, Farrar and Somervell saw its importance, while Mallory, Hinks and Longstaff were against it, on

Some of the 1922 team at breakfast. Seated l to r: Wakefield, Morris, Gen. Bruce, Karma Paul, Norton, a Gurkha, Geoffrey Bruce.

ethical and practical grounds. Hinks and Farrar had been in conflict from the start, and there seems to have been at least a lack of warmth between Mallory and Finch. Hinks wrote to Bruce: 'This afternoon we go to see a gas drill. They have contrived a wonderful apparatus which will make you die of laughing. Pray see that a picture of Finch in his patent climbing outfit with the gas apparatus is taken by the official photographer ... I would gladly put a little money on Mallory to go to 25,000ft without the assistance of four cylinders and a mask.' But thanks to the efforts of Finch, a workable, if primitive and heavy, oxygen system was devised and tested with varying degrees of willingness during the approach to the base of the mountain.

Once at Base Camp, the initial build up went smoothly with Colonel Strutt in charge, making the route to the foot of the North Col by the East Rongbuk Glacier, setting up three camps on the way, and by 18th May they had established a camp on the North Col ready for the push to the summit.

Inevitably the planning of the summit bid was dominated by Mallory on the strength of his previous experience of the mountain. Oxygen was therefore relegated to a secondary role and the plan was for Mallory, Somervell, Morshead and Norton, who were perceived to be the strongest of the climbers, to move up to the North Col then, with the support of porters, establish another camp at around 26,000ft, and make their bid for the summit. Finch, almost as an afterthought, was left with the oxygen and Geoffrey Bruce, a complete beginner, to follow in their wake.

The porters would be doing all the carrying. Very few, if any, of the Britons taking part in the pre-war Everest expeditions seemed to have carried more than a day bag, though they did all the lead climbing and, to a greater or lesser degree, took care of their porters who at this stage probably had very little mountain experience. The porters themselves, referred to as coolies by their imperial masters, were mainly Sherpas, originally from Sola Khumbu in Nepal, but settled in Darjeeling making a living from carrying or menial work. There were also some Tibetans (or Bhotias), from whose stock the Sherpas originally came, and some Gurkhas who, in the early days, had been employed as frequently as the Sherpas. They, too, were from Nepal but, while the Sherpas were Buddhists, the Gurkhas were Hindus, originating in India.

The porters were quick learners and appeared to enjoy the work, gaining the respect and, in many cases, the friendship of their British employers. The term 'coolie' quickly vanished to be replaced simply by 'Sherpa' but the relationship remained different from that with the alpine mountain guide who, although from similar peasant stock and therefore of a 'lower' social class, was venerated as an expert who knew more than the client. The high-altitude porter, on the other hand, was being taught his craft by the employer and also was of a different race and colour at a time when a sense of racial superiority permeated European society.

Mallory's party set out from the North Col on 20th May. The ground is not technically difficult, indeed little more than a plod, but they were venturing higher than anyone had been before. They had left their crampons behind because of danger from frostbite caused by tight straps, but this meant they had to cut steps in the hard snow, which exhausted them and slowed them down. The wind was fierce and it took three and a half hours to gain 2000ft. They were now at an altitude of 25,000ft. Huddled for shelter in a little notch, they were still a thousand feet short of their objective for the day, but they spotted some sloping ledges a short way above and across from where they were and decided to stop there for the night. Mallory described their decision-making:

> There never was a dissentient voice to anything we resolved to do, partly, I suppose, because we had little choice in the matter, more because we were that sort of party. We had a single aim in common and regarded it from common ground. We had no

leader within the full meaning of the word, no-one in authority over the rest to command as captain. We all knew equally what was required to be done from first to last and when the occasion arose for doing it one of us did it. Someone, if only to avoid delay in action, had to arrange the order in which the party or parties should proceed. I took this responsibility without waiting to be asked; the rest accepted my initiative, I suppose, because I used to talk so much about what had been done on the previous Expedition.

I get the feeling that Mallory enjoyed his undefined authority, and I imagine this had an influence on some of his decisions two years later. But that afternoon, they stumbled across to the broken ledges, sent down their porters and began the laborious task of building platforms for their two tents. They had an uncomfortable night, only getting away at eight the next morning, and Morshead was forced to return almost immediately. The remaining three struggled on until two that afternoon, reaching a height of 26,985ft. But they were still below the North-East Shoulder and, as it was obvious they couldn't reach the summit and get back before dusk, they decided to retreat. But they had gone a long way into the unknown, some 2500ft higher than anyone had been before.

Finch and Bruce, the forlorn hope, went up to the North Col to meet the returning summit team and to give their oxygen system a trial run. They were well pleased with the benefit it gave them, for it took only three hours on the way up and fifty minutes to get back down. Finch had worked on the system diligently, repairing the sets, most of which had been damaged in transit, modifying masks and then trying them out in a series of mini-expeditions, of which their trip to the North Col was one. It was the systematic approach of the scientist.

They were back on the North Col on the evening of 24th May, with Captain Noel, who was to film them from the Col, and Tejbir, one of Bruce's Gurkha soldiers who was to join them in their bid for the summit. Next morning Noel was feeling particularly lethargic, unable to raise the energy to get out his ciné-camera. He then decided to use his oxygen, breathing with it for a quarter of an hour or so, and immediately felt much better. Finch also gave it a try, discovering for himself the value of using oxygen at rest.

Finch and Bruce set out some time after the porters, carrying heavier loads with their oxygen sets which weighed thirty pounds, but had no trouble in catching them up. Such was the power of oxygen. They also had hoped to camp at 26,000ft but by one o'clock the wind was building up and it had begun to snow, so they stopped at 25,500ft, just a bit higher than their predecessors. It stormed through the night, the tent cracking and straining at the hammering of the wind, which blew until one o'clock the following afternoon. It is impossible to sleep in those conditions and their only means of cooking was a spirit stove whose dancing flame threatened to burn the tent down and took all too long to melt a panful of snow.

When at last the weather did improve, Finch proposed to Bruce that they stay another night to have a try for the summit, but that night the cold began to bite and it was because of this that Finch suggested using one of the oxygen sets. It had an almost miraculous effect, warming them and giving them a good night's sleep. They started cooking before dawn and were away by 6.30. Tejbir, also using oxygen but carrying two extra bottles for the Sahibs, didn't get far, turning back at around 26,000ft, but Finch and Bruce kept going, climbing unroped, picking a diagonal line over the tile-like slabs of the North Face of Everest. It is not difficult technically, indeed little more than precarious walking, but it is very exposed and they were getting very high. Finch wrote:

> Sometimes the slabs gave place to snow – treacherous, powdery stuff, with a thin, hard, deceptive crust that gave the appearance of compactness. Little reliance could be placed upon it, and it had to be treated with great care. And sometimes we found ourselves crossing steep slopes of scree that yielded and shifted downwards with every tread. Very occasionally in the midst of our exacting work we were forced to indulge in a brief rest in order to replace an empty cylinder of oxygen by a full one. The empty ones were thrown away, and as each bumped its way over the precipice and the good steel clanged like a church bell at each impact we laughed aloud at the thought that, 'There goes another 5 lbs off our backs'.

It was at 27,300ft (8320m) that Bruce's oxygen supply failed. Finch plugged him into his, and then fiddled with the set, finding that one of the glass tubes had broken, produced a spare that he was carrying in his pocket and replaced it. But it was getting late, Bruce was very tired and Finch must have been worried about how they were going to get back, particularly in view of Bruce's lack of experience, so they turned round, and slowly worked their way down.

They also were exhausted, but their progress had been faster than that of the first party. They had climbed nearly 500ft higher and a good deal further in lateral distance in twelve and a quarter hours, compared to the fourteen and three-quarters taken by Mallory's party. In terms of average speed this gave the oxygen party a climbing rate of 514ft per hour compared to 394ft per hour without oxygen.

Back at Base they took stock. Longstaff, as doctor, examined them all and declared everyone except Somervell, who seemed impervious to the effects of altitude and cold, unfit to undertake another attempt. Finch and Strutt had strained their hearts, while Morshead was suffering from severe frostbite and was to lose a toe and some finger tips. But Mallory hadn't given up and was determined to have another try. Finch also tried to return to Camp 3, but collapsed with exhaustion. Morshead had to be evacuated and it ended up with Strutt, Finch, Morshead and Longstaff setting out for home, to the grave disapproval of Hinks, who thought they should have all stayed to the bitter end. It is interesting that Mallory was sufficiently impressed by the performance of Finch and Bruce to plan using oxygen for this third attempt, but to start using it only at 25,000ft.

That one last effort met disaster almost before it had started. Mallory, Somervell and Crawford, with fourteen porters, set off from Camp 3 on 6th June for the North Col. There had been a heavy snowfall and they had given it a day to consolidate – sadly that hadn't been long enough. The Europeans were out in front breaking trail for the porter column, when an avalanche occurred. Mallory described it:

> The scene was peculiarly bright and windless, and as we rarely spoke, nothing was to be heard but the laboured panting of our lungs. This stillness was suddenly disturbed. We were startled by an ominous sound, sharp, arresting, violent, and yet somehow soft like an explosion of untamped gunpowder. I had never before on a mountainside heard such a sound; but all of us, I imagine, knew instinctively what it meant, as though we had been accustomed to hear it every day of our lives. In a moment I observed the surface of the snow broken and puckered where it had been even for a few yards to the right of me. I took two steps convulsively in this direction with some quick thought of getting nearer to the edge of the danger that threatened us. And then I began to move slowly downwards, inevitably carried on the whole moving surface by a force I was utterly powerless to resist. Somehow I managed to turn out from the slope so as to avoid being pushed headlong and backwards down it. For a second or two I seemed hardly to be in danger as I went quietly sliding down with the snow. Then the rope at my waist tightened and held me back. A wave of snow came over me and I was buried. I supposed that the matter was settled.

The three Europeans were lucky, for they ended up near the surface and were able to struggle out from the embrace of the snow, but nine of the Sherpas were swept over an ice cliff into a crevasse. They managed to rescue two of them, but seven lost their lives – the most serious accident that had so far occurred in the history of mountaineering.

The Britons were not only deeply grieved at the loss of Sherpas of whom they had become fond but also had a strong sense of guilt. Somervell wrote: 'I remember well the thought gnawing at my brain, "Only Sherpas and Bhotias killed – why, oh why could not one of us Britishers have shared their fate?'' I would gladly at that moment have been lying there dead in the snow, if only to give those fine chaps who had survived the feeling that we shared their loss, as we had indeed shared the risk.'

But the siege of Everest, and the political manœuvring that any committee-based enterprise entails, went on. General Bruce was now made Chairman of the Committee and voted unanimously to lead the next expedition in 1924, even though his medical report was even more questionable than it had been in 1922. Mallory had a little wobble about returning for a third time, but was quickly and easily persuaded to go.

Finch, on the other hand, who had not only achieved the height record on the climb, but had developed and modified the oxygen system in the field, was dropped. He had come into conflict with the Committee over some private enterprise lecturing and use of pictures, contrary to the letter of the agreement. His exclusion from the 1924 Everest expedition certainly weakened the team. The other three proven performers were Somervell, Geoffrey Bruce and Norton, while Captain Noel, once again official photographer, displayed entrepreneural flair by offering the Everest Committee £8000, a very large sum of money in 1923, for all photographic and film rights to the expedition, an offer which put the expedition comfortably into the black.

The team was made up to eight with the addition of four newcomers, Noel Odell, a geologist by profession, Bentley Beetham, a Lakeland schoolmaster, and John de Vars Hazard, experienced alpinists but with no Himalayan record, and, more surprisingly, Andrew Irvine, an engineering student at Oxford with a Blue for rowing but very little knowledge of climbing. He was selected on Noel Odell's recommendation, based on a geological field trip in Spitzbergen, on which they completed a superb ascent on a spectacular unclimbed peak. Odell was impressed by his endurance, natural ability and pleasant, easy-going manner. Another important factor was his engineering background which would be particularly useful for sorting out the oxygen system.

They had more time to prepare for the 1924 expedition, but very few innovations were made. Finch's experiments with down clothing were ignored, and the team relied on wool, protected by the windproof cotton overalls developed for Polar regions, with lightly nailed leather felt-lined boots. They set out on schedule from Darjeeling on 25th March, but almost immediately were smitten with illness. Bentley Beetham had such a severe

The 1924 expedition. Standing, l to r: Irvine, Mallory, Norton, Odell, MacDonald (trade agent); seated, Shebbeare, G. Bruce, Somervell, Beetham.

attack of dysentery that he never recovered. Mallory had suspected appendicitis, and Somervell was preparing to operate on him in the field which proved sufficient threat to ensure a rapid and complete recovery. More serious, however, was General Bruce's condition. He had gone tiger-hunting on the way to Darjeeling and had contracted malaria. Hingston, the team doctor, decided that he would have to be evacuated.

This meant that Norton was now leader. He had been appointed deputy for his administrative ability, and he naturally made Mallory deputy leader in charge of all climbing matters, in other words climbing leader. This certainly changed the balance of power, giving Mallory a much stronger influence on events. They planned their campaign during the approach march resolving that, once Camp 3 at the head of the East Rongbuk Glacier had been established, Geoffrey Bruce and Odell would move up to the North Col and establish Camp 5 on the North Ridge. Somervell with Norton would then make the first bid for the summit without oxygen and Mallory and Irvine would make a second bid using oxygen. It was Mallory's idea to climb with Irvine, even though the more experienced Odell would have been a more logical partner. Apart from having someone with him who could keep the despised 'gas' working, could it be that Mallory was attracted to a partnership in which he had undisputed seniority, which he would not have enjoyed had he climbed with Odell who was closer to him in both age and experience?

They reached Base Camp on 28th April but the tidy initial plan was to fall apart in the teeth of a violent storm that disrupted the build-up and supply of camps, leaving four porters marooned at the high point on the North Col. It was all they could do to rescue them and retreat to Base. It was now mid-May and Norton was worried about the imminent arrival of the monsoon, if it wasn't already upon them. The next attempt, therefore, was something of a scramble. The porters were tired and demoralised, so the climbers decided to abandon the oxygen and make a quick push for the summit. Mallory and Bruce were to make the first attempt, followed by Norton and Somervell, with Odell and Irvine in support at the North Col, each party with its Sherpa team. Norton seems to have run the expedition on quite democratic lines, listening to everyone's opinions but particularly those of Mallory. He was at pains not to nominate himself on the first attempt, but to leave it to his fellow team members to decide on the best order.

Mallory's attempt raises a number of questions from the way that it faded. He and Bruce set out from the North Col on 1st June with eight porters. It was a fine day but bitterly cold and windy. At 25,000ft four of the porters dumped their loads and insisted on returning. The rest struggled on another 300ft before stopping to pitch the camp. Bruce and the Sherpa Lobsang made two exhausting carries to retrieve the loads left below, while Mallory and the others built tent platforms. That night three of the Sherpas stayed with the two Europeans, but the next morning, instead of trying to establish a top camp, much to the surprise of Norton, they all came down. One can't help wondering if Mallory had decided that it was hopeless and was already thinking of returning to the original plan of making an attempt with oxygen.

Norton and Somervell, with just four Sherpas to help them, carried on the following day, to establish the top camp where their Sherpas left them to make their bid for the summit in almost perfect conditions on a still clear day. They followed a similar line to that of Finch in 1922, but continued past his high point, traversing over the scree-littered tiles below the crest of the ridge, beneath the First, then the Second Step. Each man was pushing himself to the limit. Norton was experiencing double vision, while Somervell, who had had a bad throat throughout the expedition, was racked with coughing until he could go no further. Norton kept going, higher than any man had been before, ploughing through the soft, deep powdery snow at the top of the Great Couloir that splits the face:

> Beyond the couloir the going got steadily worse; I found myself stepping from tile to tile, as it were, each tile sloping smoothly and steeply downwards; I began to feel that I was too much dependent on the mere friction of a boot nail on the slabs. It was not exactly difficult going, but it was a dangerous place for a single unroped climber, as one slip would have sent me in all probability to the bottom of the mountain. The strain of climbing so carefully was beginning to tell and I was getting exhausted. In addition my eye trouble was getting worse and was by now a severe handicap. I had perhaps 200 feet more of this nasty going to surmount before I emerged onto the north face of the final pyramid and I believe safety and an easy route to the summit. It was now 1 p.m., and a brief calculation showed that I had no chance of climbing the remaining 800 or 900 feet if I was to return in safety.

He had reached 28,126ft (8570m), alone, part blinded, in the last stages of exhaustion, and still had to get back down. Descending is always more difficult than going up, particularly on the slabby, tiled ground of the upper reaches of Everest, but he got back to Somervell and, roped together, they started down, past their top camp, past Camp 5, determined to reach the comparative safety of the North Col that night. By this time it was dark, but the ground was easier and they took off the rope. Norton even started glissading, hardly noticing that Somervell was no longer following him.

Somervell was crouched in the snow with a particularly bad spasm of coughing that actually dislodged some of the lining of his throat, blocking the air passage. He couldn't breathe and couldn't shout out to Norton who was only just a short way ahead.

> So I sat in the snow to die whilst he walked on, little knowing that his companion was awaiting the end only a few yards behind him. I made one or two attempts to breathe, but nothing happened. Finally, I pressed my chest with both hands, gave one last almighty push – and the obstruction came up. What a relief! Coughing up a little blood, I once more breathed really freely – more freely than I had done for some days. Though the pain was intense, yet I was a new man, and was soon going down at a better pace than I had done for some days.

He caught up with Norton, who, fortunately had a hand torch, and they stumbled down towards the haven of the North Col. As they neared it, Norton began to shout for help through the complex web of crevasses that barred the way to Camp 4.

At last I made myself heard, and an answering shout informed us that our escort was coming and was bringing an oxygen apparatus and cylinder. But there was something we wanted far more than oxygen for we were parched and famished with thirst. I remember shouting again and again, We don't want the d–d oxygen; we want drink. My own throat and voice were in none too good a case, and my feeble wail seemed to be swallowed up in the dim white expanse below glimmering in the starlight.

That night Mallory explained to Norton the idea that must have been forming in his mind during his abortive, almost half-hearted, attempt with Bruce. He wanted to revert to the original plan and make one more attempt on the mountain with Irvine, using oxygen. Norton, who was now totally snow blind and in considerable pain, welcomed it but did question whether it would have been better for Odell to accompany him in view of the way Odell now seemed to be going more strongly than any one else in the team. He was certainly fitter than Irvine who was troubled with a severe high-altitude cough.

But Mallory was determined to stick with Irvine and after a day's rest on the North Col, they set off with eight porters for Camp 5, moving up to Camp 6 the day after, while Noel Odell came up behind, taking up residence in Camp 5 to act in support, not that there was much he could do directly. Their last message was typical of so many climbers on a siege climb, a bit disorganised, relying on others to clear up some of the mess or recover forgotten items.

Dear Odell,
We're awfully sorry to have left things in such a mess – our Unna cooker rolled down the slope at the last moment. Be sure of getting back to IV tomorrow in time to evacuate before dark as I hope to. In the tent I must have left a compass – for the Lord's sake rescue it; we are without. To here on 90 atmospheres for the two days – so we'll probably go on two cylinders but it's a bloody load for climbing. Perfect weather for the job.
Yours ever,
G. Mallory

Dear Noel,
We'll probably start early tomorrow (8th) in order to have clear weather. It won't be too early to start looking for us either crossing the rock band going up skyline at 8:00 p.m. [sic]
Yours ever,
G. Mallory

Mallory and Irvine set out on the morning of 8th June for the summit, though no one saw them leave their camp. It was a still day, with a cloudy mist clinging to the crest of the ridge. Noel Odell left Camp 5 at 8 a.m.

The last picture of Mallory and Irvine setting off from the North Col using oxygen.

and made his way up towards the top camp. This was the highest he had been so far, he was feeling fit, but in no hurry, making geological observations as he went and even choosing to scramble up a craggy section just for the fun of it. It was as he came to the top of this that he had a glimpse of the two climbers far above him:

> I saw the whole summit ridge and final peak of Everest unveiled. I noticed far away on a snow slope leading up to what seemed to me to be the last step but one from the base of the final pyramid, a tiny object moving and approaching the rock step. A second object followed, and then the first climbed to the top of the step. As I stood intently watching this dramatic appearance, the scene became enveloped in cloud once more.

Noel Odell was not absolutely sure whether this was the First or the Second Step, though he assumed at the time it was the Second. Mallory and Irvine were never seen again.

It is just conceivable that they reached the summit and perished, presumably from a fall, on the way down, but this seems unlikely. Even if they were at the Second Step at mid-day when Odell saw them, they were behind schedule with about 800ft to go to the summit. In addition, the weather broke shortly after Odell got back to the tent, with a squall of snow that lasted about two hours. This surely would have encouraged them to turn back. The loss of such heroes as Mallory and Irvine has all the ingredients of legend and is probably the best known and most written about disaster in the history of mountaineering, especially as it can never be proven whether or not they reached the summit of Everest and is still keenly debated.

After 1924 the Everest Committee fell foul of Indian government bureaucracy. There were Tibetan objections to the defeated expedition straying from their permitted itinerary into Nepal on their way back home; and further complaints about Captain Noel's unseemly importing of Gyantze lamas to add local colour to the film show he had running for ten weeks at the Scala Theatre. Howard-Bury had known how to handle prima donna political agents. His successors lacked this skill and the Everest Committee application for 1926 was turned down.

This seems to have left a hiatus in British Himalayan climbing and there was comparatively little activity for another nine years, but with the recovery from the war of the central European countries, others were beginning to look to the great peaks of the Himalaya.

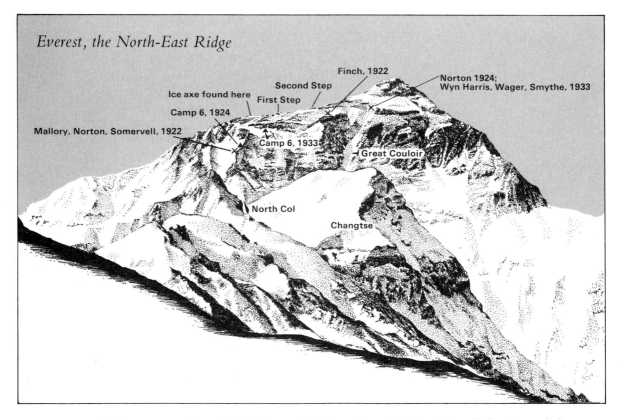

Everest, the North-East Ridge

British attempts on the north side of Everest in the 'twenties and 'thirties. Various high points reached in 1922, 1924 and 1933 are marked x. In 1924 Odell last saw Mallory and Irvine somewhere in the vicinity of the First or Second Step. An ice axe belonging to one of them was found by Wager in 1933. Neither the 1935 nor 1936 expeditions managed to get onto the ridge.

THE INVISIBLE BARRIER

Attempts on the 8000m peaks in the 1930s

•

The British had had the Himalaya to themselves for most of the 'twenties, while the rest of Europe recovered from the First World War. Paul Bauer was one of the young men whose lives had been interrupted. Born in 1896 in the Palatinate, today's Rhineland, he had ended the war as a prisoner in England.

> We had gone out to battle as soldiers of the king, but on our return we found that the monarchy had been abolished and that people spoke ill of an ancient and honoured institution. We had fought for our people and many of my friends had followed the classic example and laid down their lives. But now we found that love of Fatherland, heroism and self-sacrifice were looked down upon and denigrated. The things we had looked up to had been dethroned. My refuge was the mountains. From Munich you can see them in all their beauty on the southern skyline.

It wasn't long, however, before he started looking further afield. In 1928 he went to the Caucasus, and the following year to the Himalaya to attempt Kangchenjunga. Bauer was a brilliant organiser and his expedition differed greatly from those of the British to Everest in that a single individual, Bauer, conceived the idea and pushed it through. Admittedly he gained the support of the Akademischer Alpenverein, but it was he, and not a committee, who controlled the expedition which contributed to both the efficiency and cohesion within the team. Bauer wrote:

> Our undertaking had to be based upon a kind of military discipline and unquestioning obedience. Even though the spirit of good-fellowship overshadowed this stringency, yet in the years 1928 and 1929 anything even suggesting military discipline was cried down. Well known mountaineers declined to fall in with such ideas, and their refusal to accept the discipline I required of them found a ready support in the spirit of the times.

The kind of obedience that Bauer expected was much stricter than anything encountered in the British Everest expeditions and was given him on his merits as organiser, strategist and climber. The Germans seem to work better within this kind of disciplined team situation than the British who have always tended to be more easy-going and less systematic, the zealously guarded amateur ethic being all too often an excuse for downright inefficiency.

Bauer's team of nine experienced alpinists had all climbed together before, pushing the limits on the steep ice walls of the Eastern Alps. Having assessed the equipment and techniques used by the British Everest expeditions, they developed their own gear, based on experience in the Alps and chose the post-monsoon season to make their attempt. The British had discovered in 1921 how difficult it was to climb during the monsoon and on their two subsequent expeditions had gone out earlier. But this also had presented problems with high winds and cold in the initial stages of the expedition and pre-monsoon storms in the latter part. Bauer hoped to avoid this by climbing into the Himalayan autumn.

With Nepal still closed, they were limited to the eastern, Sikkimese, aspects of the mountain. These certainly looked formidable and they did not have much route choice. A steep crest, known as the Eastern Spur, led up to the North Ridge of the mountain, joining it at a height of around 7750m. It gave much steeper climbing than anything on Everest, and was by far the hardest climbing tackled in the Himalaya up to that date. The route crept up the rocky side of the spur and then wormed its way around a series of huge ice towers, even tunnelling through one of them. They dug snow caves for camps and kept going with considerable tenacity. Bauer's account sounds very much like a modern siege-style expedition, but it must be remembered that they were using the minimum of fixed rope, had no jumars and, given the scale of the challenge, were a comparatively small team. Their porters, many of whom had been on the British Everest expeditions, accompanied them on the ridge, but their communications were badly stretched.

They had needed six staging camps just to reach the foot of the Spur so that Camp 6, at 4700m was, in effect, their Base Camp. They were also plagued by the afternoon snows of the dying monsoon. By 3rd October they had reached only 7020m, their Camp 10, but at last the ridge was beginning to broaden and the way seemed easier. They were also running out of weather. Heavy snowfall on 4th October cut off all the camps. In a brief intermission they managed to reach 7200m (23,623ft) but then a savage storm rolled in and they were forced to abandon the attempt with a desperate retreat down the snow-plastered ridge.

Left, Paul Bauer, a firm but capable expedition leader who welded his team behind him. Right, Professor G. O. Dyhrenfurth who led the 1930 Kangchenjunga expedition.

The following year Professor G.O. Dyhrenfurth, a German scientist and mountaineer based in Switzerland, tackled Kangchenjunga with an international expedition of eleven. Hermann Hoerlin and Erwin Schneider were the most accomplished climbers and had made first winter ascents of the Aiguille Noire de Peuterey and the Aiguille Blanche de Peuterey. Frank Smythe, who was to take an important part in the 1933 and 1936 British Everest expeditions and capture the romance of mountaineering in over a dozen successful books, had had some good alpine seasons and was of the post-First World War generation. None of them had any Himalayan experience and, though they seemed to have got on well together, they lacked the cohesion of Bauer's team. Their gear certainly left a lot to be desired. Dyhrenfurth, in common with many German climbers until very recent times, believed in solid bulk and, as Smythe records, supplied the team with : 'A tricot coat weighing six pounds; breeches, three pounds six ounces; sweater two pounds ten ounces; outer wind jacket, three pounds. I can only describe the boots as portmanteaus. They weighed six and a half pounds a pair and each was nailed with sixty clinker and tricouni nails.'

This was in complete contrast to the thinking of Bauer's expedition or that of the British Everest expeditions. Smythe took the precaution of taking a selection of lightweight wool sweaters to wear under a windproof outer, following the well tried layer principle.

Dyhrenfurth reverted to the pre-monsoon period and had managed to get permission to go into Nepal, though this entailed a very long, if beautiful, approach over the Kang La, to the south of Kangchenjunga, in a wide sweep round the west of Jannu to follow the north side of the Kangchenjunga Glacier. It is not surprising that it was 26th April when they at last established Base Camp. Dyhrenfurth was following the advice of Freshfield who had first explored this aspect of the mountain in 1899, indicating that there might be a route up the North-West Face, leading up towards the North Ridge, which was the line that Bauer was trying to reach from the other side.

From photographs the route looked attractive, and their first appraisal was optimistic. The face itself was guarded by a series of steep sérac walls, but there seemed to be a possible line through the bottom wall at its left-hand end. At this stage they had no concept of how difficult or dangerous it was going to be. They established a camp on the glacier just below the wall and started trying to force a route up through it. The going was hard; they were feeling the altitude and becoming increasingly aware of the potential danger. Smythe commented: 'I have experienced fear many times on many mountains, but never quite the same dull, hopeless sort of fear inspired by this terrible wall of ice.'

They managed to push a route up the first step of the ice wall in the course of several days but his fears were justified a few days later. Dyhrenfurth described it:

> A high cracking sound was the first thing I heard. Then I saw at the very top of the cliff – somewhat to my right – an ice wall perhaps one thousand feet wide was toppling forward quite slowly. It seemed minutes, though I'm sure it only lasted a matter of seconds, before the huge face broke and came crashing down in a gigantic avalanche of ice ... I ran towards the left – if running is the right word for moving quickly in deep powder snow at 20,000 feet – with little hope of escaping. I could be knocked out by ice blocks, suffocated by the snow dust or swept away by the avalanche and hurled into the great crevasse.

Fortunately for Dyhrenfurth he was only caught by the edge of the avalanche but Chettan, one of their most experienced Sherpas, was hit by an ice block and killed outright. Schneider had been immediately beneath the ice wall, and the avalanche had thundered over him. It was a miracle more lives were not lost. There was no question of going on with that route. Smythe would have liked to admit defeat and then tackle a more realistic objective like the 7420m (24,344ft) Jongsang Peak, but the others were still determined to try to find a way up Kangchenjunga.

They now turned their attention to the North-West Ridge which led up from the West Kanchenjunga Glacier towards the summit of Kangba-chen. It was a forlorn hope, the ridge being even steeper than the Eastern Spur attempted by the Germans the previous year, with a long way to go from the 7902m (25,925ft) Kangbachen to the main summit. In addition the rock was frighteningly loose. It is not surprising that they only reached 6400m (21,000ft) before turning back. Could Kangchenjunga be climbed? Smythe's reply was, 'The answer is yes, but most likely not in this generation and not by present day mountaineering methods.'

His assessment was right but in 1931 Bauer returned to try to prove him wrong. He chose the same post-monsoon period and the same route – the devil he knew – as in 1929. They resumed the siege with the same determination and level of organisation they had displayed before, but started earlier. This meant the East Spur was more dangerous, with the cockscomb of snow bosses being less well frozen and the weather even more unpredictable than on their first attempt and, as a result, they fell behind schedule. Later expeditions would probably have fixed ropes all the way up the ridge, but it did not seem to have occurred to Bauer to take this precaution. They were moving up to establish Camp 8 on the crest of the spur. Two were out in front finding the route, while Hermann Schaller was following on behind with a group of porters. Bauer, with another group, was bringing up the rear. As he came round a corner, he saw just how dangerous was the ground ahead. Should he call them back? It's a dilemma which every expedition leader must face.

> More than once I raised the whistle to my lips to call them back; we must find a new route somewhere else and postpone our advance. But I always dropped the whistle again ... If I had called them back they would have all had to cross the difficult section. The retreat would have caused confusion and annoyance.

And then:

> Suddenly a black form – Pasang? flew out, Schaller's tall figure with rucksack streaming out behind, followed as silently.

Both were killed in the fall but they were able to retrieve their two comrades' bodies and buried them at Base Camp. There was never any question of abandoning the expedition. Bauer felt:

> For me, personally, the prosecution of our attack on Kangchenjunga was a foregone conclusion. From the very beginning we had all weighed the possibility of an accident. Each man wished that at any rate the others should reach the goal, even should his own life be prematurely ended.

One cannot help wondering how the Sherpas felt about their 'goal', though they continued their loyal support as they were to do after tragedy all too many times in the future.

So they battled on, slowly pushing their way up the ridge. It was 15th September when they at last established Camp 10 at the top of the worst difficulties. There were six climbers and three porters, with supplies and fuel for a fortnight, and equipment for three more camps. They were behind schedule, but a fortnight earlier than in 1929. The weather was settled, the route to Camp 11 prepared. But they had been at altitude for a long time. Almost as soon as he started, Bauer realised that he hadn't the strength to go any further. He sadly started the dangerous solitary route down, leaving the others to strive for the summit.

Hartmann and Wien reached the top of the pinnacle they called Outpost Peak on the 17th, getting a superb view of the route to the summit. It was one of those perfect days when everything seemed possible, but the following day, when they pressed on beyond the peak to establish Camp 12, the view of the final stretch of the spur towards the crest of the North Ridge was profoundly discouraging. It was dangerously avalanche-prone, and the team was over-extended and near exhaustion. Reluctantly they decided to abandon the attempt, having reached a height of 7700m (25,263ft), with some of the most difficult climbing ever undertaken at that time.

In 1932 another German group set out to the opposite end of the Himalayan chain to attempt Nanga Parbat (8125m/26,660ft). With the benefit of Mummery's 1895 explorations, they chose the long, but seemingly straightforward, approach from the Rakhiot valley. The British authorities didn't make it any easier by forbidding them to go through any inhabited areas beyond Astor. This meant they had to cut over the foothills, crossing a series of high passes, taking thirty-seven days to walk from Srinagar to the Fairy Meadow below Nanga Parbat. It must, however, have been a wonderful approach with a sense of pioneering adventure, very different from the two days it now takes from the roadhead above the Karakoram Highway to the site of their Base Camp. Soon it will be even more accessible, for sadly a hotel, reached by road, is being built at Fairy Meadow.

The leader of the expedition was Willy Merkl, a thirty-four-year-old railwayman from Munich, with an impressive list of first ascents in the Eastern Alps and a reputation for being an excellent organiser. The team was titled the German–American expedition, on the strength of the inclusion of a talented young American climber, Rand Herron, who had been storming the Alps. The others included an Austrian guide from Kufstein, Peter Aschenbrenner, Fritz Bechtold and Fritz Wiessner, who later became a naturalised American and was to lead the ill-fated 1939 American expedition to K2. Although none of them had been to the Himalaya, it was a young and very strong team of good alpinists who knew each other well. They made a mistake, however, in saving money by employing local and totally inexperienced porters for the mountain, rather than bringing over Sherpas from Darjeeling.

It was July before they started any serious climbing. Although the way from the Rakhiot Glacier is technically the easiest way to the summit, it is also long and complex, involving the crossing of several subsidiary summits. They were climbing during the monsoon, and although the full effects are not experienced so far west, Nanga Parbat, being to the south of the Karakoram, does have more unsettled weather in this period. They were frequently wading through thigh-deep snow and on several occasions nearly avalanched. They had only managed to cross round the side of Rakhiot Peak by the end of August, reaching a height of 6949m (22,800ft) on the saddle between Rakhiot Peak and the South-East Peak. From there, however, they could see that there was a route to the summit.

They had learnt a great deal, had some narrow escapes, but no-one had been killed though, ironically, on the way back through Egypt Rand Herron slipped while climbing one of the Pyramids and fell to his death. One cannot help wondering what might have happened on the 1939 K2 expedition had he survived. He was obviously a brilliant mountaineer and would have been a natural choice of partner for Wiessner.

Merkl started planning the next expedition as soon as he returned to Germany and was ready in 1934. Peter Aschenbrenner and Fritz Bechtold were joining him from the old team. Willo Welzenbach, the man who had made such an impact on alpinism over the past decade, was also available, and the party was made up by Peter Mülritter, Willy Bernard (doctor), Alfred Drexel, Erwin Schneider and Uli Wieland. The latter two had been with Dyhrenfurth on Kangchenjunga. They had learnt many useful lessons from their 1932 expedition, perhaps the most important being the need to

The 1934 party making their way through the icefall of the upper Rakhiot Glacier.

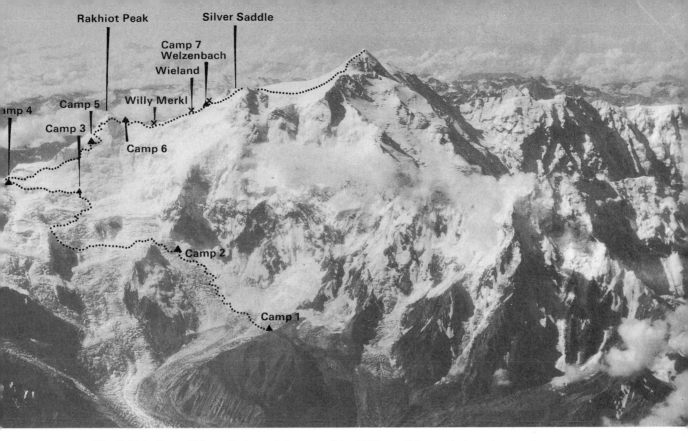

The Rakhiot Face of Nanga Parbat and the route of the 1934 expedition, with the main summit hidden from view.

recruit a strong Sherpa team, and they used many who had been with the British on Everest the previous year. They also started earlier, made faster progress than last time and set up the lower camps quickly, reaching Camp 3 at 5898m at the beginning of June. But then they had a set back. Alfred Drexel contracted pulmonary oedema at Camp 3. They managed to get him to a lower camp but his condition deteriorated and he died in his sleep.

After Drexel's burial the build-up of supplies went on. Camp 4 (6187m) at the foot of Rakhiot Peak was to be their Advance Base. They were well organised, with radio communication between camps, though news that the Sherpas' supplies of *tsampa*, their staple diet, had been delayed en route from Darjeeling meant a delay of eleven cloudless days waiting for it at Base Camp. Sherpas can be very conservative about their food.

It was 22nd June before the assault team consisting of Aschenbrenner, Bechtold, Merkl, Schneider, Welzenbach and Wieland, with seventeen Sherpas, moved back up to Camp 4. They were undoubtedly determined but there was also a sense of caution. Bernard, their doctor, made each one of them promise 'to go no further on the mountain than the point where he could retrace his steps unaided. He impressed upon us again that under the influence of altitude recognition of one's own limits goes overboard.'

This time they placed Camp 5 at 6690m on the crest of the ridge of Rakhiot Peak to avoid the avalanche danger which would have threatened the route they had taken in 1932. A traverse over steep, broken ground took them round Rakhiot Peak to the site of Camp 6 at 6955m. They could now see the summit and, even though some of their Sherpa porters were beginning to tire and three went back down, success at last seemed in sight. The weather was still fine. Though there were ominous signs of the monsoon, with an ocean of cloud sweeping in from the south, they were above it, isolated from the lower camps and the rest of the world, with just the summit ridge and their goal, the summit of Nanga Parbat, basking in sunshine, towering above them. Their seventh camp was at the foot of the Silver Saddle at 7050m. Two more of the porters were sick, so Bechtold decided to escort them down to safety and bring a replenishment group to back up what he hoped would be the successful summit team.

It was 6th July. Aschenbrenner and Schneider were away first, planning to find the route and cut good steps for their comrades and the heavily laden porters. The cloud sea stretched beneath them as they made their way up the slopes leading to the Silver Saddle. Fully acclimatised, they were feeling good, reaching the Saddle in three and a quarter hours. They had a clear view to the lower summit and could see that it was easy going all the way. Sheltering from the bitter north-east wind, they rested for a while and then set out once again hoping to find a good site for a top camp, within easy reach of the summit. Welzenbach reached the Saddle shortly after they left, but in a shouted conversation, indicated that he would wait for the rest of the team. Aschenbrenner and Schneider ploughed steadily through crusted snow to a point just below the lower summit at a height of around 7712m (25,300ft). They probably could have made it to the top that day, but they had it firmly in their minds that they were all going to the top together. Then they noticed that the others seemed to be pitching camp on the Silver Saddle. Schneider started back to try to encourage them to push on a little further, while Aschenbrenner waited for a further hour and a half but, seeing no signs of movement, also went down.

The sky above was still clear but the wind was getting steadily stronger, driving clouds of spindrift at the tents. By morning one of them had collapsed and all were filling with spindrift. Although they had six days' food with them, they were unable to do any cooking and just lay through the day in their snow-encrusted sleeping bags. The storm raged through the night and the next morning they realised they would have to retreat. It

Welzenbach pauses for breath on the way to the Silver Saddle. Inset, Willy Merkl, leader of two German expeditions to Nanga Parbat, who lost his life in the 1934 debacle.

is never easy making a move from the comparative warmth and illusory security of a sleeping bag. The Sherpas, huddled in their bags, took a lot of shifting. Ropes were like wire cables, boots frozen solid, and the wind screamed and battered as they tried to pack their sacks. Schneider, followed by three porters then Aschenbrenner, set out first with the role of making a track which filled in almost immediately. Nima Dorje was blown from his steps and fell, nearly pulling the others down with him, and losing his rucksack holding one of the two sleeping bags they had with them. They carried on, fighting their way through the screaming, driving wind. As the angle eased they took off the rope, Aschenbrenner shouted at the Sherpas that they must keep up and then plunged on down the slope.

It's easy to be judgemental at sea level, to say they should have waited for the others or, at the very least, escorted their Sherpas down, but it is less easy in practice. Aschenbrenner wrote in his diary: 'Severe fatigue overcame me and every thirty yards I sat down for a short time in the snow. The blizzard whipped the snow crystals like red-hot needles into our burning faces. We had lost sight of our porters, but presumed them to be a short distance behind. Furthermore, they would certainly be brought on by the party following.'

Wishful thinking perhaps, but all too easy in the face of the storm. In reality it was each man, or at least, each little party for themselves. Aschenbrenner and Schneider, by far the strongest pair of the expedition, fought their way back down to Camp 4, reaching it in the early evening, still convinced that the others would be on their heels, or had perhaps stopped at Camp 5 which was stocked with food and sleeping bags. The storm raged through the night and all the next day. Bechtold, Bernard and Mülritter, who had been waiting for them at Camp 4, tried to fight their way up the mountain, but it was a morass of deep powder snow and they were forced to abandon the attempt. They had a glimpse of the upper slopes through a break in the clouds: 'A fairly large party was visible, descending from the Silbersattel. Good God! Why then had they got no further? High on the ridge, at a greater distance, a solitary figure was wandering behind the descending party. Then he sat down to rest in the snow. Why did he not go on? The vision ceased, for the blizzards drove the snow clouds once more over the ridge.'

They knew they were faced with a potential disaster which they could do very little to avert. They only learnt the significance of what they had seen the following day when four of the Sherpas, frostbitten and exhausted, stumbled down. They had only got down a short way on the 8th before the three Germans decided to bivouac, even though they only had three sleeping bags between them. Merkl and Wieland squeezed into one, whilst Welzenbach, with characteristic selflessness, sat out in the snow. The eight Sherpas had the other two bags between them. One, Nima Nurbu, died during the night. The following morning, three of the Sherpas, Gay-lay, Angtsering and Dakshi elected to stay in the bivouac, when the three Germans and four porters started down. It was Wieland at the back who sat down for a rest and never got up again, while the others fought their way down, with Welzenbach taking the initiative, fixing a rope in position to enable the Sherpas to get down the final steep slope of the Silver Saddle to Camp 7. Merkl and Welzenbach reached the camp about an hour later. There was only one tent, so they told the Sherpas to push on down to Camp 6, an order which, though probably motivated by self-interest, might well have saved the lives of three of those Sherpas. This is Kitar's account of what happened:

> The blizzard was so frightful that we could not reach Camp 6, and spent the night in a snow cave. Next morning, as we were descending over the Rakhiot Peak, we met Pasang, Nima Dorje and Pinzo Nurbu, who were originally a day in advance, and had lost their way in the snow storm. While we were coming down the steep wall the blizzard came on so furiously that we could scarcely descend. Nima Dorje and Nima Tashi were at the end of their strength and died among the ropes on the Rakhiot Peak. We brought Pinzo Nurbu as far as Camp 5, where he collapsed and died three yards in front of the tents. We waited for Da Tundu, who had unroped from the two dead men, and then went down together to Camp 4.

Bald words, gleaned from the exhausted Sherpas whom Bechtold escorted down towards Base the following day, while Aschenbrenner, Schneider, Mülritter and three Sherpas struggled, unladen, through deep snows up to Camp 5. They came across Pinzo Nurbu's body just outside the tent. Aschenbrenner and Schneider tried to reach the bodies of the other two Sherpas whom they could see hanging on the ropes of the traverse, but they were driven back by the storm. No-one, surely, could have survived and they dropped back to Camp 4, planning to abandon the mountain the following morning.

Then next day, through a break in the clouds they saw three figures coming down from around Camp 7. They could even hear distant calls for help. The following morning they saw a single figure stumbling down through the snow towards them. It was the Sherpa Angtsering; this is his story:

Survivors of the blizzard. Pasang Kikuli is helped back to Camp 4 below Rakhiot Peak.

On the morning of July 9th, when the sahibs and porters left the bivouac below the Silbersattel, Gay-Lay, Dakshi and I remained behind, because we were too exhausted and partially snow-blind. We had two sleeping-sacks. During the night of the 10th-11th, Dakshi died in this bivouac. In the morning Gay-Lay and I went down to Camp 7, and found Wieland Sahib dead behind a mound of snow thirty yards from the tent. In Camp 7 we found Merkl and Welzenbach Sahibs. The tent was full of snow, and I had to clear it at the Bara Sahib's request. Our joint sleeping-sack was so plastered up with snow and ice that only Gay-Lay could sleep in it. The sahibs slept just on rubber ground-sheets. As we had nothing left to eat, I wanted to get down as quickly as possible next day, but the Bara Sahib preferred to wait until the men, whom we could see between Camps 4 and 5, should come up with provisions. Welzenbach Sahib died during the night of the 12th-13th. We left the dead Welzenbach Sahib lying in the tent, and went down towards Camp 6 that morning, Merkl painfully supported on two ice-axes. But as we could not manage to overcome the rise to the 'Moor's Head', we constructed an ice-cave on the flat saddle. Bara Sahib and Gay-Lay slept together on a rubber ground-sheet which we had brought along, and under one common porter's blanket. I myself had a blanket also, but no ground-sheet. On the morning of the 14th, I went outside the cave and called loudly for help. As there was nobody visible at Camp 4, I proposed to Merkl that I should go down. He agreed. When I set out, Merkl and Gay-Lay were so weak that they could get no further than two or three yards from the cave.

Schneider and Aschenbrenner could still hear faint cries for help from above. They made one last attempt to reach their friends but the snow was too deep and they were too exhausted. So ended the most spectacular and long-drawn-out tragedy to date in the history of mountaineering with four Germans and six Sherpas dead. It wasn't until the summer of 1974 that a similar very high-altitude tragedy occurred, when fifteen people, caught in another savage storm on comparatively easy ground, died in the Soviet Pamirs. The pattern was to be repeated on K2 in 1986, when seven climbers were caught high on the mountain by a prolonged storm. The lesson, if any, is the importance of struggling down from great heights at all costs, as fast as possible. This was why Aschenbrenner and Schneider survived in 1934 while the others died. Could the two survivors have helped the others down? There are no easy decisions taken at altitude in a state of exhaustion in a maelstrom. Another two days of fine weather and the Germans' ascent would probably have been a glorious success, acclaimed for the soundness of its planning and elegance of execution. Such is the hair's breadth between success and tragedy in mountaineering, a pattern that recurs throughout its story.

There was a delay of three years before the next German expedition set out for Nanga Parbat, but in 1936 Paul Bauer, with just three companions, returned to the Kangchenjunga region to make the first ascent of the steep and beautiful Siniolchu (6889m/22,602ft). Once again, it was an expedition ahead of its time, tackling technically difficult climbing with a small team. They had the help of porters to the glacier at the foot of the mountain, but from there they made an alpine-style push with a high bivouac and two of them, Karl Wien and Adolf Göttner, reached the summit.

The 1937 expedition to Nanga Parbat was built on sound foundations. Karl Wien was the leader, with two companions from Siniolchu, Göttner and Hepp, Hans Hartmann, with whom he had been to the high point on Kangchenjunga in 1931, Mülritter, one of the survivors of the 1934 Nanga Parbat expedition, and a newcomer, Martin Pfeffer who had a formidable alpine record. They followed the route of the previous German expeditions and, in spite of heavy snowfalls, established their Camp 4 as an Advance Base at the foot of Rakhiot Peak by 11th June. On the night of 15th June, seven Germans, which included the entire climbing party, and nine Sherpas were concentrated in the camp for the final assault, when a huge avalanche off the side of Rakhiot Peak engulfed them, destroying the camp and killing everyone in it.

Two disasters in succession on Nanga Parbat at a time when Nazi Germany was becoming increasingly expansionist and mobilising every aspect of its society in the strident call of nationalism. How far were the Germans just unlucky? Or could these two accidents be linked to a fanaticism that encouraged them to take undue risks? There was undoubtedly a sense of national awareness in the Germans that was not present amongst British climbers. Hartmann started his expedition diary in 1937 with a poem:

> Let cold and pain do what they will,
> One binding oath I will fulfil
> Which burns like fire brands
> Through sword and heart and hands –
> Whate'er fate decrees,
> Germany, I stand by thee!

I feel I must begin with these words of Flex which I heard for the first time on 11th November 1934 at the memorial service for those who lost their lives on Nanga Parbat that year. They occurred in the Sports Führer's speech and have since remained in the forefront of my mind.

German climbers were undoubtedly moved by national pride and had a sense of discipline, bordering on the professionalism decried by British climbers of the time, but their drive to climb, to find new routes, to push the limits, came from the same personal motivation that can be recognised in any modern climber. Paul Bauer and the other German climbers grieved over the loss of friends as deeply as any of the 1924 team over the loss of Mallory and Irvine. But while losses caused the British culture to question whether climbing was worth it, the Germans felt this was a price that had to be paid. There was something glorious about the climber who had died for his country and for his sport.

The German expedition to Nanga Parbat the very next year was the most flamboyant and obvious statement of national will. No expense was spared. Paul Bauer was the leader of the strongest, best equipped expedition yet. They were supported with air drops on the mountain by a three-engined Junkers 52 and were using radio. But this was of no avail against bad weather and the expedition was forced to retreat after establishing Camp 7 below the Silver Saddle.

There is no solid evidence that the resumption of the British interest in Everest was kindled by the German expeditions to Kangchenjunga, but in March 1931 the Mount Everest Committee was reconstituted and negotiations were opened once more with the Indian and Tibetan governments. Neither was keen, but it is possible that Indian Government officials were influenced by the growing pressure from other countries, particularly Germany and, as Younghusband put it: 'Attention should be called to the fact that this country should have a priority in view, among other things, that her countrymen lay at or near the top.'

The British gained permission for 1933. Although there was some fresh blood, from a post-war generation of climbers with an alpine background, the structure of the organisation was very much the same, with the same personalities in charge of the Everest Committee. There was also the influence of British attitudes to climbing in the Alps which decried the extreme technical climbing on ice and rock undertaken by the climbers from central Europe. The climbing team chosen for 1933 was perhaps stronger in technique than those of the 'twenties but it did not have the cohesiveness or drive of the German expeditions.

Nine years had passed since the 1924 expedition, so there would be little continuity. Norton and Geoffrey Bruce, either of whom would have been an obvious choice as leader, could not get away. Finch, even if he had been acceptable, had almost given up climbing. Odell was invited but was forced to drop out and, in the end, only Colin Crawford, who had been with the 1922 expedition, and E.O. Shebbeare (1924) were able to join. There were not many climbers around with a Himalayan background. Frank Smythe was perhaps the most experienced from his part in the 1930

Kangchenjunga expedition and in leading the successful expedition to Kamet (7756m/25,447ft), the highest peak to be climbed at that time. He was, however, slightly suspect in the eyes of the establishment, because, as a popular writer, he earned a living from mountaineering. He also had a reputation for irritability and impatience. In the end the Committee took a safe political course, appointing Hugh Ruttledge, a civil servant in the government of India, who was more a trekker than climber, as expedition leader.

His team had some talented climbers. Eric Shipton was a coffee planter from Kenya who had made his mark on the mountains of East Africa and gone to the summit of Kamet with Smythe, while Raymond Greene, the expedition doctor, and Captain E.St J. Birnie had made the second ascent. Hugo Boustead also had some Himalayan experience, while Jack Longland was the hero of Clogwyn Du'r Arddu West Buttress and Laurence Wager, another newcomer, had climbed in the Alps with Longland and been expeditioning in Greenland.

They set out earlier than previous expeditions, leaving Darjeeling at the end of February. They used the same tactics as in 1924 but the weather was constantly bad with high winds and heavy snowfall and they made little progress. The organisational structure of the expedition could not have helped, with Ruttledge, the leader, and Shebbeare, his deputy, being the least experienced climbers. As a result, the unspoken leadership seems to have fallen on the two soldiers, Birnie and Boustead, who organised the Sherpas until, that is, Birnie turned back with a group of Sherpas because he considered conditions were too bad for them to go on. Wyn Harris, who had no previous Himalayan experience, was strongly opposed to the retreat and the disagreement turned into a full scale row back on the North Col, with Ruttledge having to stagger up to settle the dispute.

They never tried to use oxygen, partly because of the difficulty of getting sufficient supplies in place to use it effectively, but largely because the majority had little sympathy with its use. In this respect the lessons of 1922 and 1924 were ignored. When finally there was a break in the weather in the latter part of May, the attempts lacked co-ordination and, although they managed to place a higher top camp, they got no further than Norton had in 1924, with Wyn Harris and Wager reaching the same spot in a first attempt and Smythe, on his own, in a second, after Shipton had been forced to turn back. On a slab below the First Step Wager found an ice-axe which must have belonged to Mallory or Irvine.

Because the Everest Committee had managed to get permission for 1935 and 1936, but had insufficient time to organise a full-scale expedition to Everest in 1935, Shipton took out a small reconnaissance expedition, which was an excuse to carry out the kind of exploratory lightweight mountain travel he most enjoyed. The previous year he and Bill Tilman, his climbing partner from East Africa, had tried to find a way into the Inner Sanctuary of Nanda Devi with the help of just three Sherpas. They travelled light, ate local food and enjoyed the freedom from the trappings of a formal expedition. The 1935 expedition developed into a magnificent peak-bagging jamboree with twenty-six peaks of over 6100m(20,000ft) being climbed. They even made an attempt on Everest itself but only reached the North Col. Several of the team, including Tilman, were sick, the weather was unsettled, with deep snow impeding progress, so they abandoned the attempt. This expedition was an indicator of Shipton's strength and weakness as an expedition leader. He was essentially a mountain traveller and in his restless urge to explore would never have the single-minded drive of the goal-orientated climber to solve a major mountaineering problem. One of their young Sherpas on his first expedition was called Tenzing; nobody at that stage could have predicted his future career.

And so to 1936. Both the leadership and the administration of the expedition were already being questioned, particularly by the younger members of the 1933 expedition. Longland, Wyn Harris and Wager favoured a change of leadership and espoused the cause of Colin Crawford, while Shipton and Smythe, who carried more weight, favoured Ruttledge. There was manœuvring within the Committee, a lot of lobbying, and conservatism had its way with Ruttledge in charge once more. In the aftermath Ruttledge refused to take Crawford; Longland withdrew on principle and Wager dropped out for career reasons. Two seemingly obvious contenders were barely considered, Odell being overlooked because of his age and Tilman because he had had problems with the altitude the year before on the reconnaissance to Everest. In the event, neither the leadership nor composition of the expedition made much difference, for it was a particularly bad season, with the monsoon arriving so early they failed even to reach the North Col.

That same year the French made their first serious attempt on an 8000m peak. They chose Gasherbrum I (8068m/26,470ft), also known as Hidden Peak. It was a compact but strong team led by Henri de Ségogne, with seven climbers and two scientists, of whom Marcel Ichac, who was to go on to Annapurna in 1950, and Pierre Allain, inventor of the specialist rock shoe, were members. They had a Sherpa team of thirty-five, more than many Everest expeditions, but they also were caught by the early monsoon and only reached 7070m, though this appeared to be above the main difficulties. Had they had better luck with the weather that year, they might well have been successful.

Had Bauer's Kangchenjunga teams or Willy Merkl's Nanga Parbat expeditions been on Everest, would they have stood a better chance of success or simply a higher chance of accident? I suspect that they might well have succeeded where the British failed. Their greatest strength, particularly of Bauer on Kangchenjunga, was the cohesive quality of the team, combined with the fact that Bauer, as leader, was fully capable of climbing with the best of his team and had their complete respect and loyalty. In addition they had that extra focus, nurtured on steep walls in the Alps, which could have made that bit of difference.

But they also failed to reach their summits. There seemed to be an invisible barrier, be it psychological, physiological, logistical or probably a combination of all three, that stopped climbers from attaining the elusive goal of an 8000m summit.

CHAPTER NINE

COULD WE HAVE MADE IT?

*Himalayan attempts to the outbreak of the
Second World War*

•

Charles Houston had his seventy-eighth birthday at the Nanga Parbat Base
Camp, when we made our pilgrimage to the site of Mummery's last
climb in the summer of 1990. He is a compact, tough American with a
twinkle in his eye and a sharp, but essentially kind, sense of humour. He is
also one of a small surviving handful of mountaineers who took an active
part in pre-war Himalayan climbing. His first climb was in 1924:

> I have a memory so vivid it is almost real: far below in utter silence I see the scarce
> twinkling lights of Chamonix. Cold pre-dawn air stings my nose. Warm in my belly
> is the midnight hot chocolate, the hard bread with honey. I stumble along in the
> deceptive shadows cast by my guide's candle lantern, which smells of hot smoky wax,
> all of me tingling with the excitement of night and adventure. It is my first climb. I
> am twelve, intoxicated to be living Geoffrey Winthrop Young's *On High Hills*.

*The young Charles Houston on the Mer de Glace in 1925. The moving spirit of the 1936 Nanda
Devi expedition, he went on to lead two American K2 expeditions before and after the Second
World War.*

Houston was the son of a successful lawyer who enjoyed the mountains and could afford to take his family to Europe to go walking in the Alps. Charlie studied medicine at the Columbia University Medical School, and continued climbing in both Europe and America. He went to Alaska in 1934 to make the first ascent of Mount Foraker, where he learnt a great deal about self-sufficiency and climbing in a big mountain environment without the help of porters. With Bradford Washburn as his mentor, he started building the close-knit team of friends who were to accompany him on his expeditions to the Himalaya.

Houston had a very special drive and was the catalyst that made a series of bold ventures possible. Still at Harvard, he and his friends were already planning their first Himalayan expedition and chose the East Spur of Kangchenjunga as their objective. They knew little about the Himalaya and as there was no suitable gear available in the States, Loomis, one of their group, was dispatched to England in February 1936 to equip the expedition and learn what he could. He met Shipton and Tilman at the Alpine Club, and they, in the nicest way, suggested that the East Ridge of Kangchenjunga might be too much for four undergraduates without Himalayan experience. This inspired Loomis to think of strengthening the team with some British experts. Houston remembered: 'Loomis cabled me about this – I was the de facto organiser – and I said, "Well let's invite them." And looking back on it, it's really pretty precocious for four college kids in the United States to invite the cream of British mountaineering to go on an expedition with them.'

Shipton was already committed to Everest, but Tilman and Odell had been left out, so Houston invited them, together with Graham Brown, who had been on the first ascent of Mount Foraker, and Peter Lloyd who had a strong alpine background. Since it seemed very possible they would be refused permission for Kangchenjunga, Tilman suggested they chose Nanda Devi (25,645ft/7816m) as an alternative. He and Shipton had penetrated its Inner Sanctuary in 1934.

The expedition had a delightfully casual quality that was distinctly modern. There was no formal leader; they travelled out in dribs and drabs, Tilman going first with part of the expedition gear and food. Fighting a forlorn battle for Kangchenjunga but finally settling for Nanda Devi, he commented wrily: 'If the pen is mightier than the sword, the type-writer is mightier than the ice axe. All Himalayan expeditions should carry one, even if it means leaving their ice axes behind.'

The Anglo-American 1936 Nanda Devi party, small, informal and harmonious. L to r: Tilman, Loomis, Graham Brown, Houston, Lloyd, Odell, Emmons, Adams Carter.

Having obtained permission for Nanda Devi he went off trekking in Sikkim, to put himself 'well beyond the reach of any cables', before returning to Darjeeling in mid–May to meet up with Loomis and carry what gear they had into the Sanctuary. One has the feeling that Tilman was making the most of the time when the team was still of minimum size. He writes with relish that, 'the party consisted of two Sherpas, a 10lb Cheddar cheese and ourselves'.

The rest of the team assembled spasmodically, with Odell going off to Simla to collect some scientific instruments and Ad Carter coming direct from Shanghai. It was early July 1936, and the height of the monsoon which had arrived early, before they were ready to ascend the Rishi Gorge. It took them a month just to ferry their gear up the gorge and establish a Base Camp. They then laid siege to the mountain.

They had no fixed ropes and only six Sherpas, who were the leftovers from the British Everest expedition, and whose performance was disappointing. By far the best was Pasang Kikuli, who was one of the survivors of Merkl's Nanga Parbat expedition, but he became snow blind and was forced to drop out before the top camps were established. At this time British climbers rarely carried any loads; they certainly didn't on Everest, leaving this to the Sherpas. The Americans, on the other hand, and for that matter Graham Brown, were used to humping their own loads in Alaska, while Tilman in his climbs in Africa and more recent explorations in the Himalaya always preferred to be self-sufficient. They had all been

H. W. Tilman, Pasang Kikuli and Charles Houston. Tilman, who began his climbing in Kenya, had already explored the Nanda Devi Sanctuary with Eric Shipton, been a member of the British 1935 Everest reconnaissance, and explored into Sikkim before he reached the summit of Nanda Devi with Odell in 1936. He led a further Everest expedition in 1938 and was involved in the postwar exploration of the newly opened Nepal. But after the 'fifties he turned more to adventurous small boat sailing and was lost in the Southern Ocean in his seventy-ninth year.

carrying sixty-pound loads up the Rishi Gorge and ended doing all the load-carrying on the mountain for the upper camps.

The team worked well together, taking turns in front, ferrying up the mountain twenty-five days' food and fuel, and slowly pushing out the route in the face of monsoon weather. It was only at Camp 4 on 21st August that they felt the need of a formal leader to decide who should go for the summit. They elected Tilman by a secret written ballot and he in turn selected Odell and Houston as the fittest for the summit bid. It was a question of establishing one last high camp and then going for the top. They set out on 25th August, with Loomis, Lloyd and Tilman carrying their tentage and food to the top of a rock tower at around 23,000ft. It was steep ground, plastered in snow, and there were no obvious campsites. The three load-carriers dropped back while there was still time to return to the lower camp in daylight, leaving Odell and Houston to find a spot for the night.

Next day Tilman, Loomis and Lloyd descended to Camp 3 for some more loads. On the morning of the 27th, they were startled to hear a yodel, 'rather like the braying of an ass', from above. At first they thought it was a victory yell, then realised it was a call for help. They were just able to make out, 'Charlie is killed.' In a state of shock, they struggled up towards the high camp full of conjecture as to what had happened, only to find both climbers alive but Houston very weak and sick. The call that morning had been 'Charlie is ill.'

It was probably some corned beef they had eaten the previous night. Either just one bit was contaminated, or Odell had a cast iron stomach, but only Houston was affected with violent cramps, diarrhoea and sickness. There are few things so speedily debilitating, particularly at altitude where there is always the risk of dehydration. The previous day they had made a reconnaissance, climbing about 500ft to find a good site for the top camp, and had then pushed on over steep broken ground to a point where the angle began to ease with a snow ridge sweeping towards the summit. It had seemed in the bag.

Houston knew he should go down immediately and suggested Tilman should take his place, so that the summit bid could go on as planned, but they all accompanied him until they met up with Graham Brown and Ad Carter. Odell and Tilman then turned round and went back to the top camp. Next day they shifted it to the better site at 24,000ft and on 29th August went for the summit. There was some initial hard climbing, and they were very nearly involved in a wind slab avalanche that could have resulted in a tragedy as mysterious as that of Mallory and Irvine, but they pressed on and reached the top at three in the afternoon. Odell, the scientist, had brought a thermometer and recorded a mild 20°F as they basked on the highest summit by far that had been reached to date, before returning to their top camp.

It had been a wonderful expedition, close-knit and harmonious, with such a strong sense of shared achievement that they even planned to withhold the names of the summiters, feeling that this was a team effort. But the popular demand for heroes proved too great and they were coaxed into releasing the names of Odell and Tilman, whose achievement was especially remarkable in a year in which the British on Everest failed to reach even the North Col.

Like all too many climbers, Houston continued to have to juggle the demands of a career with expeditioning. Two years later, while still a medical student, he was given the chance to lead an American expedition to K2. The American Alpine Club had been trying to get permission for the world's second highest mountain for some time and received it for 1938 and 1939 from the government in India. They first offered the leadership to Fritz Wiessner, who had recently emigrated from Germany and had already made his mark as a mountaineer. He had also taken part in the 1932 Nanga Parbat expedition and had made a series of remarkable first American ascents, including the Devil's Tower in Wyoming and Mount Waddington in the Canadian Coastal Range. These two routes, one a rock climb the other a major mountaineering challenge, were the hardest climbs to have been completed in North America. He had the technical expertise and single-minded drive, combined with a high level of risk acceptance, that characterised the approach of central European climbers in the 'twenties and 'thirties. He was, however, in the throes of establishing his own business in the aftermath of the Recession and was unable to get away in 1938. So Houston, in view of his success on Nanda Devi, was invited to lead this expedition, very much on the understanding that it was to be just a reconnaissance, and that Wiessner would lead a more serious attempt the following year.

Unlike the British establishment, who retained firm control of every aspect of Everest expedition organisation, the American Alpine Club simply appointed a leader and left him to get on with it, something I am sure the expedition members welcomed. Charlie Houston picked his team with care. He was determined to keep it small – just six climbers, including the essential transport officer supplied by the British government, and six Sherpas. His first choice was an old friend, Bob Bates, who had been with him in Alaska. He also invited Bill House, a forester from New Hampshire who had been with Wiessner on Mount Waddington, Paul Petzoldt, a giant of a man from Wyoming with a pioneering background of winter expeditions in the Rockies, combined with a double traverse of the Matterhorn, and Dick Burdsall, the eldest at forty-two, who had reached the top of China's Minya Konka (7587m/24,892ft) in 1932. Houston selected his team as much for compatibility as climbing prowess – 'five Americans full of Kipling and eager for the adventure' – but it was a good strong team and although their declared aim was reconnaissance, there was never any doubt in their minds that they hoped to climb the mountain. Their liaison officer was Captain

Norman Streatfeild, who had been with the French on Hidden Peak, and was to become an integral member of this small group.

Like all pre-war expeditions, they started their approach march from Srinagar. They had porter strikes and river crossing adventures that plague expeditions to this day, and finally reached K2 on 12th June after a month of walking through wild, unspoilt country. They were faced with a formidable challenge. Since the earlier expeditions had failed to come up with an obvious route to the summit, they were going to have to start from scratch. They spent an intensive fortnight with forays towards the North-East Ridge, to the Abruzzi Spur and to the North-West Ridge, leading up from the Savoia Saddle, which they never managed to reach because of the steepness and hardness of the ice. At this stage it was not at all clear which route gave the best chance of success. The South-East Ridge, with its Abruzzi Spur, was very steep and seemed to have a serious shortage of campsites.

On 28th June, realising that they were running out of time, they had a conference and settled democratically on the Abruzzi Spur, even though Houston and Burdsall still favoured the North-East Ridge which looked less rocky, but was obviously long and complex. (In fact, its lower and middle parts were only climbed in 1977 by a Polish expedition and the final pyramid is still unclimbed.)

At first they despaired of finding campsites on the Abruzzi Spur, but Petzoldt and House persevered and discovered a pocket of snow, fully twenty feet across, which could take all their tents. This was the breakthrough and, from establishing their first camp, they slowly, systematically worked their way up the Spur, despite unsettled weather and continuous technical difficulty, using fixed rope, anchored by pitons only on a few of the steepest sections – tactics similar to those used in modern siege-style climbing.

Some friendly argument arose about the use of pitons. Houston, whose apprenticeship had been served under British alpine influence, deplored their use and had only included twenty in the expedition stock. But Petzoldt, who had developed his climbing in the Rockies with an attitude more akin to that of the central Europeans, had quietly purchased another fifty pitons in Paris on the way out. They were going to need them all and Houston's moral stance was torpedoed when Bates revealed that they had taken dynamite with them to Alaska to blow down the cornices on ridges. The bulk of their Himalayan equipment was based on that developed by the

British on Everest, with windproofs of Grenfell cloth, inner insulation from layers of light Shetland wool sweaters and lightly nailed, non-freezing leather boots. They also had comparatively light, double thickness down sleeping bags, and their Meade high-altitude tents were similar in design to the ones used on my first Himalayan expedition in 1960, except the poles were bamboo. Aluminium alloy had yet to be introduced.

They used a kerosene pressure stove, very like a Primus, for cooking and their food was modelled on the spartan rations espoused by Bill Tilman — pemmican, tea, chocolate and porridge. Despite, or maybe because of this, they had voracious appetites throughout the expedition, a tribute to the length of their acclimatisation period during the approach and reconnaissance. Petzoldt was the greatest eater of the team, a man of huge appetite and immense strength, though he was plagued with recurrent bouts of fever, which, fortunately, he managed to throw off every time.

It was on reaching a height of around 21,500ft that they evolved a system similar to the modern 'capsule' method of climbing. Burdsall had volunteered to go back to Base and help Streatfeild survey parts of the Baltoro and Godwin Austen Glaciers. This left the four younger climbers with the three best Sherpas, led by Pasang Kikuli, to force the Spur. They worked in pairs, one out in front, climbing from their top camp, the other pair and the three Sherpas ferrying supplies to the top camp, until they were ready to move and exchange lead and support roles.

They now had a spell of settled weather and steadily pushed the route out, weaving their way through rocky buttresses and ice chimneys. The crux was what has become known as House's Chimney. Here is his account of it:

> Ten feet from the base of the crack was a tooth of rock three feet high standing a foot away from the cliff. Bates cut large steps for his feet below this, tied himself firmly to it and passed my rope behind it. It was an excellent belay, but would be of little use to me when I got higher in the crack. Traversing from his perch to the crack was tricky. Once there, I was glad to drive a heavy piton in and loop my rope to it. This was the only crack that could be used for such a purpose for the first 50 feet.
>
> While Bates held my rope tight I rested, for the sides of the gash above were smooth and I would need all my strength. With feet and hands gripping both sides, I climbed up 20 feet to where the walls flared outward and became so smooth that I had to put my back against one and feet against the other to hitch myself.
>
> At this point I discovered that I had neglected to leave my crampons with Bates, for they were in my rucksack, pressing into my back and catching on the rock. This carelessness cost me dear, but after a while I was able to use feet and hands on both sides of the chimney. A little ledge 40 feet up gave me a timely rest, for any progress

under such conditions is exhausting. I remember spending precious strength trying to drive in another piton so I could loop my rope through it and slide down, but the metal only crumpled up after penetrating a half-inch of rock. I felt I was pretty close to my margin of safety, but there were no piton cracks and I thought anything would be better than climbing down without some protection from above.

Most climbers reaching House's Chimney today clip into the old fixed ropes that are festooned down it, and they are universally impressed by its steepness and difficulty. At the time it was a remarkable lead. By 19th July they had reached the top of the Abruzzi Spur, but were still below the great shoulder that is such a strong feature on this side of the mountain. All seven of them were at their sixth camp at about 23,294ft. Effectively they were on their own, for there is little that Burdsall and Streatfeild, with the remaining three Sherpas, could have done had there been an emergency high on the mountain.

They were very aware that the period of perfect weather they had enjoyed for several days must come to an end, and just how difficult a retreat would be in storm conditions, but the camps below them were well stocked. They decided to have one tentative attempt on the summit, which at least would confirm that the route was there. Houston observed:

> Our first objective had been the establishment of a safe and direct route to the summit. Our second objective far overshadowed the first – to bring the entire party home unscathed. We felt that in reaching the great snowfield below the summit cone we had well completed our first objective. Abruzzi Ridge, though far from an easy route, was a direct one and if discretion was used, a safe way to the summit.

Since Houston and Petzoldt had already made a reconnaissance of the route onto the final Pyramid, House and Bates agreed to support them, helping to establish a final camp at its foot, so that they could make their summit attempt. It was characteristic of them that they decided it would be unfair to ask the Sherpas to make this carry, in view of the altitude and difficulty of the climbing. The irrepressible and loyal Kikuli, however, persuaded Houston to let him go.

The extended period they had been working above Base Camp without a rest now took its toll. House and Bates felt obliged to turn back with Kikuli at 3.00 p.m., when they were just short of a steep ice traverse at around 24,700ft. Houston and Petzoldt ferried the loads across the traverse and camped just beyond, still below the crest of the shoulder. That night they discovered a dreadful omission – they had left the matches behind. Searching every pocket they came up with:

Four safety matches and five strike-anywhere matches, all of dubious value. The latter, brought all the way from New York, carefully dried in the sun at many of the lower camps, had persistently failed to function well above 20,000 feet, and only with extreme care and preparatory rubbings with grease did they even glow. The safety matches, on the other hand, were made in Kashmir and were very fragile.

Petzoldt struck the first one. It fizzled – and went out. I tried one of the safety matches. It broke off at the head. Petzoldt, in desperation, seized a strike-anywhere match and struck it almost casually. It burst into flame and the stove was lighted.

Next morning they made their push for the summit, but they were too far gone, the weather was showing signs of change and by the time they had reached the foot of the Pyramid, Houston was exhausted:

Every inch I gained in altitude was an effort. My legs were so weak I was forced to rest every five or six steps, and soon fatigue made me forget all danger from above. I struggled on – why I do not know, for it was foolish to try to gain a few more feet, and yet something within me drove me to go as high as I possibly could. Had I ever been so tired before? Would I be less tired with another day of acclimatisation at this altitude? Could Bob or Bill have done better?

Fifty-two years on, sitting in the meadow below Nanga Parbat, Houston was more sanguine:

Could we have made it? I think so, I think so. Petzhold was very strong. I not quite as strong, but we had no matches left. It would have been taking a giant risk. What puzzles me, even today, is why we didn't go back down to the next lower camp and then send the next team back up or go back ourselves. I'm not sure why we didn't do that – may be we were burnt out.

I'm quite sure they were! It's a moment in an expedition when there is an unspoken acknowlegement of exhaustion, of a loss of will to go on. They had pushed themselves to the limit on technically difficult ground that was unknown. They were the pioneers. In addition they had a strong safety ethos, developed from the traditional British approach and from their own roots in American climbing. There had been an element of the forlorn hope in Houston and Petzoldt's attempt, for they knew they really needed another higher camp. They therefore unanimously took the safe decision and returned a united and happy team.

Wiessner was already beginning to put the next attempt into place. All the signs were hopeful but the seeds of potential disaster were sown in the way his team was put together. For a start there was a very limited choice. He had wanted House and Petzoldt, but neither was available. House couldn't take a second year off work and, it seems, had doubts about joining Wiessner, while Petzoldt could not return to India. He had stayed on after the 1938 expedition, joined a sect and had got into a fist fight which resulted in his opponent's death. It had taken a lot of fast talking from the members of his team and the American Alpine Club to get him back to the United States without facing prosecution. Neither Bates nor Houston was invited but they, too, would have found it difficult to take extended leave again.

Unfortunately, the two most experienced climbers Wiessner invited, Al Lindley and Bestor Robinson, backed out at the last minute. Their withdrawal seems linked to an elusive feeling sometimes experienced about a companion. Both they and House had climbed successfully with Wiessner, but Lindley and Robinson had not been comfortable with him. How far this was the difference in background, the quality of foreignness that Wiessner must inevitably have had, or his forcefulness and single-minded drive, it is difficult to tell.

This left him with O. Eaton Cromwell, a wealthy forty-two-year-old who had climbed extensively in the Alps with guides. As the most experienced he became deputy leader, but he had only ever ventured on standard routes and was used to others taking all the decisions for him. The team was completed by two twenty-one-year-old Dartmouth students, Chappel Cranmer and George Sheldon, who had a few climbing seasons behind them and Dudley Wolfe, a forty-four-year-old wealthy socialite who had done some sailing and a bit of climbing, once again on classic easy routes in the Alps with at least two guides. He had also helped fund the expedition.

It was therefore with a very weak team that Wiessner set sail for India. A few days after the start of the voyage he received a radio message that some senior members of the Board of the American Alpine Club had chosen and funded an extra team member, Jack Durrance, a talented climber, about to start in medical school, who had worked as a guide in the Tetons on some of his vacations. Not only had Wiessner not been consulted about this addition to his team, but he apparently had doubts about the man which he made all too obvious when Durrance boarded the ship at Genoa.

But they were on their way and, at first, everything went smoothly, under their British transport officer, G. Trench. They had a strong Sherpa team of nine, led by Pasang Kikuli who had performed so well the year before. They set out much earlier than previous expeditions, and reached Rawalpindi on 14th April, giving themselves a fortnight's ski-ing at the Kashmir resort of Gulmarg to help their acclimatisation. The approach also went well, admittedly with the usual porter strike, but they all arrived at Base Camp on 31st May. In a letter back to a friend in the American Alpine

Durrance (left) meets Wiessner and Wolfe (right) at Genoa en route for K2.

Club, Wiessner wrote: 'They all are such a nice lot, taking everything from the easy side and hitting hard when necessary. It is fun to be a member of such a congenial group. I feel quite certain that they will do well on the mountain, and that I will have no difficulties whatsoever in the running of a careful, efficient and co-ordinated climb.'

But it was early days. Most approach marches pass off amicably. None of the inherent weaknesses of the group had been tested. Wiessner's planning was very methodical. With the knowledge gleaned from the 1938 expedition he was able to plan out his camps better. He intended to stock each one with three sleeping bags, air mattresses, stoves, fuel and food for two weeks. He spurned oxygen and radios however, explaining this later to the author, David Roberts: 'My ideal has always been free climbing. I hated mechanical means. I didn't even want walkie-talkies on the mountain.'

There seems to be a contradiction in this statement, for he was using siege tactics with fixed ropes anchored by pitons. As with all ethics, in the end it comes down to choosing rules which suit you, though, had he used a radio, the outcome might have been very different.

As they gained height on the mountain, establishing Camp 6 and almost reaching the site of Camp 7 above the top of the Spur on 5th July, the inexperience of the climbing team was becoming apparent. Everything depended on Wiessner's superb fitness and determination. He was out in front the whole time preserving the momentum of the climb through a series of violent storms, while his fellow team members were beginning to drop out from exhaustion or sickness. Sheldon had been forced to return to Base Camp with frostbite and the others were ferrying supplies between Camps 1 and 2 and on to a dump at the site of Camp 3, which Wiessner had been able to miss out, running the route straight through to Camp 4 at 21,000ft, just below House's Chimney.

He returned from his high point on 8th July to find that his companions were tired, pessimistic and already planning their return home, having ordered the porters to come to Base Camp on 23rd July. The expedition had become polarised between Wiessner, single-minded, superbly fit and optimistic, stimulated by the excitement of being out in front with the summit now seemingly within his grasp, and the others, tired and discouraged from the endless slog of ferrying loads, with little or no communication with their leader. Even if Wiessner had had some stronger lead climbers, I suspect he would still have stayed out in front. He was that kind of man, attracted by the stimulus of finding the route, and certain, probably quite correctly, that he would be quicker than anyone else. He also assumed, having made a good plan, which indeed it was, that it would be carried out by the rest of the team. This made no allowance for their lack of experience, enthusiasm, or the weakness of the group as a whole. It was not necessarily a Teutonic approach, as suggested by some of his critics. Paul Bauer on Kangchenjunga had been amongst the most accomplished climbers in the team, but had taken his turn in support and ensured, as leader, that his lines of communication were working. A siege climb, depending on a flow of supplies from camp to camp up a mountain, needs co-ordination and it has been shown time and again that an overall leader cannot carry out his role effectively from the front, especially when he has no radio communication with the rest of his team.

Wiessner described the arrangement he came to with his support climbers in an article in the *American Alpine Club Journal* immediately after the expedition: 'It having been agreed that Wolfe and myself, with some of the Sherpas, could stay on the mountain for somewhat longer, as we had ample provisions, the party being, meanwhile, divided into two groups – Durrance, Wolfe and myself on high, Cromwell and Trench at Camp 4 or lower, ready to go out with Sheldon and Cranmer on July 24th, even if we were still up on the mountain.'

With that agreed, Wiessner, Wolfe and Durrance, with seven Sherpas moved up to Camp 6 on 12th July. It was an ill-balanced team. Dudley Wolfe, enthusiastic and totally supportive of Wiessner, was not only inexperienced but very clumsy, needing constant supervision on the rope. It was like taking an awkward client on a guided climb. It was a responsibility that Durrance, who had guiding experience, was getting increasingly worried about. Durrance had been limited in what he could do by the fact that he had inadequate footwear. He had ordered a pair of high-altitude boots on his way through Europe, but they had failed to catch up with him. As a result he had set out with an old pair of inadequately nailed boots and suffered constantly from chilled feet. Even so, he had been the strongest, and certainly the most dedicated, of the support climbers up to this stage. But, like the others, his morale was now low; a series of hard carries had tired him, and he was suffering from insomnia. He was the last to reach Camp 6 that night. Even so, Durrance strongly advised Wolfe against going any higher. Dudley Wolfe inevitably appealed to Wiessner who sided with him, appreciating Wolfe's cheerful support and feeling that he was going much more strongly than Durrance. Wiessner also suspected that Durrance was jealous of Wolfe, clear signs of the way the expedition had divided into two camps.

The following day they set out to establish Camp 7 , the highest camp of the previous year. Wolfe's comment seemed justified when Durrance could go no further and was forced to turn back. That night Wiessner and Wolfe, Pasang Lama, Pasang Kitar and Tendrup, stayed at Camp 7, while the rest, including the Sirdar, Pasang Kikuli, went down to Camp 6 with instructions to make another carry the following day. But Durrance felt so ill next morning, with what seems to have been the symptoms of mild cerebral oedema, that he dropped back down to Camp 4 with Pasang Kikuli and three Sherpas, thus removing the only effective leader amongst the Sherpas. Sheldon and Trench, tired, ill and probably disillusioned, had already abandoned Camp 4, returning to Base Camp. Durrance struggled on down the mountain back to Base Camp with Kikuli, so that now the only Americans left on the mountain were Wiessner and Wolfe.

On the 14th, the same day that the lower part of the mountain was being evacuated, Wiessner, Wolfe and the three remaining Sherpas pressed on towards the crest of the shoulder to establish Camp 8 at a height of 25,300ft. Pasang Lama stayed with them, while Pasang Kitar and Tendrup descended to Camp 7 with instructions to make another carry the following day. It snowed, however, on the 15th and 16th and there was no movement on the mountain. The 17th dawned clear. They had been above the worst of the storm and the snowfall had been comparatively light. The summit, 3000ft (900m) above them, looked quite close and attainable. The view across to Broad Peak, still above them, and through Windy Gap to the Shaksgam valley, was magnificent. Wiessner felt well satisfied with his position. He seemed much better placed than Houston had been the previous year. He was in a higher camp, had the capacity to place another before making his summit bid, and had a string of fully stocked camps behind him.

They left at 9 a.m. with a tent, sleeping bags, food and fuel for seven days, but it was slow going through soft thigh-deep snow. At last they came to the bergschrund guarding the slopes of the summit Pyramid. The snow seemed bottomless and it took Wiessner two hours just to flounder up the twenty-foot slope across it. Both he and Pasang Lama were lithe and lightly built, but Dudley Wolfe was like a huge clumsy walrus and, although strong, had a poor power-to-weight ratio. It was too much for him. However hard he tried he could make no headway, so he abandoned the attempt and said he would wait for them back at Camp 8. The other two Sherpas, Pasang Kitar and Tendrup, should be coming up that day to keep him company.

Wiessner and Pasang Lama camped just beyond the bergschrund, but the following day shifted the camp to a better and higher site at the foot of a rock ridge at 26,050ft (7940m). They were poised for the summit. Wiessner felt fit and confident. The 19th dawned fine and they picked their way up a series of rocky buttresses to the side of the summit cone. Inevitably progress was slow and it was 6.30 in the evening before the difficulties seemed to relent and a traverse across a steep wall led to a snow gully rising towards the summit ridge. It was at this point (27,430ft/8365m) that Pasang Lama refused to go any further that night, saying he preferred to return to their camp and attempt the ice couloir immediately above it, which looked as if it would give an easier route onto the summit snow ridge. Wiessner did his best to persuade Pasang Lama to keep going through the night but without success. It is hardly surprising. Even the best Sherpas, and Pasang Lama was outstanding, had limited experience of steep, technically difficult climbing. In addition, pushing on through the night without head torches could have been fraught with risk. They could not know for certain that all the difficulties were over.

It was not an easy descent. They had to make a free abseil over an overhang and I wonder if the Sherpa had done anything like that before.

In the process of abseiling the rope became tangled in the spikes of their two pairs of crampons which were strapped to the back of his rucksack. In trying to free the rope, he unstrapped the crampons and dropped them. It was 2.30 a.m. before they got back to Camp 9. Wiessner wrote: 'Many times during that descent I regretted intensely that I had not insisted over that last short traverse.'

Miraculously, the weather held and they were able to laze through the following day in the sun-warmed tent, to make their second attempt on 21st July. They set out at 6 a.m., heading for the gully that skirted the sérac wall barring the route to the summit Pyramid. Not only must they have been tired, but because they did not have any crampons, Wiessner had to cut steps in the hard snow all the way up the gully. Their progress was too slow and they had no choice but to retreat. But Wiessner had not given up. He now resolved to drop back to Camp 8, restock their supplies, get some spare crampons, and return for another attempt.

They descended to Camp 8 the following morning, Wiessner leaving his sleeping bag at the top camp, but Pasang taking his with him. Had Pasang Lama decided he had had enough of this obsessive drive for the summit? They had now slept for four nights above 26,000ft (7925m), pushing themselves to the limit on two separate days, yet Wiessner was still convinced he could reach the top. It is a dangerous illusion that can affect people at altitude, particularly when the weather is good, the sun is hot and you are going down, rather than up.

Dudley Wolfe was relieved to see them when they reached Camp 8. The Sherpas had not returned and he had been on his own for five nights. Supplies were low so they had no choice but to go down to Camp 7. They set out that same afternoon. Wolfe, probably affected by the altitude, tripped over the rope, pulling them all off and they went hurtling down the slope. It was little short of a miracle that Wiessner managed to slow their fall with an ice axe brake and hold all three of them.

They reached Camp 7 late in the evening and found, to their consternation, that it was empty, with one tent damaged from the weight of snow that had settled on it and the food scattered untidily, but most serious of all, the spare sleeping bags and air mattresses had been removed. Dudley Wolfe had lost his sleeping bag in the fall, so they had to share Pasang Lama's between three. They had a bitterly cold, uncomfortable night and next morning resolved to retreat to the camp below, pick up provisions and sleeping bags and restart their ascent.

Can one surmise their states of mind at this stage? Wiessner, still obsessed with the summit, with that single-minded drive that can blank out reality and the condition of your companions; Wolfe, tired to the degree that all he wanted to do was lie down and sleep; Pasang Lama, probably the only one aware of the dangers, wanting to get back down to safety, but used to obeying and respecting the Sahibs who were always right. Wolfe stayed at the camp, using Pasang's sleeping bag and mattress while the other two went on down to get more supplies from Camp 6. Should the alarm bells have been ringing in Wiessner's mind? Perhaps, but they were living in a cloud-cuckoo land induced by lack of oxygen, summit obsession and a clear blue sky. There was no question in Wiessner's mind but that they should resume the assault. Yet it is most unlikely, given his deterioration from long exposure to altitude, that he could by now have made another attempt and probably would have failed even to regain his high point.

There was no-one at Camp 6, no sleeping bags, no mattresses. Baffled, raging about betrayal, increasingly exhausted, he descended through the camps to find each one stripped. They struggled down to Camp 2 that evening and could go no further. Wrapped in a tent, they shivered through the night and next day staggered to Base Camp, where Wiessner remonstrated with Tony Cromwell, his deputy leader, in a hoarse, angry whisper, having lost his voice, threatening legal action for what he felt was deliberate treachery. Cromwell angrily responded justifying his actions.

It was Tendrup and Pasang Kitar who had stripped the upper camps. On 17th July, instead of making the carry up to Camp 8 as ordered by Wiessner, they had retreated to Camp 4, where they were stopped by Pasang Kikuli and sent back up the mountain, to resume their support role. On 19th July, they reached Camp 6, where Phinsoo and Tsering had stayed, and the following day, the one on which Wiessner and Pasang Lama were resting at Camp 9, they went up to Camp 7. Once there they shouted up the mountain and, getting no reply, convinced themselves that an accident had occurred, that all three in the higher camps were dead, so took all the sleeping bags and did the same on their way past Camp 6, arriving at Base Camp on 23rd July just a day in front of Wiessner. Just why the lower camps were stripped is more obscure and was to be the subject of an acrimonious controversy after their return to the United States.

More important than any recrimination was the retrieval of Dudley Wolfe, waiting at Camp 7. Amazingly, Wiessner still did not comprehend how serious the situation was or how exhausted he was. He was still talking of having a few days rest, going back up the mountain, picking up Dudley Wolfe and making another attempt. Durrance, on the other hand, was very clear that this was a rescue operation. He set out with three Sherpas the very next morning and reached Camp 4 on the 26th, but he was still weak from his illness, felt the symptoms of pulmonary oedema returning and retired to Base Camp with the Sherpa Dawa, who was also ill, while the other two Sherpas, Pasang Kitar and Phinsoo pushed on up to Camp 6. On arriving at Base none of the other Americans was fit enough to go back on the mountain, and so Kikuli volunteered to go up with Tsering, setting out on the 28th to make a magnificent push straight through to Camp 6 in the day. The next morning they went up to Camp 7 to find Dudley Wolfe lying in his sleeping bag, conscious but very weak and incapable of cogent thought. The tent was a chaotic mess of food and his own body waste. He was too far gone, told them to come back the next day, and they, used to total obedience, took him at his word. They dropped to the lower camp but three of them, Pasang Kikuli, Kitar and Phinsoo, set out in a storm the following morning to bring him down. They were never seen again. Only Tsering, who had stayed in the camp, returned. In a lull in the storm, on 3rd August, Wiessner, now realising just how serious things were, tried to return to the mountain with Dawa and Tsering, but the weather worsened again and he was exhausted. On the 7th he abandoned the attempt, having got no higher than Camp 2.

Inevitably there was controversy after this tragedy and Wiessner was made a scapegoat. Kenneth Mason in his classic history of Himalayan climbing, *The Abode of Snow*, wrote: 'It is difficult to record in temperate language the folly of this enterprise. From 11 July until the end of the month each day added to the errors of judgement. The weather was never to blame.'

A committee of enquiry by the American Alpine Club came up with an inconclusive judgement, which disappointed Wiessner, but opinion generally combined with anti-German feelings of the time to condemn Wiessner and he resigned from the AAC. He never gave up climbing, though, continuing to play an important part in the development of American rock climbing, and becoming so far rehabilitated that he was later, and deservedly, made an honorary member of the American Alpine Club.

Wiessner, indisputably, was a superb technical climber and performer at high altitude. He also had an engaging personality and a wonderful enthusiasm for climbing which lasted into his eighties, but the quality of

Fritz Wiessner in later life, a brilliant climber and performer at altitude, but not the best leader for a siege-style attempt on a complicated route with a less able team.

his leadership on the K2 expedition must be questioned. It is no good having a brilliant logistic plan that has no relevance to the personalities or frailties of the team. The leader of a siege-style expedition, with groups of climbers scattered up the length of the mountain, must take responsibility for the enterprise as a whole and care for the welfare of each individual member.

I cannot help comparing the 1938 and 1939 expeditions. In each case there was a small group of climbers high on the mountain, with no-one else above Base Camp. The big difference was that in 1938 Houston's team was a mutually supporting group, who took care of their Sherpas, even refraining from using them to load-carry to their highest camp. (It was only after a very strong plea from Pasang Kikuli, that they allowed him to make that carry with the four Americans!) They had been self-sufficient throughout the climb, and therefore knew exactly what had been left at each camp. Taking into account that they had pioneered almost the entire Abruzzi Spur, their achievement was no less than that of Wiessner. The big difference was that they had been able to retreat in good order.

There had been a strong cross-fertilisation between American and British climbers on Nanda Devi and the 1938 British Everest expedition was to have the same philosophical approach as Houston's K2 expedition with the Everest Committee's appointment of Bill Tilman as its leader. This was fortuitous because the Committee were still reeling from the costs of the 1936 expedition and also because there was a sense of scepticism about the entire project among the climbing community and the public as a whole. The concept, therefore, of a lean expedition was attractive. The core of the team comprised Tilman, Smythe and Shipton, with Odell and Lloyd who had been with Tilman on Nanda Devi, Peter Oliver and Charles Warren as doctor. It was a compact, experienced and compatible team, organised on a tight budget of £2,360, and left to get on with it, with the minimum of interference from the Committee. The only controversial area was the question of food. Tilman's frugal diet of pemmican and porridge was to lead to near malnutrition on the mountain.

Nevertheless it was probably the strongest expedition so far to approach Everest. They set out early to give themselves plenty of time, leaving Gangtok on the Sikkim border on 3rd March, and reached the Rongbuk Base Camp by 6th April. Unfortunately, it was a particularly cold, windy spring and they had to retreat to the Kharta valley to await warmer weather. By the time they returned in early May, they were hit by bad weather. The monsoon had arrived unusually early. The snow slopes leading to the North

Col were so dangerous they were forced to find a route from the main Rongbuk Glacier up the west side. It was much steeper, but there was less danger of avalanche and less snow to wade through. Shipton and Smythe succeeded in establishing a top camp at 27,200ft (8291m) but the snow was so deep they abandoned the attempt.

This expedition, with its eight-man team and twelve high-altitude porters, was compact rather than lightweight, certainly bigger than Houston's K2 team. In fact, it had a similar number of effective climbing members as any of the previous Everest expeditions and, had they experienced better weather they might have had a very good chance of success. Although Tilman was sceptical about the benefits of oxygen, he did take four sets, and these were used to advantage on the climb. Some useful foundations were laid during this expedition, particularly in working with high-altitude Sherpas, the strongest of whom was Tenzing Norgay.

The 1930s also saw an increasing number of small expeditions to the lesser peaks. Shipton and Tilman, with Michael Spender and John Auden, had explored and mapped the Shaksgam region to the north of the Karakoram in 1937, Shipton returning in 1939 with a larger team to complete the survey. This was the type of mountaineering he enjoyed best. André Roch mounted a nineteenth-century-style expedition, taking two Grindelwald guides and a cartographer to the Garhwal to climb Dunagiri, whilst a Polish expedition climbed Dunagiri East. Most remarkable of all, though, was the ascent of Chomolhari (23,997ft/7314m) in Bhutan, by F. Spencer Chapman, a young member of the Indian Civil Service. He had seen the mountain on his way back from an official visit to Lhasa. In 1937 he went there with C.E. Crawford and three Sherpas, Nima Thondup, Pasang Lama and Pasang Kikuli, who was to lose his life on K2 in 1939. Just reaching the mountain was a challenge and the ascent by Spencer Chapman and Pasang Lama was a remarkable achievement.

With the clouds of war building up over Europe, a small German team, very different from the previous Nanga Parbat expeditions, investigated its huge Diamir Face. The team numbered four and included Peter Aufschnaiter and Heinrich Harrer, fresh from his success on the North Wall of the Eiger. They did not get much higher than Mummery had, but picked out a feasible route about which Aufschnaiter wrote:

> A team of mountaineers skilled and experienced in tackling ice and rock of this kind might prefer the Diamir Face to the Rakhiot side. A party of at least seven climbers would be required, as some would have to prepare the way in order to leave a reserve

for the final assault. The climbers would have to do a lot of load-carrying in addition, as few porters would be willing, or capable, of such steep and exposed rock and ice.

A prophesy fulfilled in 1962, when an expedition led by Karl Herrlig-koffer laid siege to the face. In 1939 the team was overtaken by the war and all four were interned by the British. Aufschnaiter and Harrer made their escape to undertake the greatest adventure of their lives – seven years in Tibet.

By 1939 the foundations of Himalayan climbing had been laid. The invisible barrier preventing success on an 8000m peak could be ascribed to bad luck with the weather. Wiessner had got very close, and it is very possible that Tilman's expedition to Everest would have been successful, given better weather. Certainly all approaches had been tried, from the highly organised siege-style expeditions to compact, small teams climbing alpine-style. The full gamut of bureaucratic control, free-spirited attempts, tunnel-visioned single-mindedness or selfless sacrifice had all been seen, while the Sherpas had developed from coolies to capable high-altitude performers. The Himalaya was awaiting an explosion of activity, that was delayed by the Second World War but which was to encompass its length and breadth with an exponential increase that is continuing to this day.

CHAPTER TEN

THE LAST OF THE CLASSIC LINES

Post-war alpinism in Europe

•

The technology for war led in peace to the development of alloys for lightweight karabiners, to nylon for ropes that were stronger and easier to handle, to moulded rubber boot soles, dehydrated foods and much more. But the social changes were to have an even greater effect on every aspect of our lives, leading, in the case of climbing, to its spreading far beyond the bounds of the comfortably off middle class. This development had started in Britain before the war, particularly in the industrial towns around the Peak and up on the Clyde. The gritstone of Stanage Edge, Laddow and Kinder Scout had offered release from long hours in the factories or, during the depression, a change from the dole queues. There had been confrontations with possessive landowners that led to the mass trespass on Kinder Scout. But working a six-day week made it difficult to get beyond the crags within easy striking distance of home. Take Bill Peascod, a young miner from Workington.

> I had been on night shift. When I came out of the pit, up into God's real air, the morning was so beautiful I couldn't bear to go to bed. I cycled home, had a meal, then my bath, where my father and I always bathed – in a tub in front of the fire; got dressed and onto my old broken down bike that my father had bought me for five shillings and I set out – towards the sun.
> On that day, at seventeen years of age, I discovered Lakeland . . . it was a revelation. All my life I'd lived within fifteen miles of the Buttermere Valley. I had never seen it or thought about it or even considered going to it. Like London or Mars, I knew it existed. But there had never been any point in going to find out where . . . my discovery of Western Lakeland set my senses in a whirl.

He went on to make a series of fine first ascents in West Cumberland and became a member of the Fell and Rock Climbing Club, but there was no question of travelling further than the Lakeland Fells. The introduction of a five-day week after the Second World War and the improvement in wages opened up a wider prospect.

Joe Brown was born in Manchester in 1930, the youngest of a family of seven. His father died when he was six months old and his mother was left to bring up the entire family at a time when there was little or no social security, and she was too proud to take it anyway. He started his climbing exploring the old mine shafts at Alderley Edge, then ventured further into gritstone quarries and onto the Edges, in the words of Tom Patey's famous ballad, 'He'd nowt but pluck, beginners luck and his mother's washing line'.

Climbing was a process of self-discovery, going on camping trips to the Lake District and Scotland in summer and winter, with equally hard-up, like-minded youngsters, hitch-hiking and walking or taking an occasional bus ride, in an ever expanding adventure.

There were many lads of a similar background to Joe, but he had a special talent. He began to attempt new routes on gritstone, tackling rock that was steeper and technically more difficult than anything tried before. His first major routes were on Froggatt, a gritstone edge near Sheffield, and in 1948 they included Brown's Eliminate, a smooth, seemingly holdless, slab of rock. Others followed, the Right and Left Unconquerable on Stanage, two steep bulging cracks which had turned back some of the best climbers of the time. He then turned his attention to Wales, to the steep cliffs of the Llanberis Pass and the dark walls of Clogwyn Du'r Arddu.

The fruits of technology took a while to filter through into austerity post-war Britain. Gym shoes were still worn on difficult rock. The cleated rubber sole did not appear until the late 'forties. Nylon rope had been introduced but there was still plenty of hemp around. My own first rope in 1951 was hemp. Protection was rudimentary, with the climber carrying two or three hemp slings round his neck, which he placed over rocky spikes or threaded behind jammed chockstones. It was a period when it was most inadvisable for the leader to fall. By 1952 practically everyone was climbing on nylon rope and carried half a dozen or so nylon slings – quarter weight to squeeze behind tiny rock flakes for purely psychological protection, three-quarter weight and full weight slings to put round large spikes.

Joe Brown's routes were all the more remarkable when one considers the strong British ethic against the use of pitons. But from an early stage he saw the value of chockstones, carrying a selection of pebbles in his pocket to jam in cracks and use as running belays, a technique that the majority of the climbing world was slow to pick up. I climbed with Joe for the first time in 1962, making the first ascent of Tramgo, on Castell Cidwm, up a continuously overhanging prow of rock. He courteously let me try leading,

Joe Brown on the first ascent of Tramgo, Castell Cidwm. Inset, Doug Belshaw, Nat Allen and Joe Brown after the first ascent of the Corner on Clogwyn Du'r Arddu.

but I retreated after struggling up a few feet. He then slowly drifted up it, inserting chockstones with an ingenuity that I had never dreamt of.

As the number of climbers in Britain increased, so did the local clubs, formed by people who climbed together and enjoyed meeting in the pub mid-week. The Valkyrie Club, which Joe Brown joined, had started off as a cycle club. It lasted a few years and gently faded away to be replaced by the legendary Rock and Ice, a casual grouping of working-class lads from both sides of the Peak.

Don Whillans came on the scene in 1951. Four years younger than Joe, he was an apprentice plumber from Salford. He quickly grasped the rudiments of climbing and very soon emerged as a peer to Joe Brown. They formed one of the strongest partnerships in British climbing history, yet were very different in character. Joe has a whimsical, easy-going manner that conceals a strong competitive drive, while Don, short in stature but powerfully muscled, had a much harder edge. With a quick, acerbic sense of humour, he tended to be dogmatic and developed a reputation as a fighter. Their styles of climbing mirrored their personalities. Joe was prolific in making new routes and had an eye for a subtle line up a crag, while Don

A youthful Don Whillans at Stoney Middleton, before he met up with Joe Brown and forged one of the most famous partnerships in British rock climbing.

19 (previous page): Ed Webster on the world's loftiest Tyrolean traverse high on the Kangshung Face of Everest. After the four-man team made a new alpine-style route up this sheer East Face, Stephen Venables completed the climb alone to the summit without oxygen.

20 (above left): Catherine Destivelle, outstanding rock athlete who turned her back on sport climbing and soloed a new route on the West Face of the Dru. 21 (left): Wanda Rutkiewicz, first European woman to climb Everest, and first woman to climb K2, has led many Polish expeditions to the Himalaya. 22 (top right): For two decades Reinhold Messner pushed back the boundaries of the possible in both climbing style and altitude survival. 23 (above): Tomo Česen whose solo first ascents of the North Face of Jannu and the South Face of Lhotse point the way forward for extreme alpine-style climbing in the 'nineties.

24 (facing): The North Face of Jannu.

25 (second double spread back): The notorious South Face of Lhotse. Messner called this a route for the twenty-first century, Kukuczka died on it, and it was soloed by Tomo Česen in 1990, climbing mostly at night to avoid rockfall.

26 (previous double spread): The South Ridge of Kunyang Kish, one of the Karakoram's challenges taken up by Andrzej Zawada's Polish team in 1971. The mountain was not climbed again until 1988.

27 (above): An unclimbed Himalayan challenge, the West Face of Makalu, lying between the left-hand skyline (line in part of the 1955 French first ascent) and the West Ridge (toward the camera). The difficulties are on the headwall below the 8481m summit.

favoured natural lines that were steep, obvious and hard. His climbs have stood the test of time. Sentinel Crack on Chatsworth Edge, a brutal overhanging off-width crack line through a roof, Extol on Dove Crag in the Lake District, or Slanting Slab on Cloggy have all maintained a reputation for seriousness.

It was a partnership of convenience that never extended into friendship off the crag, yet between them Joe and Don made the greatest advances in technique of any Britons to date. It was ten years or more before some of their routes were repeated and not until the early 'sixties that a fresh generation of climbers were putting up new routes of a similar standard and beyond.

Whillans had his first alpine season in 1952. It meant foregoing trips to North Wales to pick off any remaining lines on Clogwyn Du'r Arddu, for he had to save every penny throughout the year for just one short holiday, his first ever abroad. It was that summer that Joe Brown climbed Cenotaph Corner, the great square-cut corner of Dinas Cromlech, the most obvious feature in the Llanberis valley. In doing so he showed a level of pragmatism, using two pitons on the final smooth corner that had defeated an earlier attempt (when he had pounded in five with a slater's hammer and then dropped the hammer onto the head of his second, whose thick skull fortunately survived the onslaught). When Don heard of the successful ascent, he commented, 'It'd better be worth it in t'Alps.'

It was. That first season, under the tutelage of Don Cowan, a member of the Rock and Ice who had already had half a dozen seasons, they tackled some of the classics, routes like the Ryan/Lochmatter route on the Aiguille du Plan, and Don was hooked on greater mountaineering. This was always to be his first priority.

A larger team, which included Joe, went to the Alps in 1953, driving to Chamonix on motor bikes and staying in the Biollay campsite, the place that was to become the focal point for British climbers in the next few years. At the same time the conservatism of the Alpine Club was being challenged by an independent body, the Alpine Climbing Group. Formed to revitalise British alpinism, they were tackling the difficult rock and mixed routes in the Mont Blanc massif that their predecessors had tended to deride.

In France things were also moving. The pre-war advances in climbing had mainly derived from Germany, Austria and Italy, while French climbers had adopted a slightly more conservative stance, opposing the use of pitons and artificial aids. Many of them came from Paris, where the sandstone pinnacles of Fontainebleau had a record of free, pitonless climbing very similar to that encouraged in Britain. Pierre Allain, who invented the specialist climbing shoe which took his initials, had put up a series of demanding rock routes around Chamonix. These were essentially free climbs, all the more impressive, considering he just used a hemp rope, a couple of slings, nailed boots (with PAs for the hardest pitches) and an ice axe. His equipment was still not very different from that of Mummery, who had used tennis shoes on the first ascent of the Grépon. One of Allain's finest routes was the North Face of the Petit Dru, up the side of the magnificent rock pinnacle that is supreme of all the rock towers around Chamonix. The route ascends a series of steep grooves and corners, often gummed with ice in a bad season and, although not as long and remote as the North Wall of the Grandes Jorasses, still a major challenge. But looking down on the sheer smooth walls of the West Face, he had commented:

> On the right, one's gaze plunges into the abysms of the West Face. Here is absolute verticality, broken only, from time to time, by enormous overhangs; over fifty or a hundred metres, immense slabs of protogine present a smooth faultless surface, the very model of the impossible. Alpinism here loses its rights; only embedded rungs or some such device would enable one to win through; and that would no longer be Alpinism but a job of work on the mountain. Treating it in that spirit, everything is feasible – even an internal railway on a spiral ramp.

It was a statement of ridicule not dissimilar to those of Colonel Strutt, but it touches on a fundamental question, the conflict between the purist, who is happy to leave stretches of rock unclimbed, and the ambitious climber who wants to venture onto new ground and is ready to use artificial techniques to get there. There have been arguments about climbing ethics throughout the development of our sport. At one stage the use of crampons was considered cheating. There had always been a powerful lobby against the use of pitons and this had not been confined to Britain and France, since Paul Preuss had also opposed their use and the Saxon climbers had evolved a strong climbing ethic on their sandstone towers. But the desire to step into the unknown is strong, an ambition inspired both by the spirit of discovery and also of competition, of wanting to make a mark, to be first. This had led to the extensive use of pitons in the Eastern Alps and the same approach was now to be used in the Mont Blanc massif.

With the end of the Second World War the young French climbers, like those from Britain, wanted to tackle the big north walls climbed by the Germans and Italians and were now prepared to try out the techniques dismissed by the pre-war generation. The West Face of the Petit Dru, so visible from Chamonix and seemingly so invincible, was a natural challenge. There had been attempts in 1939 and in 1945, but these early efforts barely made an inroad. The first serious attempt was made in 1949 by Marcel Schatz and Jean Couzy, two of the most brilliant French mountaineers of the immediate post-war era, and Georges Livanos and Robert Gabriel, who had been stretching their limits on Dolomite limestone.

The next year saw the start of Guido Magnone's campaign. He had discovered the method and the men he needed on the smooth bulging limestone cliff of Le Saussois, south-east of Paris. Le Saussois lent itself to artificial climbing techniques and it was here that the French developed their aid climbing, drifting away from the strong free climbing ethic established at Fontainebleau. Three of the best climbers were a high-spirited trio, Lucien Berardini, Adrien Dagory and Marcel Lainé, who had already

Guido Magnone (right) and his team-mates, Marcel Lainé, Adrien Dagory and Lucien Berardini who took six attempts to master one of the hardest challenges of the time in the Alps, the West Face of the Petit Dru.

been thinking of trying the West Face of the Dru. Magnone joined them and seems to have provided a driving force within the group. They refined their aid climbing techniques, planned their attempt and kept it a secret from any potential competition.

They made four attempts in the summer of 1950, each time getting a little higher. On their third attempt they met with some competition, a team from Lyons, which included Gilbert Vignes and Louis Dubost. The lower part of the route crept over a series of huge interlocking blocks that felt as if the dislodgement of a single capstone could bring the entire edifice down on them. Beyond it became even harder, up steep or overhanging cracks and corners. Shared risk and discomfort united the two teams after initial mutual suspicion, and this unity was further strengthened when they had to cope with a series of violent thunderstorms, which eventually forced an epic retreat. They joined forces again in early August with Vignes and Dubost climbing with Berardini and Dagory, since Magnone and Lainé had to return to work in Paris. Magnone could have been forgiven for feeling relieved when another storm cut short their attempt. Also, at the end of the summer, the middle section of the route that they had so painfully worked out was swept away by a massive rockfall that carved a huge scar out of the centre of the face.

They returned in 1951, though Magnone had to stand down once again, having badly sprained his ankle while training on the ice of the Bossons Glacier, but the attempt was quickly abandoned for the ledges were piled high with terrifyingly loose blocks, the debris of the rockfall. That winter Magnone went off to Patagonia and with Lionel Terray made the first ascent of Fitzroy, a magnificent obelisk of granite battered by some of the fiercest winds found anywhere in the world. This experience gave him an extra perspective on the challenge of the West Face of the Dru and the following summer it was the original team that set out on 1st July to try it yet again.

The lower part was terrifying. Magnone describes his progress:

Loose stones trickled like water over the slabs. Every step on this terrain set off interminable torrents of them, which poured with a frightening rumbling into the couloir. Bitter dust enveloped us, taking us by the throat and covering our faces with a greyish mask . . .

I tested a few holds which remained firm in my hands. With infinite precautions I tried to drive a wooden wedge into a large fissure. Suddenly I noticed with terror that its lips were widening with each blow of the hammer and that I was loosening a block of several tons. With all speed I doubled the assurance by a piton a few inches further up. On these two ludicrous supports, I tried to calm the violent thudding of my heart.

At last the rock became sounder; they had passed the rockfall, but the angle was much steeper. There were the relics of previous ascents, bits of tatty fixed rope and old electron ladders, that had to be handled with care. They had a bad first bivouac but a slightly better second one above their previous high point. They might have been using artificial techniques, but this was a very fundamental, and certainly very high-risk, adventure. Being early in the season, the backs of the cracks were running in water. They plunged into some deep, slime-filled chimneys and were soaked to the skin by the torrent pouring down them. Their third bivouac was below a threatening impending groove, which the following morning took them up to the great roof overhang that bars this part of the face. There was no way through, but they thought they could perhaps get round it by making a series of diagonal abseils across some steep slabs. They made a tentative attempt, but it was too daunting.

Dehydrated and exhausted after four days on the face, they decided to retreat, but that was no easy matter. The shoulder of the North Face was a mere fifteen metres above them, but the rock was blank and overhanging and they could make no progress. The line of descent was intimidating. The groove they had just climbed both overhung and was at a diagonal. There was a risk of ropes jamming, a frequent problem before the days of special abseiling devices, and the constant worry of an anchor coming out.

They were forced to bivouac on the way down, had to recross the area of the rockfall, something they had hoped to avoid, and weather a final storm, before reaching safety and the waiting French press. Like the Eiger, the Dru is a wonderful stage and the imagination of France had been inflamed by their adventure.

They allowed themselves just ten days to recuperate and wait for a spell of settled weather and then went back. They can't be blamed for missing out the section they had already climbed by scaling the North Face to the little notch they had tried to reach from their high point. From there a precarious abseil put them back on the route. Fresh, with plenty of rope and equipment, the situation no longer seemed quite so frightening. The climbing was not as hard as they had anticipated and the final push was almost an anticlimax. Another bivouac on the upper part of the face and they reached the top. Their ascent had shown the effectiveness of combining techniques developed on Dolomitic limestone with an expedition approach and for a short time the West Face of the Petit Dru had the reputation of being the most difficult climb in the Western Alps.

The British were still catching up. Don Whillans and Joe Brown resolved to spend the entire summer of 1954 in the Alps, which meant saving a lot of money and it is noticeable that there are no new routes in Wales or the Lake District ascribed to them for that year. They gave up smoking, cycled everywhere and limited their climbing to Derbyshire, but also used this period to polish up their artificial technique, putting up a series of peg routes on the limestone crags. They had saved about a hundred pounds each but had chosen one of the worst seasons for years.

The first few weeks were spent in the Chamonix campsite in soggy tents under dripping trees. But they snatched every available spell of fine weather and in the course of the summer made two ascents that brought them to the forefront of alpinism. They returned to the West Face of the Blaitière to make a new route on which their crack climbing technique, learned on Peak grit, came into its own. The route followed a series of cracks up the side of the scar left by a rockfall and gained them a reputation amongst continental climbers less accustomed to crack climbing without aid or protection. They went on to make the third ascent of the West Face of the Dru in unsettled weather, soaked by melt-water running down the cracks and afternoon storms. Their equipment was rudimentary – Pacamacs to keep them dry, and a route description translated by Donald Snell, the Chamonix climbing shop proprietor who has been a good friend to the British over the years.

When they got back to Chamonix, Joe commented how, when Hamish Nicol, who with Tom Bourdillon had made the first British ascent of the North Face of the Dru, congratulated them on doing something 'for the old country', he felt a pride in the underdogs from the campsite at last doing their stuff and catching up with continental alpinism. Joe went on:

> Louis Lachenal, one of France's foremost guides, came to pay his respects. He was dressed immaculately and was escorting a gorgeous girl. He found the party lounging on the ground in filth and squalor, like a band of brigands. Goodness knows what he thought of us. Homage from one so exalted in the mountaineering élite was indeed a surprise. After this the Chamonix guides came up to us in the street to shake our hands.

On getting back from the West Face of the Dru, Joe received an invitation to join Charles Evans on Kangchenjunga. It was Joe, easy-going and diplomatic, who tended to receive the invitations, while Don felt he was being left out in the cold. But they continued climbing together for a couple of years after Joe got back from Kangchenjunga, putting up some of their hardest routes to that time: Woubits on the Far Left Buttress of Clogwyn Du'r Arddu, a magnificent challenging climb; the Thing on Dinas Cromlech, a short but savage overhanging groove, followed by the Girdle on the same cliff, a wonderful devious route, picking its way across the great, and at that time blank, walls on either side of Cenotaph Corner. Then they drifted apart, Don becoming less interested in British rock and progressively attracted to the Alps and soon the further ranges, while Joe maintained his enthusiasm for pioneering on British crags, climbing with Pete Crew, one of the outstanding representatives of the next generation of climbers.

The great difference, perhaps, between Joe and Don was that Joe has used his supreme natural ability to the full, but never forced it. He regards climbing as a pastime to be enjoyed alongside a host of other activities. He has always been happy to sit back and let opportunity arrive, and it has. Don, on the other hand, seemed to feel he was owed opportunity, based on his ability. He told me as we sat below the North Wall of the Eiger in the summer of 1961, 'I'll meet any bugger half way, but don't expect me to go further.' It didn't make for an easy partnership.

Back in the Alps, the Petit Dru remained a focus of attention, for the most obvious line of all, the South-West Pillar that soared above the end of the Mer de Glace, was still unclimbed. It became the target of Walter Bonatti, who was to have such an impact on the development of alpinism in the 'fifties and the first half of the 'sixties. He also was a product of the post-war social explosion in mountaineering, son of an Italian factory worker, who learnt to climb on the crags around his home town of Bergamo. Bonatti had known what it is to be permanently hungry during the war. His mother died while he was still very young and his father believed he should learn to look after himself. In the words of his friend, Carlo Mauri: 'Each did their own thing. Living together, but leading independent lives. It wasn't a relationship of father and son, or of love; basically, it was a matter of "you're a man; I'm a man and we are together but let's live without emotion."'

Could this have shaped his approach to mountaineering? 'It is a reason for struggle and for self-conquest, for spiritual tempering and enjoyment in the ideal and magnificent surroundings of the mountains. The trials, the hardships, the privations with which an ascent of the peaks is always studded, become, for that very reason, valid tests which the mountaineer accepts to temper his powers and his character.'

Fun very rarely comes into Bonatti's vocabulary. From the beginning there is a driving intensity in his desire to test his own limits. Like Whillans, he dreamt of climbing the Walker Spur in his first alpine season. At the age of nineteen he was turned back on his first attempt, but succeeded a few days later with a team of four, which included Andrea Oggioni who was to be his most trusted climbing partner in the future. Other climbs followed, including the first ascent of the East Face of the Grand Capucin in 1951. Today this granite monolith is a high-level rock gymnasium which takes a few hours in 'sticky' rubber climbing shoes, a rack of 'quick-draws' and a line of linked bolt placements for abseil points on descent. It is difficult to appreciate the quality of challenge it offered in 1951. After one attempt in 1950 was repulsed by bad weather, Bonatti had no hesitation in using artficial techniques to complete the climb. Preuss's strictures were long forgotten. None of the big walls could have been climbed without pitons and Bonatti used over sixty in 450 metres of sheer or overhanging rock. But this in no way diminished the spirit of adventure:

> Towards evening, when I was trying to plant the nth piton in the vertical rock, the already insecure one to which I was suspended suddenly came out of the rock and fell into space. Clawing with my hand against the rock face, partly instinctively and partly by luck, I managed, a foot or two below, to catch hold of a little protuberance as I fell and I remained hanging with the tips of my fingers embedded in the stinging granite crystals.

Bonatti and his partner, Luciano Ghigo, were overtaken by storm, had a cold precarious bivouac and fought their way out over snow-plastered rocks.

Wanting to test himself to the full, Bonatti was naturally attracted to winter climbing. The mountains are empty and, with every ledge plastered in snow, the backs of cracks filled with ice, they assume a Himalayan scale. With Carlo Mauri, a warm-hearted, gregarious man from Lecco who was to become a close friend and climbing partner, he made the first winter ascent of the North Face of the Cima Ovest di Lavaredo, the climb put up by Riccardo Cassin and, at the time, thought to be one of the most committing routes in the Dolomites. As a result of these ascents, Bonatti was invited to join the Italian K2 expedition in 1954.

He had attempted the South-West Pillar of the Petit Dru in 1953, but had been beaten back by bad weather. On K2 he had sacrificed his own chance of being in the successful summit team. In 1955 a further attempt on the South-West Pillar with Mauri, Oggioni and Aiazzi had failed. Bonatti was in a self-confessed spiritual crisis which had already lasted too long. It was in this mood that the idea of attempting the South-West Pillar solo began to formulate itself.

Soloing is the ultimate expression of the sport, for the climber is staking his life on his judgement. Although there are techniques of self-belaying, it is laborious, time-consuming and, in the event of a fall, of very dubious value. Most of the time the climber is moving unroped, his life literally in his hands, which gives the sense of mastery over one's destiny that Bonatti urgently needed at that moment.

But while the best climbers frequently climbed solo, it was usually on routes that had already been climbed. Bonatti was now thinking of tackling, alone, a climb that was not only unknown but probably the most technically demanding in the Western Alps. He set out on 17th August 1955, abseiling from the crest of the Flammes de Pierre into the head of the dangerous gully that leads up to the foot of the South-West Pillar, and took six lonely days to reach the summit. At one point he came to a dead end in the crack line, suspended from his top piton. The thought of retreat to the foot of the overhang was appalling. In desperation he gazed around him and noticed a long thin crack curling up the wall to the right. If only he could reach it – but the rock in between was smooth, sheer and blank. Perhaps he could swing across on the end of the rope?

He threaded his double rope through the top piton and descended, removing the others he had put in place, until he had rejoined his sack. Then he started to pendulum back and forth until he was very near the crack. But his troubles were not over; the rope jammed when he tried to recover it, forcing him to climb and swing back along the line of the rope until he was able to pull it free, then work his way back. He was nearly there; just twelve impossibly sheer metres now separated him from the crack line. He could not climb any higher to get an anchor for another pendulum and there was no way he could get back the way he had come, for he had now pulled the rope from behind him. If he went down, he would have dangled in space. Alone, at the end of five days of struggle, he was on the point of panic, but then he saw, at the foot of the crack he was trying to reach, a small rock outcrop shaped like a hand with five fingers extended. It was his last chance. If only he could lasso it and then swing across. He made a kind of bolas, with a series of nooses and his entire stock of fifi hooks and metal rings, so as to catch in the rock encrustations sufficiently firmly to take his weight. It took a dozen casts before the bolas settled on the outcrop, only to break loose at the first trial tug. He tried again, and again.

At last it held, but he could not pull really hard – he'd only know if it was secure once he started swinging: 'A last unnerving delay, a last inner prayer for safety, and then, as an uncontrollable tremor ran through me, before my forces grew less, I closed my eyes for a second, held my breath and let myself slip into space, holding the rope with both hands. For an instant I had the feeling of falling with the rope and then my flight slackened and in a second I felt I was swinging back. The anchor had held.'

He heaved himself up the rope, muscles aching. Some more hard climbing, another bivouac and he was on the top of the Dru. This ascent put Bonatti in a unique position in the climbing world. More alpine first ascents followed: the East Face of the Pilier d'Angle, the Red Pillar of Brouillard and Mont Maudit by a direct route up its South-East Face, expeditions to Patagonia and Peru, back to the Himalaya to reach the summit of Gasherbrum IV – it was an incredible list of achievements. Then, in 1961, he went through an experience that was to scar him permanently.

The Pillars of Frêney tower above the Frêney Glacier, the wildest and most inaccessible of any glacier in the Alps, on the south side of Mont Blanc. The Right-Hand Pillar had been climbed by the great Italian climber, Giusto Gervasutti, in 1940, but the central one was untouched. By 1961 most of the major features in the Alps had been climbed and the Central Pillar of Frêney was certainly the most impressive that still remained inviolate. Bonatti had had his eye on it for the previous nine years and had made an attempt on it with Oggioni in 1959. He was not the only climber aware of its challenge, for that same year, two young and little known Scottish climbers, Robin Smith and Dougal Haston, were sniffing around its foot.

It was on the 7th July 1961 that Bonatti, with Oggioni and a client, Roberto Gallieni, who was also a close friend, reached the Col de la Fourche bivouac hut, below the Brenva Face of Mont Blanc. It was early in the season and so they were surprised to find four French climbers, Pierre Mazeaud, Antoine Vieille, Pierre Kohlman and Robert Guillaume in residence. Bonatti immediately guessed from their equipment and reputation that they could only have one objective. They talked it through. Bonatti even offered to stand down but Mazeaud insisted that they should join forces and so at midnight they set out for the Central Pillar. Just to reach it involves a major climb, traversing below the Brenva Face, across the Col Moore and the upper part of the Brenva Glacier to the Couloir de Peuterey which sweeps with some 762m of steep ice and snow to the Col de Peuterey. The base of the Frêney Pillars is higher than most of the other peaks in the Alps.

At first everything went well. The rocks were encrusted with snow and their progress was slow but steady as they picked their way up the steep buttress. It was classic climbing. They stopped that night about two-fifths the way up and continued the following day to reach a little shoulder just below the final barrier, a smooth monolith of granite. They seemed to have success in their grasp, but they had hardly noticed the scum of high grey cloud that had crept in from the west. The storm took them by surprise as it tumbled over the top of Mont Blanc and engulfed them in a cataclysm of lightning, thunder and snow. Kohlman was hit by lightning and almost paralysed, but recovered after gulping down some Coramine.

Their way was barred by about seventy metres of steep rock. Beyond that they knew the angle relented, making it easier and safer for them to reach the Vallot Hut on the other side of Mont Blanc than try to get back the way they had just come. So they decided to sit out the storm and hope it wouldn't last too long. After the lightning came a dense and continuous snowfall which threatened to suffocate the Italians in their tiny tent and got under the French plastic sheeting. They could not cook or melt snow for drinks in their cramped surroundings, and on the morning of their fourth day, with the storm raging as furiously as ever, they realised that if they were to survive, they had to retreat.

Just getting started in those circumstances is an agonisingly slow, painful process, made no easier by the size of the party. Bonatti took the lead and made the first abseil; there were long frustrating waits and the constant threat of getting a rope jammed. At last they reached the bottom of the Pillar. They could now all move together, but their problems were by no means over. The wind was as fierce as ever, the fresh snow was thigh-deep and they were in a white-out. Without Bonatti's guidance they would probably never have found the Col de Peuterey, their key to survival. That night, their fourth in the storm, they found a crevasse in which to get a little shelter. By this time the plastic sheets of the French had disintegrated. They put Kohlman, who was obviously in a bad way, into the little bivvy tent. His hands were blue and swollen with frostbite, so Bonatti handed him the flask of cooking alcohol to rub on them. But before Bonatti could stop him, Kohlman had snatched the flask to his lips and started to gulp the alcohol. It was the worst night yet, bitterly cold with the wind driving through the part-open crevasse.

Next morning they decided that their only hope of survival was to reach the top of the Rochers Gruber, a buttress dropping down onto the Frêney Glacier from the Col de Peuterey. Once again Bonatti led the way, digging a trench through deep soft snow. Avalanche was a constant threat. Vieille was now weakening rapidly and near the top of the Rochers Gruber he collapsed and died. The others struggled on, making seemingly endless abseils down frozen ropes in the driving storm to reach the Frêney Glacier. Here the snow was deeper than Bonatti had ever experienced it, even at the height of winter. But the visibility improved slightly, and they were able to pick their way through the labyrinth of crevasses barring their way to the foot of the Col de l'Innominata which, at last, would lead them to safety. Bonatti was still leading the way, while Oggioni brought up the rear. The group became spread out and Guillaume sat down. He could go no further. By this time it was each man for himself and he was left behind. The gully leading up to the Col de l'Innominata was steep and heavily iced. Oggioni was now so far gone he could not climb it, even on a tight rope.

Mazeaud stayed behind with Oggioni, while Bonatti took Gallieni and Kohlman, who was now delirious, on the rope. They reached easier ground, but Kohlman was getting worse and he attacked Bonatti and Gallieni who, finally in desperation, untied from the rope and fled to get help from the Gamba Hut below. A rescue party immediately set out to recover the rest of the team but only Mazeaud survived.

Thus ended one of the most harrowing tragedies in the Alps. Bonatti was near to death and had a long spell in hospital. 'The day we left hospital Mazeaud and I promised each other to return to the Central Pillar and to finish off those remaining eighty metres. For us the project was like a religious pilgrimage to complete a monument to the courage and sacrifice of our dead friends. It was hoping too much.'

Only two weeks later a Franco-Italian pairing of Pierre Julien and Ignazio Piussi stretched ethics by flying to the top of Mont Blanc by helicopter and descending the Peuterey Ridge but, even so, failed to make the summit. Meanwhile that same summer, Don Whillans and I had been sitting below the Eiger at Alpiglen, wanting to be the first Britons to climb this great North Face which seems such a supreme test of mountaineering competence. But the weather was bad and we had lingered over six weeks.

We only had forty pounds between us to last the whole summer and so could do little travelling, but now it seemed time to move.

It was Don who suggested the Central Pillar. We were more aware of the attempt by the two Scots in 1959 than the tragedy that had recently taken place. To us it was just another exciting unclimbed line. We had become friendly with four Polish climbers who had also been waiting below the Eiger, and one of their number, Jan Djuglosz, asked if he could join us. In Chamonix we brought our team up to four with Ian Clough, a young Yorkshire climber who had just completed the Couzy route on the Cima Ovest di Lavaredo.

We made the same approach as Bonatti had earlier that summer, by the Col de la Fourche bivouac hut, reaching the Col de Peuterey at dawn on 27th August and climbing through the day to reach their fateful high point in the early evening. Being late in the season, the rocks were clear of ice and snow, giving superb climbing at a very reasonable standard. The ledge at the foot of the final tower had a few sad reminders of the previous occupants – an empty gaz cartridge and a few tins. I was uncomfortably aware of how little we knew of the routes off the south side of Mont Blanc and how difficult would be a retreat in the event of a storm. But the weather was settled and the night bitterly cold.

Don had climbed to the start of an overhang the previous evening which appeared to be the high point of Julien's attempt. The following morning he prusiked up the rope he had left in place and, belayed by me, started climbing round a huge impending nose that barred the way into a square-cut corner leading to a massive overhang. It was Whillans at his best – bold, fierce free climbing. The rope began to drag so he brought me round to the base of the corner, and then continued up the crack to the over-hang which was split by an undercut chimney. He could get his shoulders into it, but could neither heave himself up nor retreat. Inevitably he fell off, dropping about forty feet, until he was held on his top peg, dangling about three feet out in space, but level with me. His only comment was, 'I've lost my bloody 'at' and then the dreadful realisation, 'My fags were in the 'at.' He wasn't bothered that all our supply of cash was in it as well.

Meanwhile a team of four, who had arrived the previous evening on the Col de Peuterey, had caught us up by climbing the gully to the side of the Pillar. They turned out to be Pierre Julien, with René Desmaison, Yves Pollet-Villard and Ignazio Piussi. They were trying to find a way up the Pillar on its left-hand side.

It was now my turn to have a try. I knew I could not free climb something that had beaten Whillans, and the corner crack was too wide for our pitons, yet too narrow for the wooden wedges we were carrying. I relayed a request through Ian to the French to borrow some suitable gear from them, but they, quite justifiably, said they needed everything they had for their own route. I then reverted to British climbing techniques, finding some small pieces of rock in the back of the crack, jamming these in suitable spots, threading a sling round them and standing in it, thus establishing myself in the undercut chimney through the overhang. Wriggling out through the overhang, pulling out over iced rocks, I reached a ledge and saw that the rocks were now more broken and the angle easier. Don and I had been on the two pitches all day. We dropped a rope down to Ian and Jan for them to prusik up and the other team, who had reached a dead end on their side of the Pillar, asked Ian to take up one of their ropes and fix it for them, so that they could follow up the next day.

After another chilly bivouac we topped out on the Pillar, climbed the easy snow slopes to the top of Mont Blanc de Courmayeur and on to the summit of Mont Blanc. It had been a superb climb, certainly one of the most beautiful that I have pioneered and it brought the personal and creative satisfaction that comes from having completed a climb obviously destined to be a classic. I can sympathise with Bonatti's disappointment, but either of us could be caught out in a storm and have to pay the price. I sympathised with their loss, but reserved the right for me or any other climber to attempt the route.

Bonatti had recovered sufficiently by the end of September to return to the mountains, picking out a classic line between the Right-Hand Pillar of Frêney and the Peuterey Ridge. In the next few years he put up a series of major new routes, completing a trinity of climbs on the Grand Pilier d'Angle, the first winter ascent of the Walker Spur, and an impressive direct line on the Whymper Spur. He was less fortunate on the North Wall of the Eiger, where in the early 'sixties a race had developed to be the first person to solo it. He tried in July 1963, but was caught in one of the huge rockfalls that are a hazard of the face and was lucky to survive it with an injured back and part cut through ropes. It was finally to fall to a young Swiss guide, Michel Darbellay later that summer.

Bonatti faced the problem that confronts everyone who wants to devote his life to the mountains. Unless you have a private income, you have to earn a living. You can either follow a career and devote all your free time to your sport or you can try to make a living around it. Every serious mountaineer has grappled with this problem. Whymper had used the mountains as a source of inspiration for his etchings and writing; Smythe earned a living as a writer and lecturer. Others, particularly after the Second World War, became mountain guides. Bonatti had tried guiding but it was not something that suited his temperament. He now began to get commissions from *Epoca*, Italy's top picture magazine, to carry out adventure assignments in distant places. The previous winter he had been to the coldest place on earth in the middle of Siberia. I can remember seeing the picture story in one of the British colour magazines. He was beginning to think of a change of direction in his life and it was in 1965 that he made his swansong.

It was the centenary of the first ascent of the Matterhorn. He had seen the possibility of a new route up the side of the huge overhanging nose that flanks the North Face. He tried it in the New Year, first making the attempt with two friends, but they were turned back by bad weather. It was then he decided to make a solo attempt, setting out secretly on 18th February. The climb stretched him to the limit. It was bitterly cold; the rock on the Matterhorn is appallingly loose and, after he had climbed the first overhang, there was no way of retreat. Though he craved privacy, he needed to sell the story and pictures of his ascent to the media. The light planes buzzed around him daily, and the whole of Europe watched. It was a very public swansong. At the end of the climb he was awarded the Gold Medal for Civil Valour by the President of Italy.

But while Bonatti could overcome climbing problems, he could not withstand the glare of media attention and the ill-informed criticism that is the penalty of success. After the Matterhorn, he renounced what he described as 'the now worked-out world of mountaineering, rotten with mediocrity, incomprehension and envy'.

It's a decision I have always found difficult to understand. I enjoy the process of climbing too much ever to think of giving it up, but with Bonatti there is little mention of enjoyment in his description of climbing. A man of extremes, who placed a high demand on friendship, insecure in the face of criticism, he was still essentially a romantic in his approach to mountaineering with a love for solitude and wild places. Of all the immediate post-war climbers, the mark he left was the strongest.

René Desmaison's life has many parallels with that of Bonatti. He also lost his mother as a child and, because his father who had been wounded during the war could not look after him, he was sent to Paris to be brought up by his godfather through whom he was introduced to the sandstone outcrops of Fontainebleau, and then during his military service he discovered mountaineering. Back in Paris in the mid-fifties he formed a climbing partnership with Jean Couzy, who had been on Annapurna and had reached the summit of Makalu with Lionel Terray. Together they made the first ascent of the North-West Face Direct of the Olan, the first winter ascent of the West Face of the Dru in 1957, and attempted a direct route up the huge overhanging wall on the left side of the Cima Ovest di Lavaredo. Next year Couzy was killed by a falling stone, so when Desmaison completed his route on the Cima Ovest with Bernard Lagesse, Pierre Mazeaud and Pierre Kohlman, they named the route after their friend, Couzy.

Like Bonatti, Desmaison took the guides' qualification but he had problems in being accepted by the Chamonix company of guides, partly because he came from outside the valley, but also because of his success as an extreme climber and the way in which he was earning a living through lecturing, writing and sponsorship. It came to a head in 1966 when he was involved in a spectacular rescue on the West Face of the Dru. Two young Germans, who arguably should never have attempted the route, came to a halt at the end of the tension traverse near the top. The official rescue operation, which is organised by the gendarmerie and calls upon the Company of Guides for help, went into action, attempting to reach the beleaguered pair by climbing the normal route and coming down to them from above. But a small international group of climbers, led by Desmaison, decided the best way to reach them was to climb the West Face itself and bring them down it, which they did successfully. But Desmaison was expelled from the Company of Guides.

It was in the 'sixties that most of the major unclimbed lines left in the Alps were finally picked off. Desmaison took a leading part, particularly in winter mountaineering – the Walker Spur in 1963, a few weeks after Bonatti, the Central Pillar of Frêney in 1967, the Shroud, the steep icefield to the left of the Walker in 1968 and then in 1971, he attempted a line on the left flank of the Walker Spur that had achieved the reputation of being the current 'last great problem'. It followed a tenuous line of ramps creeping up the side, and had repelled summer attempts because of stonefall.

Desmaison's partner was Serge Gousseault. The twenty-three-year-old was making a reputation in Chamonix with a series of bold fast ascents and had just completed the guides' course with top honours. But from the start Gousseault declined the lead on the grounds that Desmaison was more

Walter Bonatti, the most outstanding and prolific alpinist of the postwar era, crowned his career with a solo first ascent of a new route up the North Face of the Matterhorn.

experienced and would be faster. It suited Desmaison but perhaps it should have made him pause. The climbing was slow and difficult, but they made steady progress, clawing their way up the long ramp. The North Face of the Jorasses is a stark, sunless place, surrounded by jagged peaks and tumbling icefalls, set at the head of the Leschaux Glacier. The serrated crest of the Aiguilles de Chamonix blocks any view of the valley.

On the sixth day the weather closed in and their one link with the world, their walkie-talkie, packed up. By the tenth day they were only a hundred metres below the cornice at the top of the Spur, but Desmaison was unable to persuade Gousseault into any further effort. Held in a cocoon of rope, they had no choice but to wait for helicopter help. Incredibly, a rescue helicopter failed on two consecutive days to interpret Desmaison's gestures as needing help. By then it was too late for Gousseault who died on the twelfth day of the climb. Desmaison himself was now sinking fast and it was the fourteenth day before a helicopter from Grenoble picked a point to land below the summit ridge and Desmaison was hauled the last few metres up the Walker Spur, nearly dead of hypothermia and dehydration. Very few people could have survived what he had gone through.

Desmaison suffered the same criticism as Bonatti had, but at least he was able to bury his resentment in completing the climb to which he had sacrificed so much. He returned the following year, to be beaten back once more by bad weather but was at last successful, in January of 1973, when he and Giorgio Bertone fought their way out in yet another storm.

It was near the end of an age, for Bonatti and Desmaison between them had completed many of the major unclimbed lines in the Alps. They exemplified an ethic of adventure in climbing, renouncing the use of bolts or siege tactics and fixed ropes. But they also attracted controversy, primarily because of the way they needed, and used, publicity to earn a living to pursue the sport they loved.

Perhaps by the act of reaching out beyond the confines of the climbing fraternity to a wider audience they were seen as betraying the confidentiality of a freemasonry. At the same time they were courting danger. The popular media have a tendency to build someone up, only to knock him down and do not really understand the delicate balancing act between success and disaster, the adrenalin of risk or the individual responsibility accepted by each climber. But however the wider world saw Bonatti and Desmaison, their ascents and the climbing philosophy they propagated are their long-lasting contributions to the development of mountaineering.

It was around this time, in the mid-to-late 'sixties, that another young climber was beginning to make his mark. Reinhold Messner, the second in a family of eight boys and one girl, was born and brought up in the village of Villnöss, in the Süd-Tirol amongst the peaks of the Dolomites. It is the region that Italy took from Austria after the First World War but, although its inhabitants carry Italian passports, their culture and language has remained firmly Germanic.

Messner's father was the village school teacher. A firm, fair man he introduced his children to the joys of the mountains and allowed them the freedom to develop their own potential, even though it meant they put themselves at some risk. At the same time he seems to have built within them a strong competitive undertow, of comparison or exhortation of one against the other. But it was a strong, happy and very secure family upbringing. Money was short, but there was enough for their simple needs. They had one of the most wonderful adventure playgrounds in the world on their doorstep. Introduced to climbing by his father at the age of five with an ascent of the highest of the Geisler peaks, his younger brother, Günther, became his main partner and their first serious route, when Messner was only sixteen, was on the biggest local crag, the North Face of the Sass Rigais, first climbed by Fritz Wiessner and Emil Solleder back in 1925. By the mid-sixties they had climbed many of the classic Dolomite routes and had even ventured to the bigger peaks of the Western Alps on the 'helicopter', the old motor scooter loaned them by their father.

Messner built his climbing ambition on very solid foundations, a progressive evolution of experience through the climbing grades, tackling bigger and steeper climbs, progressing onto new routes, first winter ascents, and then exploring his own thresholds by climbing solo. This was to be not only the secret of his success, but also of his survival – an analytical approach that meant, in aspiring to the seemingly impossible, he had clearly defined a game plan that brought the challenge within the realms of the possible.

His first major solo ascent was the Soldà route on the South Face of the Piz-de-Ciavàces. It was a classic Grade VI. More challenging climbs followed; the first solo ascents of the ice-bound North Face of the Droites; the huge and complex North Face of the Langkofel, or the soaring line of the Philipp/Flamm route on the Punta Civetta. There were new routes and amazingly fast ascents of climbs like the Central Pillar of Frêney in a single day. He was building a very sound base for his next step forward, to the greater ranges of the world, where he was to establish a unique position.

By 1970 he had shown himself to be among, if not the most, talented climber in the Alps, but he had come onto the scene just those few years after all the great unclimbed lines had been completed by people like Desmaison and Bonatti.

He was also formulating a climbing philosophy that was to serve him well in the Himalaya. Through the 'fifties and 'sixties there had been a growing divergence between the climbers who wanted to maintain a high level of adventure, which is all about risk and uncertainty, and those who wanted a greater certainty of success at a lower level of risk. The way the equipment used for protection was becoming the means of upward progress was at the heart of the argument. It was the same argument ventilated rationally by Paul Preuss at the beginning of the century and tetchily by Colonel Strutt in the 'thirties, but made more acutely relevant now by the introduction of the expansion bolt, where a hole is drilled in the rock and a bolt is driven into it. With the use of this new device the climber could go anywhere, ignoring all natural features. In Messner's words, this was the 'murder of the impossible', the murder too of some of the strongest and most important ingredients of adventure.

The North Face of the Cima Grande, one of the most dramatically beautiful faces in the Dolomites, provides a stage to examine this development. The original route, made in 1933 by Comici and the Dimai brothers, follows the right-hand side of the face, is steep, technically challenging and used pitons for protection and the occasional pull up. At the time it was one of the hardest climbs in the Dolomites. In 1958 four Germans, Lothar Brandler, Dieter Hasse, Jörg Lehne and Siegfried Löw, made a direct route up the centre. Much of the lower part of the climb gave magnificent, and thinly-protected, free climbing. They were heading for a series of overhanging corners that led into a deep chimney crack system, but to reach the corner they had to cross a blank space. The only way they could do this was to put in a short bolt section to link and complete a fine and very committing climb. Can it be justified? I made an early ascent in 1959, was stretched to the limit, and revelled in the climbing. But it was also the opening of a door; once you accept a few bolts on a route, it is too easy to put in a few more and then a complete bolt ladder from bottom to top of a face. This was the case in the two routes that followed; the Saxonweg in the winter of 1963 and the Camilloto/Pellisier route in the summer of 1967, both of which used a huge number of bolts in a long drawn out siege. Messner commented:

Today's climber doesn't want to cut himself off from the possibility of retreat: he carries his courage in his rucksack, in the form of bolts and equipment. Rock faces are no longer overcome by climbing skill, but are humbled, pitch by pitch, by methodical manual labour; what isn't done today will be done tomorrow. Free-climbing routes are dangerous, so they are protected by pegs. Ambitions are no longer built on skill, but on equipment and the length of time available. The decisive factor isn't courage, but technique; an ascent may take days and days, and the pegs and bolts counted in hundreds. Retreat has become dishonourable, because everyone knows now that a combination of bolts and singlemindedness will get you up anything, even the most repulsive-looking direttissima.

It is a conflict that is with us to this day.

Another important phase in this period was a cross-fertilisation of techniques and ideas that took place in the mid-sixties between European climbers and the Americans, nurtured on the huge smooth walls of Yosemite valley. In almost complete isolation they had been evolving their own solutions to the climbing problems presented by Yosemite granite. It brought out the best of the American psyche, though they also went through the same ethical dilemmas as the Europeans on the use of pitons and bolts, siege tactics and free climbing. The development of the chrome molybdenum piton, alloy bongs (wedges) for wide cracks, nylon tape to replace the étrier and a methodical technique for aid climbing and sack hauling took them ahead of their European counterparts. There was a comparatively small group of climbers in the forefront; Warren Harding, a wild iconoclast, anarchic, hard-drinking, hard-living, who couldn't care less about the ethics imposed by others, was the driving force behind the first ascent of the Nose on El Capitan, the first route to be made up this magnificent wall. Yvon Chouinard and Tom Frost not only featured in some of the best early ascents but also designed and manufactured the hardware that made them possible.

They refined artificial climbing to extraordinarily high levels but they also developed a strong free climbing ethic. This was aided by exchanging ideas with the British and continental climbers who were beginning to visit Yosemite in increasing numbers in the early 'seventies. The British influence was particularly strong, encouraging the introduction of nuts (metal wedges of different sizes), developed in Britain from the chockstone of the 'fifties, and then increasingly refined alloy wedges. They had the aesthetic advantage that they did not damage or mark the rock and, like chockstones, needed some ingenuity to place. But the flow of climbers and ideas from Europe was preceded by that of the Americans going east.

The catalyst who helped intermix the European and American climbing cultures was John Harlin, an American pilot who stayed on in Europe after a spell with the U.S. Airforce in Germany. He taught at the International School in Leysin, Switzerland, and in 1965 founded there the International School of Mountaineering. He had the physique of an American football star combined with a charismatic presence that earned him the title of 'the Blond God'. Some of the top American climbers came over to Europe in the 'sixties. One of the most talented was Royal Robbins; lean, intense, with a serious, almost pedantic manner, he was a brilliant rock climber who had pioneered some of the hardest routes in Yosemite. In 1962 he made a direct start to the West Face of the Dru with Gary Hemming who the previous year had won himself European notice for his part in Desmaison's controversial rescue on the same face. The following year Hemming, Tom Frost, John Harlin and a Scot, Steve Fulton, climbed the impressively steep South Face of the Fou on the Aiguilles de Chamonix and that same year Harlin and Frost climbed the Hidden Pillar of Frêney, a smooth column of granite lying to the side of the Central Pillar. Most impressive of all was the West Face Direct of the Dru in 1965 when Robbins and Harlin climbed the impending grooves and tenuous cracks between the West Face route and the South-West Pillar. This was in the region of the huge rockfall that had swept the face in the early 'fifties. It was technically hard and frighteningly loose.

A natural end to this period came in 1966 with the death of John Harlin in an attempt to make a Direct route on the North Wall of the Eiger. This had become the current last great problem of the Alps. Harlin had been trying it for a couple of years in both winter and summer. That winter of 1966 he brought Layton Kor, a brilliant rock climber from Colorado, over from the States and recruited Dougal Haston, a Scot in his early twenties, who was rapidly building a reputation as one of the best climbers in Britain. He and Robin Smith, while studying philosophy at Edinburgh University, had dominated Scottish climbing in the late 'fifties, putting up a series of technically hard routes in summer and winter and, establishing a laconic, yet vivid, writing style which was to have considerable influence on climbing literature. The partnership was broken in 1962 when Smith, climbing with Wilf Noyce, was killed in the Pamirs.

Harlin's team arrived at Kleine Scheidegg in February, planning to make an alpine-style ascent, but the weather was unsettled and they had no choice but to wait. Everything changed, however, with the arrival of an eight-man German team, one of whose members was Jörg Lehne. They

Royal Robbins, above left, was one of the most talented American rock climbers who brought the big wall techniques developed in Yosemite to the Alps in the 'sixties and became a heeded custodian of climbing ethics. Gary Hemming, right, another American who took a prominent part in the Dru rescue and became a cult figure on the French climbing scene, with some of the chrome molybdenum pitons, angles and bongs which revolutionised Chamonix climbing. Below left, Dougal Haston was making his name as one of Britain's leading alpine climbers and was to go on to build an even greater reputation in the Himalaya.

were prepared for siege tactics and wasted no time in running a line of fixed rope up the face. It was a case, once again, of the greater chance of success being weighed against the more adventurous spirit of uncertainty which an alpine-style attempt would have involved. Harlin was faced with a dilemma — if he waited for the settled weather an alpine-style attempt needed, the Germans could very nearly have completed the climb before he started. He was forced to abandon his sound ethical stance to stay in the race, and start a siege with a team that was uncomfortably small for such an enterprise.

This was how I became involved, for I had been taking photographs for the *Telegraph Magazine*, who had sponsored the climb, and I now joined the team to help as a climber as well. It was an extraordinary media circus of great contrasts. The line of fixed rope meant that you could be poised on a thin film of steep ice half-way up the face in the afternoon and back in the Kleine Scheidegg Hotel, drinking, eating and dancing in the cellar bar that evening. And yet the risks were very real. The fixed rope was 7mm perlon which, with hindsight, was much too thin and unsuitable for long jumar ascents. An accident was almost inevitable, and it happened when the climbers seemed to be in sight of success. The two competing teams had joined forces. Dougal Haston and four Germans were in the White Spider and John Harlin was jumaring up the final rope to join them, when it parted, worn through over a sharp edge. The climbers in the White Spider decided to continue, completed the route in a violent storm and named it after Harlin.

Other routes up the North Face followed, some like the Japanese in 1969, making extensive use of bolts, and others bold adventurous routes climbed alpine-style, as that of the Czechs in 1976. It was a brilliant young English climber, Alex MacIntyre, climbing with the American, Tobin Sorenson, who made the fourth ascent of the Harlin route in 1977, but the first alpine-style.

The mountaineer who wanted to find virgin faces and unclimbed peaks now had to go further afield than the Alps. The Alps, however, still provide a foundation for climbing in the greater ranges and certainly in the 'sixties and even 'seventies, changing techniques and ethics were to form a basis for making the Himalaya into a gigantic, super-alpine playground, a process which was to witness some extraordinary achievements, tragedies on a larger and more harrowing scale than anything in the Alps, and to introduce environmental problems whose longterm effect is still incalculable.

CHAPTER ELEVEN

LADDERS INTO THE SKY

The first ascents of the 8000m peaks

•

ive years elapsed after the turmoil of the Second World War before climbers started looking to the highest peaks once again. The French were quick off the mark with their expedition to Dhaulagiri (8167m/ 26,795ft) and Annapurna (8091m/26,545ft) in the spring of 1950. It was the drive of one man, Lucien Devies, that made this possible. A talented pre-war climber, he was a brilliant organiser and committee man, determined to see France take a leading part in post-war mountaineering and in a position to make it happen. During the war men like Lionel Terray, Gaston Rébuffat and Louis Lachenal had been able to keep up their skills and, immediately after the end of hostilities, tackled some of the big north walls, Terray and Lachenal making an early ascent of the Walker Spur and the second ascent of the North Wall of the Eiger, while Gaston Rébuffat was also putting up a series of hard routes, including a new line on the Aiguille du Midi.

They were three obvious candidates for the Dhaulagiri expedition but Lucien Devies appointed Maurice Herzog as leader. Although not one of the top climbers of the time, he was a good organiser. The climbing team was completed by Jean Couzy and Marcel Schatz, two gifted amateurs based in Paris. Only Marcel Ichac, their climbing cameraman, had been to the Himalaya before.

This was a time when Tibet, about to be engulfed by its neighbour to the north, looked unpromising for expeditions and Devies achieved quite a coup when he persuaded the Nepalese government to open its frontiers to foreigners. Hitherto only Kangchenjunga had been opened up to a few expeditions and very little was known about the mountains of Nepal. The only maps were ones made surreptitiously by the Survey of India and there were no photographs available.

The first glimpse of their chosen peak was awe-inspiring:

An immense ice pyramid, glittering in the morning sun like a crystal, rose up more than 23,000 feet above us. The south face, shining blue through the morning mists, was unbelievably lofty, not of this world. We were speechless in face of this tremendous mountain; its name was familiar to us from all our talk about it, but the reality so moved us that we couldn't utter a word. Then slowly the reasons for our being here at all took precedence over our own emotions and our aesthetic response, and we began to examine the gigantic outline from a practical point of view.

Dhaulagiri, the sixth highest mountain in the world, was their prime objective, It was a magnificent sight but from that aspect obviously too difficult. They made a series of reconnaissances but failed to find any chinks in its armour and therefore turned their attention to Annapurna. It was a case of 'first find your mountain'. What appeared on their map bore little relation to the ground. A complete ridge seemed to be in the wrong place and they spent a month trying to find a way to the foot. Consequently it was 23rd May before they managed to establish a Base Camp immediately below the North Face of Annapurna, which appeared to offer a feasible route to the top. The North Face is huge and complex but relatively easy-angled, a bit like the North Face of Mont Blanc writ large. They tackled the climbing with élan, taking their turn with the Sherpas at load-carrying, and alternating the lead across the dangerous basin below the Sickle ice cliff and up the steep gully that led into the upper reaches of the mountain. Herzog, probably the least capable technical climber of the six, emerged as an extremely strong performer at altitude and the other driving force of the team was Lionel Terray.

At last, on 2nd June, they were poised for their summit bid. Who goes for the top depends as much on their position on the mountain at the time as their fitness. Herzog had hoped to make his attempt with Terray, but they had got out of phase with each other through Terray doggedly stocking Camp 4, knowing it had to be done, even though it would mean he would lose his chance with Herzog. So it was the restless, volatile Lachenal who teamed up with Herzog and two Sherpas to climb above the Sickle ice barrier, across the long slope that stretched towards the summit. They plodded on above 7300m through the afternoon, until the ice-plastered rock of the summit ridge loomed up in front of them.

Here the Sherpas left them, after helping to hack out a tiny ledge for a tent. All night the spindrift, building up against its wall, threatened to dislodge them down the slope and in the lethargy of altitude they just brewed tea and swallowed some pills. By morning the tent had nearly collapsed on them and it was too much trouble to light the stove. So they

Lionel Terray, left, arguably the strongest member of the Annapurna team, took a support role in the summit bid, playing an important part in helping the exhausted, frostbitten summiters back to safety. Louis Lachenal, right, one of the first men to reach the summit of an 8000m peak when he climbed Annapurna with Maurice Herzog in 1950.

set out having had only a cup of tea the previous night and nothing at all to eat or drink that morning.

The slope looked straightforward so they left the rope behind and struggled upwards through the day, panting heavily at each step. At last a short gully led through the summit rocks and suddenly a savage wind was tearing at their clothes and faces and the slope dropped away on all sides. They had reached the summit of Annapurna and in doing so were the first men to climb a peak of over 8000m, that magic height that was to become such an obsession to so many climbers in the future.

Looking around they could see the shapely, fish-tailed summit of Machapuchare nearly engulfed in an angry tide of dark clouds, marching in from the south. It was time to escape. Lachenal started to descend immediately, but Herzog followed more slowly. He took off his gloves to get something out of his sack and watched in dawning horror as they blew away down the mountain. The storm they had seen from the summit was now upon them as they staggered separately down to their top camp. Lachenal survived a fall but his feet were badly frostbitten. Herzog lost all his fingers. It was a price he was willing to pay. Concluding his expedition book, he wrote: 'Annapurna to which we had gone empty handed, was a treasure on which we should live the rest of our days. With this realisation we turn a new page: a new life begins. There are other Annapurnas in the lives of men.'

For Herzog there were. He is an urbane, relaxed man, has been a Minister of Sport in the French government, and gives the impression of having led a deeply satisfying life. He and Lachenal had also broken a barrier that somehow made all the 8000m peaks seem accessible.

That same spring, on the other side of Nepal, two old friends, Charles Houston and Bill Tilman, were invited by Houston's father on an historic trek to the home country of the Sherpas with whom they had worked before the war. They were the first westerners to explore Sola Khumbu, so it is not surprising that with so much to claim their attention they spared only a brief glance at the approach to Everest. They scrambled most of the way up Kala Patar to peer round the shoulder of Nuptse into the Icefall and Western Cwm. From here they could only see the steep buttresses of the South-West Face, which appeared to stretch to the South Col. As a result, their report was discouraging.

But back in Britain, an unknown medical student called Michael Ward was not deterred. Inspired by Herzog's success he was making the first moves that were to lead to Britain's return to Everest. The Himalayan Committee, which had been resurrected from the old Everest Committee to support Himalayan expeditions in general, gave Ward's notion of a reconnaissance expedition half a blessing and Eric Shipton was promptly invited to lead it. The President of the New Zealand Alpine Club mentioned that four of his countrymen were climbing in the Garhwal and asked if two of them could join the team. Shipton agreed, and it was a beekeeper called Ed Hillary and the New Zealand expedition leader, Earle Riddiford, who joined them in Kathmandu in September 1951.

They reached the Khumbu Glacier at the end of September and confronted the 2000ft Icefall. It must have been a daunting moment. The Khumbu Icefall is a gigantic frozen cataract of tottering walls, towers and blocks, all being pushed inexorably from above by the weight of ice in the Western Cwm. They had to pick a way through it which could then be used over an extended period of time by heavily laden porters. It is a place of constant movement, of groaning ice interspersed with the dull crash of collapsing séracs and towers. Icequakes regularly occur, caused by the changing pressures being built up.

It was 19th October before they reached the top of the Icefall, but their way was still barred by a huge crevasse that stretched across the entire Cwm.

Above left, Michael Ward, prime mover of the postwar British return to Everest: right, Eric Shipton, pre-eminent climbing explorer with Tilman in East Africa and the Himalaya; after three Everest expeditions, in 1936, 1938 and 1951, he was generally expected to be given the leadership of the 1953 team, but the Mount Everest Committee suspected his climbing drive and organisational ability were less developed than his exploratory instincts and they badly needed to get to the top of the mountain. Below, climbers in 1953 at the top of the Khumbu Icefall, the major hazard of the southern approach to Everest.

Tired, nerves taut from the constant threat of shifting ice, they decided they had seen enough, even though they had not penetrated the Cwm itself, so they turned back. It is indicative of Shipton's prime motivation that he was much more successful exploring the environs of Everest. On the way back to Kathmandu, he and Michael Ward even trespassed into Tibet, crossing the Menlung La to drop into the valley going between the beautiful unclimbed peaks of Menlungtse and Gauri Sankar. It was here that they photographed the controversial tracks that have been ascribed to the yeti, and had a frightening brush with Tibetans, who might have arrested them and handed them over to the Chinese.

The British had drifted too casually into their return to Everest. They had even omitted to apply for permission to be on the mountain the following year, giving the Swiss an opening to snatch the precious government permit without which no foreign expedition may climb on the major Himalayan mountains. The Swiss were very nearly successful, making the route up through the Icefall into the Western Cwm and then up its huge headwall, the Lhotse Face, to establish a camp on the South Col at 7986m (26,200ft). Raymond Lambert and Tenzing Norgay, who had been a young Sherpa on the pre-war expeditions from the north, made a determined bid for the top, being turned back about 165m below the South Summit. They returned in the autumn, but, battered by the post-monsoon winds, were only able to reach the South Col.

The British, meanwhile, were having to sit it out. It was decided to mount an expedition to Cho Oyu, (26,750ft/8153m), to broaden out a potential team and build up altitude experience in the hope the Swiss failed on Everest. Eric Shipton was leader and the 1951 team was somewhat expanded. The expedition however was a fiasco. Cho Oyu is on the frontier and, like many peaks on the Himalayan watershed, the northern or Tibetan aspect is by far the easier. To reach it the expedition would have had to cross into China and Shipton, perhaps mindful of his experience the previous year, was not prepared to do so, even though it was most unlikely that any Tibetan, let alone Chinese, would have detected their invasion. It was indicative, perhaps of the level of priority he placed on the official objective of the expedition. They sited a Base Camp low on the Nepalese side, made

The Lhotse Face of Everest, with the summit of Lhotse right. The Swiss reached the South Col, on the horizon left, above the Geneva Spur, from where Raymond Lambert made a summit bid with Tenzing Norgay.

a half-hearted attempt on the South-West Ridge, and then scattered to do what Shipton, and for that matter the others, enjoyed most – exploring this treasury of unmapped mountains. Ed Hillary and George Lowe demonstrated their lack of respect for Chinese territory by crossing the Nup La to reach the West Rongbuk Glacier and cutting up the East Rongbuk to have a look at the north side of Everest. They then joined Eric Shipton and Charles Evans to explore the mountains around Makalu. It was all great fun and geographically useful, but it did not demonstrate the single-minded drive that was necessary to succeed in climbing Mount Everest.

However, the British were now in with a chance, for they had permission for 1953, but it was their only chance, for the French had a permit for 1954 and the Swiss for 1955. There was a growing pressure for success and an increasing disquiet about Eric Shipton's style of leadership. There was the same kind of lobbying and intrigue that had been so prevalent in the pre-war expeditions and, as a result, Shipton was eventually placed in a position where he had no choice but to resign, leaving the Committee to appoint Colonel John Hunt, the man they had come to favour, to the leadership of the expedition.

John Hunt, the unexpected but highly effective leader of the 1953 Everest expedition, with Dawe Thondup, survivor of Merkl's disastrous 1934 Nanga Parbat expedition.

John Hunt was a career soldier who had spent most of his time before the war serving in India, where he had undertaken a series of small but adventurous climbing expeditions. He then had a distinguished war career, ending up in command of an infantry brigade in Greece. In no way the stereotype of the professional soldier, he had chosen to work with the Indian police during much of his time in India, even though this had been slightly looked down on by class-conscious army officers of the time.

It was a challenging appointment, for Eric Shipton was popular with his team and the best known mountaineer in Britain, while John Hunt was practically unknown, even among the climbing fraternity. The organisation of the expedition was pressured since it could not get fully under way until November 1952, when it was known that the Swiss had not been successful. But once the decision had been taken, with John Hunt in command, everything fell into place. It was Hunt who ran the expedition, chose the team, allocated responsibility to the right people and left them to get on with it. The principles of running a brigade and laying siege to a mountain are very similar and Colonel Hunt was to demonstrate that he was good at both.

Members of the Everest Reconnaissance and Cho Oyu expeditions obviously had a strong priority for Hunt's team because they represented the small handful of younger British climbers with Himalayan experience. The New Zealand connection was also retained. Ed Hillary and George Lowe had been outstanding in their performance around Cho Oyu. Charles Evans, a brain surgeon, had also been impressive for his performance and his maturity of outlook. He was to be deputy leader. Michael Ward, who had initiated it all, was now qualified, and chosen as team doctor. Tom Bourdillon had been on both expeditions, was exceptionally strong and certainly the best technical climber, while Alf Gregory, a Blackpool travel agent and only non-Oxbridge northerner, had performed particularly well at altitude on Cho Oyu and had the added advantage of being a first-class and dedicated photographer. The newcomers were all from a very traditional public school/Oxbridge background – Mike Westmacott, a statistician and ex-President of the Oxford University Mountaineering Club, George Band, a geologist and ex-President of the Cambridge University Mountaineering Club, and Wilfrid Noyce, a schoolmaster at Charterhouse (echoes of Mallory), who was a talented rock climber and alpinist of the immediate pre-war years. The team was completed by Charles Wylie, a thirty-two-year-old Gurkha officer, and Griffith Pugh, a high-altitude physiologist who had done much to investigate the effects of altitude and through this had a considerable influence on the planning for the expedition.

The team, both in social background and terms of balance and experience, was very similar to the pre-war British expeditions. The big difference was to be its leadership. John Hunt had formulated a carefully thought out plan. All the ingredients of specialised equipment, training, co-ordination of Sherpas and climbers were to be brought together in a harmonious whole. It was this quality that was to give them success where previous expeditions had failed. Another important change in concept was in making Tenzing, who had been so near the summit of Everest the previous spring, a full member of the team. This was a huge jump from pre-war attitudes where the Sherpas were perceived clearly as members of a servant class.

The expedition reached the Thyangboche monastery, spiritual centre of the Sherpa community, on 27th March. It is an idyllic spot, nestling amongst rhododendrons and birch, on a shoulder high above the fast flowing Dudh Kosi. Everest, like the keep of a Norman castle, is guarded by the outer ramparts of Lhotse, fourth highest mountain of the world, and Nuptse. John Hunt's orchestrated siege of the mountain started with a relaxed, yet effective, acclimatisation programme and then developed successive waves of activity – reconnaissance, securing the route to the next camp, establishing the camp, moving into it and then pushing forward again. It was a blueprint for expedition planning, each stage being secured, supplies being checked and maintained, and the potential summit teams carefully rested before moving into position. Hunt led by example, ferrying loads when necessary, positioning himself on the mountain at the camp from which he could have a feel for what the climbers were doing out in front and see how the supplies were flowing. He was earning the respect of his team, even though there was always a degree of distance between them. Hillary commented, 'I learnt to respect John, even if I found it difficult to understand him. He drove himself with incredible determination and I always felt he was out to prove himself the physical equal of any member.'

From the start Hunt had thought Hillary and Tenzing were potentially his strongest pair. Another forceful pairing was that of Evans and Bourdillon. They had been the two members of the team closest to Eric Shipton. Bourdillon actually resigned from the trip when Shipton was replaced, and only came back in after a great deal of persuasion. Hunt had been very touched on the walk in when Bourdillon had told him how happy the expedition seemed to be. He wanted to keep it that way.

The tents and boxes of the first Base Camp are unpacked near Thyangboche monastery.

Although Bourdillon was younger than Evans and had climbed at a much higher standard in the Alps, they had a great deal in common and Evans, though initially sceptical, became deeply involved in Bourdillon's brainchild, the closed-circuit oxygen system which his father had specially developed for the expedition in the hope of avoiding the wastage of the conventional open-circuit set. In theory it should have been the better system, but in practice it proved to be less reliable and the other members of the team were not impressed. Hillary simply preferred the look of the open-circuit system and felt that too much time was being expended in trying to prove the closed-circuit equipment. Privately, Hunt felt the same way, but gave his support to the closed-circuit trials all the same. At 6.30 a.m. on 2nd May, Hillary and Tenzing set out from Base Camp, using the open-circuit set, carrying a load that totalled forty pounds. They reached Camp 4, the Advance Base in the Western Cwm, after 3300ft of climbing and about four miles in lateral distance, breaking trail most of the way through soft snow. It was as much an affirmation of their fitness and suitability for the summit as a vindication of the open-circuit system.

With Advance Base established Hunt announced his plan of assault on the summit. Once fixed ropes were in place up the Lhotse Face, Evans and Bourdillon were to make a first attempt on the summit from the South Col and Hillary and Tenzing were to make the second bid from a higher camp placed on the shoulder of the South-East Ridge. Hunt himself was planning to take part in the carry to place the second summit pair in position, an understandable indulgence of the leader wanting to check personally that everything had been done to ensure a good chance of success. Inevitably, there was disappointment and criticsm among those not included.

Ward came out strongly against Hunt's plan on two counts. He could not understand the logic of making an initial bid from the South Col, when only a slightly greater porter effort would be needed to establish a high camp for Evans and Bourdillon's attempt which could be used by Hillary and Tenzing as well. He also challenged Hunt's decision to take charge of the carry to the top camp himself on the grounds that he was not physically fit for it. The latter doubt proved quite unfounded. But I myself have always been surprised at John Hunt's decision to allow Bourdillon and Evans to make their attempt from the South Col which meant, in effect, that there would be only one strong attempt on the summit itself. Had they been allowed to place a top camp, it is very likely Bourdillon and Evans whose names would have gone into the history books as the first men on top of Everest. It is easy, however, to be wise after the event. Hunt was probably the only member of the team fully aware of just how thin was the ferrying capability of his Sherpas, particularly once they were above the South Col. Had Hillary and Tenzing failed, and the British team not climbed Everest in 1953, no doubt the post-mortems would have been long and furious – but no-one is too interested in a post-mortem after success.

Whatever reservations some members of the team might have had, they all settled into their roles and worked themselves to the limit in the next three weeks. But things began to go wrong almost from the start. It needs ruthless determination and, at the same time, some flexibility to keep the momentum of a climb going. The Lhotse Face proved tougher than predicted and they were begining to fall behind schedule. George Lowe spent ten exhausting days at altitude but still had not reached the South Col, and it was Wilfrid Noyce, with the Sherpa Annullu, a delightful, hard-smoking, hard-drinking bull of a man, who finally made it.

Hunt was also forced to use Hillary and Tenzing to help bully and cajole a carrying team of Sherpas, led by Charles Wylie, to get all the supplies needed for the summit bids up to the South Col. It was then up to Bourdillon and Evans. They came so close to success, reaching the South Summit early in the afternoon of 26th May. Now higher than any man had ever been before, they were able to inspect the final ridge to the main summit. It was not encouraging. Looking at it head-on made it appear steeper, longer and more difficult than it actually was.

With the summit within reach Evans and Bourdillon were now faced with the classic dilemma – to go on or retreat. They could get there, but could they get back? Bourdillon was for risking all for the summit. Evans was for prudent withdrawal while the oxygen held out, and after as fierce an argument as one can conduct through oxygen masks, it was deputy leader Evans who prevailed.

Evans and Bourdillon retreat from the South Summit. Maybe they could have made it to the top, but could they have returned safely?

It was now up to Hillary and Tenzing. The expedition barely had the time or the resources to mount another bid. John Hunt and Da Namgyl had made a carry towards the shoulder but had not managed to get all the way. Alf Gregory, George Lowe, who had already done so much on the Lhotse Face, and the Sherpa Ang Nyima, were going to help Hillary and Tenzing up to their high camp. The big difference between this effort and that of any of the pre-war expeditions was the strength of the high support and the fact that the climbers were taking a full part in load carrying. Hillary was carrying the heaviest load of all, at sixty-three pounds. They pitched a tent at 27,900ft and the next morning the pair started for the top, reaching the South Summit some hours earlier than their predecessors, with plenty of spare oxygen in hand. They picked their way steadily along the steep corniced ridge until they were stopped by a sheer step barring their way:

> In front of me was the rock wall, vertical, but with a few promising holds. Behind me was the ice wall of the cornice, glittering and hard but cracked here and there. I took a hold on the rock in front and then jammed one of my crampons hard into the ice behind. Leaning back with my oxygen set on the ice, I slowly levered myself upwards. Searching feverishly with my spare boot, I found a tiny ledge on the rock and took some of the weight off with my other leg. Leaning back on the cornice, I fought to regain my breath. Constantly at the back of my mind was the fear that the cornice might break off, and my nerves were taut with suspense. But slowly, I forced my way up – wriggling and jamming and using every little hold. In one place I managed to force my ice axe into a crack in the ice, and this gave me the necessary purchase to get over a holdless stretch. And then I found a solid foothold in a hollow in the ice, and next moment I was reaching over the top of the rock and pulling myself to safety. The rope came tight – its forty feet had been barely enough.

This was the final sting in the tail. From above what has come to be known as the Hillary Step, the ridge broadens, and in a series of gentle undulations leads up to the highest point on earth. They reached the summit at 11.30 that morning, 29th May, embraced and gazed down the north side of Everest, scene of all the desperate pre-war struggles, and across the great sweep of brown and purple hills of the Tibetan plateau. Hillary photographed Tenzing holding the British, Indian, Nepalese and United Nations flags aloft, and then they returned to civilisation. The evacuation of the mountain was like the ascent, disciplined and well ordered. Thanks to some luck with the weather, but most of all to John Hunt's meticulous planning and a very high level of teamwork, the first ascent of Everest remains a model for siege-style climbing.

To the general public in Britain it was a fitting national victory to coincide with the coronation of Queen Elizabeth II. Even today, Ed Hillary

Edmund Hillary and Tenzing Norgay, the first men to reach the highest point on earth.

and Sherpa Tenzing are the two mountaineering names best known throughout the world. There are few statements stronger or more easily understood than being the first men to reach the highest point on earth. Hunt and Hillary received knighthoods, Tenzing the George Medal – a touch of class distinction there for, as a foreign national, he could have been awarded an honorary knighthood. Since Everest each man has given society a great deal in return for his fame: Hillary devoting his life to the well-being of the Sherpa community with his Himalayan Trust; John Hunt going into public service, helping to found the Duke of Edinburgh's Award Scheme and chairing the Parole Board; while Tenzing worked as chief instructor of the Himalayan Institute in Darjeeling and became the unofficial ambassador for the Sherpa community.

Even as the British started work on the Lhotse Face a German expedition was approaching its Base Camp on the north side of Nanga Parbat, also bent on settling an old score. The leader was Dr Karl Herrligkoffer, a general practitioner from Munich, who was to have a profound and continuing influence on post-war Himalayan climbing. Nanga Parbat offered a special challenge to Herrligkoffer for Willy Merkl, who had lost his life on the 1934 expedition, was his half-brother, and the young Herrligkoffer resolved that he would see the mountain climbed to fulfil 'a sacred trust'. His chief problem was that, though he had read everything about Nanga Parbat he could lay his hands on, Herrligkoffer was playing out of his league. He was not a climber. Unfazed, he allotted himself the role of organiser and enlisted a veteran of the 'thirties expeditions, Peter Aschenbrenner, as climbing leader.

An important member of the team was Hermann Buhl. Coming from the same sort of working-class background as Brown and Whillans, he had the geographical advantage over them of living in Innsbruck, and by 1942 had already made his mark as a rock climber in the Eastern Alps. He ended the war as a Russian POW, but survived to return to the Alps and make some impressive climbs, including the first traverse of the Aiguilles de Chamonix. Buhl was a determined rather than a technically brilliant climber, and it was to be a quality which served him well on his first trip to the Himalaya.

Inevitably, friction developed between the lead climbers and the organisation. It is easy enough for the man out in front to think he's the only one doing any work on an expedition. The climbers fretted at the delay in stocking the higher camps, Herrligkoffer's instructions were ignored, Aschenbrenner went home, and climbers and organisation became entrenched physically as well as mentally apart. It was a recipe for defeat out of which emerged an incredible individual success when Hermann Buhl set out from Camp 5 at 6900m in what became a solo bid for the summit.

First he had to climb 1220m on the undulating ridge, then cover five miles over the Silver Saddle, up and down the Fore Peak, to the Bazhin Gap. He experienced some difficulty on the pinnacles before the final shoulder, but eventually crawled on all fours to the summit of Nanga Parbat at seven o'clock in the same evening. On the way down he had to survive a forced bivouac with no tent or proper clothing at nearly 8000m and he staggered back into Camp 5 next morning badly frostbitten and looking like a wizened old man.

Left, a drained Hermann Buhl, on return from his remarkable solo push to the summit of Nanga Parbat. Right, Dr Karl Herrligkoffer, the abrasive leader of a succession of postwar German Himalayan expeditions. Not a serious mountaineer himself, he was obliged to direct operations from Base Camp which exacerbated the difficulties of dealing with ambitious climbers like Hermann Buhl or Reinhold Messner.

The other major attempt on an 8000m peak in 1953 was very different from either of the two already described. Charles Houston wanted another try at K2 and obtained permission for 1953. He took Bob Bates, who had been with him in 1938, and five other like-minded Americans, and the team was completed by Captain Tony Streather as transport officer, a British link with pre-war days but, in Streather's case, Houston recognised his experience of having climbed Tirich Mir (7706m) with a Norwegian expedition in 1950, by making him a full climbing member of the team.

At first things went well. They all got on together, were fit, capable and acclimatising steadily, pushing the route out on familiar ground on the Abruzzi Spur, seeing all too many sad reminders of the disastrous 1939 expedition. The weather began to break up in mid-July, with high winds and heavy snowfall, but they just kept going, using the same capsule-style approach that had been so successful in 1938.

On 1st August Schoening and Gilkey established Camp 8 on the shoulder below the summit pyramid at around 7770m and by 2nd August all eight of them, including Streather, were there, ready for their push to the summit. The weather was still wild and unsettled and that night a storm raged, tearing at their tents, with the snow crushing in upon them. But they had enough food and were determined to sit it out, to snatch a fair spell when surely it must occur. Unless you've experienced it, it is difficult to imagine the debilitating discomfort of life in a storm, packed into a small tent, with sleeping bags getting progressively wetter from the condensation and the spindrift, the battering of the tent material, the effort needed to make a recalcitrant stove work, the time it takes to melt snow, and the horror of going out into the storm to relieve yourself. But their morale and will to reach the top remained high as they planned their summit bid.

Charlie describes his approach as leader:

> The philosophy of our expedition had avoided one-man decisions, and I was reluctant to choose by myself the men who might have the great chance for the crowning effort. We took a secret ballot, therefore, selecting our two best men by vote of all. Each of us thought carefully and long, and when I crawled back from the other tents through the blizzard, I was prouder than ever before of my party. When the ballots were counted, Bell and Craig were to be the first team, Gilkey and Schoening the second. But I asked Ata [liaison officer] not to tell their names to the porters when I radioed him that night, for one of our cherished hopes was to preserve the anonymity of the summit pair – if they succeeded. We hoped to report, 'Two men reached the top' – no more, no less.

This level of consultation was made easier by their style of ascent with the team rarely dispersed between more than two adjacent camps. It is interesting to conjecture whether the same approach could have worked on the 1953 Everest expedition, when there were so many more different permutations and priorities.

At last on 7th August the storm relented and they started thinking of the summit but as Art Gilkey crawled out of his tent, he collapsed unconscious in the snow. Houston diagnosed thrombophlebitis, a clot of blood formed in the veins of his left calf. Quite apart from the danger to his leg, bits of the clot could break away and be carried up to his lungs with fatal consequences. His only chance of survival was for them to get him down from altitude quickly.

So they started down, ploughing through the deep new snow, hauling Art in his sleeping bag, wrapped in a tent, as if he were a sledge, no easy feat, even with seven to do it. Their first attempt led them into an avalanche zone from which they had to struggle back to their starting point.

The storm returned; their position was desperate and yet, amazingly, they were still discussing the possibility of snatching the summit, while they waited for Gilkey's condition to improve, but there was little hope of that, and in fact it was worsening. His lungs were affected and clots had appeared in his other leg. On the 10th, even though the weather was as bad as ever,

Houston announced they had to retreat if Gilkey were to have any chance at all of survival.

They had now been ten days at over 7700m, and quite apart from the effects of altitude, had been on short rations and were badly dehydrated. Lowering a helpless man down steep ground is a slow precarious business, requiring careful co-ordination of effort, even at sea level. At altitude, in a storm with an exhausted team, it was a nightmare. They were hit by one avalanche on the ridge but survived it and then came level with, but to one side of, the site of Camp 7. To reach it they had to cross a slope of bare ice and somehow swing Gilkey across. They were all roped together, belayed by Schoening and most of them had crossed the slope when Bell slipped and catapulted down, pulling Streather off, who in turn pulled down Molenaar, Houston, and Bates. They went hurtling down the slope, dependent on the strength of one man and his ice axe belay. Somehow Schoening held them and miraculously no one was seriously hurt, though Houston was badly concussed, hardly aware of where he was or capable of helping himself. Bates got through to him by saying with great intensity, looking straight into his eyes, 'Charlie, if you ever want to see Dorcas and Penny [his wife and daughter] again, *climb* up there right now.' It worked, though Houston kept asking, 'What are we doing here?'

Leaving Gilkey anchored to the ice axe that had saved them all, they got themselves sorted out, prepared a campsite and returned to bring their friend across, only to find that he had vanished. There was no trace of the axe or rope, but there was a slight groove in the snow, indication of an avalanche, that must have swept everything away. A salvation and grievous loss all at the same time. They knew that not only had their chances of getting Art Gilkey down alive been minimal, but the effort would, in all probability, have cost them their lives as well. Yet they had never thought of abandoning him.

This remains one of the great stories of how a group of people working in unison can come through the most testing ordeals. It took its toll on those individuals, however. In 1954 a strong Italian party reached the summit, which was fitting because of the Duke of Abruzzi's pioneering expedition. Houston took this news hard because he had already received permisson to return in 1955. Whether he would have gone or not is unclear because his feelings were mixed. He relived the trauma, feeling the responsibility for Gilkey's death for many years, and he did no serious climbing after 1953. Instead he turned to altitude research on Mt Logan in the Canadian Yukon from 1967 to 1979, and subsequently in a decompression chamber in the Colorado Rockies. He also became director of the Peace Corps in India. In the summer of 1990 he was a fit and active seventy-eight-year-old who relished being amongst the mountains once again on the walk in to the Diamir Base Camp. If there was a tiny hint of regret that he had not reached any of those major tops, there was a much stronger joy and satisfaction in the full life he has led.

In the race for K2 the Italians, with their early expeditions, had a stake almost as strong as that of the Americans. Professor Ardito Desio, who had been a geologist on the Duke of Spoleto's 1929 K2 expedition, now organised the 1954 venture. Unlike Houston's effort, it was very much a national expedition with state funding. In the tradition of previous expeditions it was also hierarchic in structure, with a strong scientific research element and within the twelve-man climbing team a number of mountain guides who had a high standard of technical expertise (greater than that of the British on Everest), and were used to obeying orders. The expedition needed 500 porters to carry its gear into Base Camp.

Setting out much earlier than the Americans, they enjoyed good weather initially, making a steady build up on the Abruzzi Spur, but in mid-June they were hit by tragedy when Mario Puchoz developed pulmonary oedema and died before they could get him down. They resolved to continue the climb, but the weather deteriorated and it was the end of July before two of the strongest climbers, Achille Compagnoni and Lino Lacedelli went for the summit. Their nomination as the summit pair, and their eventual success, was to take a heavy toll on another member of the team. Walter Bonatti at the age of twenty-four had already emerged as one of Italy's most forceful alpinists. Ambitious, yet introverted, he had performed well on K2, and was determined to go to the summit but, like Houston on Nanda Devi before the war, he was struck down with food poisoning at the wrong moment to be included in the summit push.

Bonatti recovered fully, moved up in support and did his best to resign himself to this role, which was particularly difficult, since he felt he was stronger than either Lacedelli or Compagnoni. As so often happens, in even the most systematic expeditions, things have a habit of going wrong on the upper reaches of the mountain. The summit pair were planning to use oxygen for the final push, but the climbers carrying the respirators had failed to make it to the penultimate camp, so Bonatti had no choice but to go back down and collect them.

It ended with a harrowing experience that made his failure to reach the summit even more bitter. He collected the respirators and together with Mahdi, one of the Hunza porters, started back up the mountain, trying to get all the way to the top camp which Lacedelli and Compagnoni had set up. Bonatti and Mahdi failed to make it in the gathering dark and had a gruelling unprotected bivouac on a ledge Bonatti carved in the snow. Mahdi was not only bitterly cold but also terrified and hysterical. Bonatti called out over and over again to Lacedelli and Compagnoni, whom he was convinced were only just round the corner, but without response, until at last a light glimmered on the other side of the slope and he heard Lacedelli's voice clearly. He called for help but Lacedelli claims he could not understand and returned to the warmth of the tent.

Next morning, half frozen, Bonatti descended, while the summit pair crossed over to pick up the respirators and went on to the summit and their share of glory. This was the experience which, on his return home, drove Bonatti to his most remarkable solo ascent of the South-West Pillar of the Dru.

Herbert Tichy's expedition to Cho Oyu that autumn could not have been more different. Tichy, an Austrian anthropologist, was more a mountain traveller than a climber. He enjoyed the company of the Sherpas, and for choice travelled with them alone. To his seven Sherpa companions he added just two Europeans, Sepp Jöchler and Helmut Heuberger. His Sherpa leader was Pasang Lama who had been so close to the top of K2 with Fritz Wiessner in 1939.

Tichy had none of Shipton's inhibitions about encroaching on Chinese territory, but crossed the Nangpa La and established his Base Camp below the north side of the mountain inside Tibet. Gazing up into the vastness of the sky he saw his mountain. 'There before my eyes was Cho Oyu, and its ridges were ladders into that longed-for sky. Suddenly I had become a fanatic to climb them.' On their first attempt they were caught by a violent storm which threatened to rip their tent to pieces. In rescuing it Tichy plunged his gloveless hands deep into the snow and was so badly frostbitten his chance of contributing much more to the climb seemed over. But Tichy would not give in and, while Pasang went down to Namche Bazar for more food, he set about his recovery in the autumn sunshine. His recuperation was rudely interrupted however by the arrival of a Swiss expedition looking for something slightly easier to climb after giving up on Gauri Sankar. True, they had no permission for Cho Oyu. But why, suggested the pragmatic

Pasang Dawa Lama, left, a survivor of Wiessner's 1939 K2 expedition, made phenomenal speed to resupply Tichy's small team and keep alive their chance of climbing Cho Oyu ahead of the interlopers. Right, Tichy's frostbitten fingers made climbing an agony, but he reached the summit with Jochler and Pasang, determined not to be beaten by a rival Swiss party.

Swiss, looking meaningfully at Tichy's swollen fingers, did they not join forces? How about if they started establishing their camps but did not make their summit bid until Tichy's team had had another try from their top camp?

Tichy, the philosopher, was now spurred into competitive action. Without waiting for Pasang, the Austrians returned to the site of their Camp 3, a snow cave at 6590m, where they were pinned down by the first of the autumn storms. To their horror they saw some figures coming up out of the driving spindrift. It must be the Swiss, stronger in numbers, much fresher, and about to move past. Then with amazement they saw it was Pasang with two of their Sherpas. On learning of the arrival of the Swiss, he had travelled, heavily laden, from 4000m on the other side of the Nangpa La and some thirty miles away, getting back to them in two days.

His first question was:

'Have the Swiss done it?'

'No.'

'Thank God; I'd have slit my throat if they had.'

Tichy announced he would just go as high as possible to do what he could to help them. He could barely hold anything and certainly would have been unable to hold a fall by anyone else or stop himself. And yet he had it in the back of his mind that he could go to the summit. It was something that was becoming increasingly important to him. On that one climb he had all the competitive drive of a Desmaison, a Bonatti or a Messner, and yet combined with this obsession to reach the top was a profound spiritual experience: 'The world seemed to me to be instinct with a hitherto unknown benevolence and goodness. The barrier between me and the rest of creation was broken down. The few phenomena, sky, ice, rock, wind and I which now constituted life, were an inseparable and divine whole. I felt myself – the contradiction is only apparent – as glorious as God and at the same time no more than an insignificant grain of sand.'

Tichy, Jöchler and Pasang reached the summit of Cho Oyu at three o'clock in the afternoon of 19th October. In some ways it was the most remarkable ascent of all, not just because of the smallness of the team, but because of the spirit in which the climb was completed. Although the others nursed Tichy to the summit, it was his indomitable will combined with his warmth and compassion, that got them there to see how 'the endless blue sky fell steeply all around us like a bell. To have reached the peak was glorious, but the nearness of the sky was overwhelming.'

In 1955, Kangchenjunga, the third, and Makalu, the fifth highest mountains in the world were climbed. Charles Evans, the quiet brain surgeon from Liverpool, led the expedition to Kangchenjunga (28,208ft/8598m). His team of nine had a distinctly northern flavour, and included Joe Brown who had made such an impact on the British climbing scene. They were selected on a similar basis to that used by Charles Houston – of being capable mountaineers who could get on together. George Band, who had acclimatised poorly on Everest, was the only Oxbridge man.

They chose the Yalung Face, the route attempted by Crowley in 1905. It presents a huge complex of hanging glaciers, shelves and icefalls leading up to the summit rocks. The team worked well together, made steady progress and it was Joe Brown and George Band, using oxygen, who made the first ascent on 25th May from a top camp at 26,903ft (8200m). Joe Brown even managed to find a hand jam crack near the top, though Streather and Hardie on the second ascent did not have the same appetite for technical rock climbing at 8500m and found a way round it, sticking to the snow.

George Band a few feet below the summit of Kangchenjunga. He and Joe Brown refrained from standing on the top out of respect for the local belief that the summit was the abode of the gods.

The French meanwhile had targeted Makalu (8481m/27,825ft) and, after being repelled in 1954, succeeded triumphantly in 1955 with all nine climbers in the team, as well as the sirdar, reaching the summit. Lionel Terray and Jean Couzy, neither of whom had had the chance of reaching Annapurna's summit in 1950, were the first summit pair.

The height of 8000m was beginning to have a magic significance which has captured the imagination of continental climbers to a much greater degree than the British and Americans, brought up on feet. In the Alps there was the attraction of the 4000m peaks, and the symmetry of 8000m perhaps increased the magic. There are fourteen 8000m peaks in the Himalaya and by 1955 just six had been climbed. The rest seemed to fall more easily. In 1956 the Swiss returned to Everest and not only made the second ascent, but also turned right from the South Col and climbed Lhotse (8511m/27,923ft).

In 1957 an Austrian team of four set out for Broad Peak (8047m/26,400ft). It consisted of Hermann Buhl, of Nanga Parbat fame, Marcus Schmuck, Fritz Wintersteller and a young alpinist who was beginning to make a name for himself, Kurt Diemberger. In many ways they were the first modern-style expedition, for they had no high-altitude porters and, although they established three camps on the mountain, they used no fixed ropes. Their success in all four reaching the summit was all the more remarkable because of their disunity. Buhl fell out with Wintersteller and Schmuck. He had perhaps taken too much out of himself on Nanga Parbat, but he never went strongly on this expedition and maybe resented the fact. He naturally turned to Diemberger, who idolised him, and they climbed together throughout the trip. Wintersteller and Schmuck went to the summit first; Buhl and Diemberger followed, with Diemberger reaching the top far ahead of Buhl, going back for him, and accompanying his friend to the summit in the failing light at the end of a long hard day. Buhl was thus the first man to climb two 8000m peaks. Success did not unite the expedition. Schmuck and Wintersteller went off to make the first ascent of Skilbrum (7420m) while Buhl and Diemberger decided to try Chogolisa (7654m). There was possibly an element of competition in their choice, the desire to outdo the other pair. It was also the highest peak ever attempted in pure alpine-style, in other words, packing a rucksack at Base Camp and moving continuously up the mountain, bivouacking or camping on the way.

At first everything went well. Buhl had not only recovered from the climb on Broad Peak, he seemed to have a new lease of life. They were carrying heavy loads and Buhl was taking his share of breaking trail. At 450m below the summit the way seemed straightforward, but the weather was now beginning to break up. Without any markers behind them, they would never be able to find their way down in a white-out, so Buhl counselled caution and they started to retreat. Almost imperceptibly Diemberger drew ahead, picking his way carefully down the heavily corniced ridge, barely able to see where the snow-filled cloud began and the cornice lip ended. He very nearly walked through it. Shaken, he waited for Buhl and then, when he didn't appear, struggled back up the ridge, only to find a jagged gap in the cornice and a line of tracks leading into it.

What of the rest of the 8000m peaks? Manaslu (8156m/26,760ft) fell to the Japanese in 1956; the same year an Austrian expedition climbed Gasherbrum II (8035m/26,360ft). Gasherbrum I, (8068m/26,470ft) went to the Americans in 1958 in an expedition led by the lawyer, Nick Clinch, who was to be America's most successful expedition leader in the coming years. Pete Schoening, who had saved almost the entire K2 team by holding their fall in 1953, went to the summit with Andy Kauffman. Dhaulagiri

(8167m/26,795ft), sixth highest, was climbed by a Swiss/Austrian expedition using a Pilatus Porter plane to ferry supplies into Base Camp in 1960. Diemberger was one of the summitters. The only remaining 8000m peak was Shisha Pangma (8046m/26,398ft) which is in Tibet and this was climbed in 1964 by the Chinese with one of the large teams they have always favoured, six Chinese and four Tibetans reaching the summit.

The pressure of expeditions throughout the 'fifties and even the 'sixties was comparatively light, with only a few each year. Even in 1960, when I went to the Himalaya for the first time, Kathmandu had only one hotel; there were no tourists, and in the course of a walk around the Annapurna massif, we met only two fellow westerners, members of the Dhaulagiri expedition. Today you would probably see several hundred.

The unclimbed peaks below 8000m were being picked off quite slowly and the 8000m peaks, once climbed, tended to be left alone. The one inevitable exception was Everest. At first, perhaps, it was a question of patriotism, particularly in the case of the countries bordering the mountain. Both the Indians and Chinese put a considerable national effort into placing their first national on the summit. The Indians had three tries before Commander Kohli of the Indian navy finally found the right formula and weather for success, putting nine on the summit, the most of any expedition so far. The Chinese made an attempt from the north in 1960 with a huge team numbering 214. They claimed to have reached the summit, but at the time western experts tended to disbelieve them as they lacked adequate summit pictures because they got there in the dark. Their account was cloaked in Marxist rhetoric with reference to Communist party meetings at over 8000m and readings from *The Thoughts of Chairman Mao*. Since the thaw in relations with China in the 'eighties, western pundits have been more tolerant. I met one of the summitters, Wang Fu-chow, in 1981. He showed me the stumps of his fingers, described graphically how he had climbed the Second Step with bare hands and went on to the summit in the gathering night. I believe him.

The Americans also went to Everest in 1963. It was a big expedition, led by Norman Dyhrenfurth, son of G.O. Dyhrenfurth. Some of the team just wanted to get to the top of Everest by any means while others were more interested in pioneering and making a new route. Dyhrenfurth, an essentially liberal leader, resolved the dichotomy by having two objectives. Big Jim Whittaker, a guide from Mount Rainier, reached the top of Everest by the South Col route with the Sherpa, Nawang Gombu, Willi Unsoeld,

President Kennedy presents the National Geographic Society's Hubbard Medal to Norman Dyhrenfurth and the American Mount Everest team in 1963.

a dreamy philosopher, and Tom Hornbein, a sharp-eyed gnome of a man who was a brilliant academic scientist, chose the West Ridge, which they climbed with minimum support, trespassing into Tibet to cross the North Face to reach a couloir, now known as the Hornbein Couloir, which led to the top. They had a bivouac just below the summit on their way down, and then helped back to the South Col Barry Bishop and Lute Jerstad who were meant to be their support party, thus completing the first traverse of any 8000m peak. It was an amazing achievement.

The higher the mountain, the bigger the challenge. There can be no doubt about that. The debilitating effects of lack of oxygen, the greater scale of every natural obstacle, the consequences of storm, all contribute. But it is a gradually escalating scale and the higher 7000m peaks have the same attributes as the lower 8000ers. The measure is an artificial one that has protected some beautiful peaks from the obsessive attention that was to be seen in the 'seventies and 'eighties.

One of the most challenging and beautiful peaks in the entire Himalaya is Gasherbrum IV (7925m/26,000ft) towering majestic above Concordia at the head of the Baltoro Glacier. It was climbed in 1958 by Walter Bonatti and Carlo Mauri, members of an Italian expedition led by the great alpinist, Riccardo Cassin. Soaring walls of granite, steep and difficult cracks, give it a standard of climbing reminiscent of the best on the Mont Blanc massif at twice the height. Bonatti had at last reached a major Himalayan summit which, although it did not have the prestige of K2, was considerably harder.

It was around this time that I had my own introduction to the Himalaya. In 1960 I went to Annapurna II, a peak which at 7937m (26,040ft) is just tantalisingly below the 'magic number' and Nuptse (7880m/25,850ft) the following year. The latter is little more than the highest point of the long retaining wall, flung out from Lhotse to guard the Western Cwm of Everest. The easiest way to its summit is up its huge South Face, yielding a complex route seeking out the line of least resistance up crenellated spurs, across icefields to reach a gully stretching up towards the summit. Six of us reached the top. In 1962, Herrligkoffer returned to Nanga Parbat with an expedition which climbed the huge Diamir Face by a series of rocky buttresses and steep gullies leading up to the North Summit. Toni Kinshofer, Anderl Mannhardt and Sigi Löw, reached the top but Löw lost his life on the way down.

In the mid-sixties there came a respite for the mountains caused by the conflict between India and Pakistan and India and China. In addition, the Nepalese government had been embarrassed by a freelance television crew filming an attack by Khampa rebels, based in Nepal, on a Chinese convoy. As a result, the mountains were closed to climbers from the mid-sixties until the end of the decade. It was like damming a fast flowing river, and when climbers were allowed back in the explosion of energy thus engendered was to transform not only climbing techniques but the entire use, development and exploitation of the Himalayan region by the adventure-hungry climbers and trekkers of the developed world.

CHAPTER TWELVE

BIG WALLS-BIG TEAMS
Himalayan sieges of the 1970s and 1980s

•

I can remember sitting in a tiny snow hole half-way up the North Face of the Eiger, listening to John Harlin talk of his dream of climbing the South-West Face of Everest. This was the logical Himalayan progression from the Eiger and, if he had lived, I am sure he would have been one of the driving forces in the new challenge climbers found for themselves in the 'seventies on the big Himalayan walls. Among these, Everest inevitably had priority.

On the South-West Face of Everest a snow slope leads up to a huge Central Gully that ends in a sheer rock wall spanning the face at 8200m, higher than most other mountains in the world. This Rock Band was to be the crux that turned back the early expeditions. First off the mark were the Japanese with two useful reconnaissance expeditions in 1969 which gave them confidence for the following year. 1970 was the year of the Japanese as far as Everest was concerned. Not only was there a thirty-strong climbing party dividing its attentions between the South-West Face and the easier option of the South-East Ridge, but a second team was dedicated to getting a pair of skiers down the mountain from the South Col.

The climbers faced the same dilemma as the Americans in 1963. They wanted to be sure of putting the first Japanese on the summit, so the South-East Ridge team inevitably received priority. Uemura, destined to become one of Japan's leading climbers and adventurers, reached the summit by this route with Matsuura. But, despite its size, the expedition was not capable of sustaining both thrusts, particularly on a route as exacting as the South-West Face. Two climbers got close to the foot of a gully below the left-hand side of the Rock Band, but it was no higher than they had reached on their reconnaissance, and though they thought it climbable, they retreated under stonefall, content to take home to Japan an easier ascent and a somewhat spectacular ski descent (Miura launched himself on skis from the

South Col with a parachute to slow him down that failed to open and lived to tell the tale of the longest, highest fall ever).

1970 was the year of the big walls. While the South-West Face remained unclimbed, two other major routes succumbed. I led a British expedition to the South Face of Annapurna that same spring. Towering above the Sanctuary, Annapurna, like the Grandes Jorasses, has three summits and presents a magnificent buttressed wall, twice the height of its alpine counterpart. The highest point is the west summit and the route up to it seemed

the most reasonable, a cockscombed ice ridge like a flying buttress reaching up to a snow slope that in turn led to a great prow of rock guarding the summit slopes. The team was modest in size with eight lead climbers, three more in support and six Sherpa high-altitude porters.

The Annapurna team leader receives a word of advice in siege tactics before departure: l to r, John Hunt, Chris Bonington, Don Whillans, Martin Boysen, Nick Estcourt, Dave Lambert.

We very quickly learnt how few we were to maintain an effective siege on a steep face using fixed rope all the way, and recruited trekkers who visited our Base Camp to help carry loads on the lower part of the mountain. This style of climbing was outside the experience of the Sherpas and although they helped us loyally on the lower part of the mountain, it was up to the climbers to do all the carrying above 6000m. Apart from myself, only Don Whillans, Ian Clough and our American team member, Tom Frost, had climbed in the Himalaya before. But among the leading British alpinists in the party was the outstanding figure of Dougal Haston. He and Whillans formed a partnership on the climb, Dougal doing practically all the leading but learning from the older, more experienced man, who arguably was now getting beyond his prime. Whillans had always been a strong believer that training started when you left the last pub, but once on the mountain his judgement and abrasive drive made a very real contribution to our success.

So did two pieces of radical new equipment he designed which were to have a profound effect on future mountaineering. The most important was his sit-harness of stitched tape which, with modifications, has become the standard waist harness for all climbers throughout the world. His other innovation was the Whillans box. This was a box-shaped frame shelter developed from a wooden-framed structure he had designed on the Central Tower of Paine in 1963, when he and I discovered that no conventional tent would stand up to the high Patagonian winds. The Whillans box had an alloy frame which could be dug into a snow slope to withstand the pressure of the snow without collapsing as a normal tent would.

Leading a siege-style expedition in 1970 was a different matter from doing so in the 'fifties and 'sixties. The habit of obeying a leader, inculcated by war service or National Service, was no longer there and the climbers themselves were becoming more skilled, competitive, individually ambitious and deserving of their chance to succeed. So when there is probably only an opportunity for making one summit push, the leader finds himself in an invidious position. My team relations were severely tried at times, especially when I appeared to be favouring Whillans and Haston as our best bet for the summit. But it was certainly heroic team effort that got them there, with Tom Frost and the irrepressible climbing cameraman, Mick Burke, outflanking the rock prow that guarded the upper part of the face, and Martin Boysen, Nick Estcourt, Ian Clough and myself carrying to high camps so that Whillans and Haston could make their push to the

Tom Frost, top left, one of America's outstanding rock climbers; below left, Ian Clough trying to thaw out with Don Whillans at Camp 6. His tragic death in an avalanche below Camp 2 destroyed the joy of a successful ascent of Annapurna by Haston and Whillans. Right, Chris Bonington on Annapurna, the first Himalayan big wall to be climbed.

summit, climbing unroped, with great billowing clouds, outriders of the monsoon, piled around them. It was the first of the Himalayan big walls to be climbed.

As we returned to Kathmandu, our initial joy at success shattered by the death of Ian Clough near the bottom of the face, a German expedition, led by the inevitable Dr Herrligkoffer, was just starting on the huge Rupal Face of Nanga Parbat which, extending for 5000m, is bigger, though not as steep, as the South Face of Annapurna. Reinhold Messner and his brother, Günther, were members on their first Himalayan expedition.

Reinhold had taken a leading part in the climbing and was determined to make a fast solo bid for the summit from their high camp at 7350m before the monsoon closed in. As he climbed he realised there was someone coming up behind him. It was Günther. Together, as they had done so many times in the Dolomites, the brothers climbed to the summit. But the scale of the Himalaya was too severe a test for the younger Günther. Reinhold realised that his brother would never be able to climb back down the steep walls of the Merkl Gully without a rope, so they settled in for a chill enforced bivouac to wait for some support. Attempts next morning to communicate their dilemma to two other members of the team on their own way to the summit failed as inexplicably as Desmaison's on the Walker Spur. Now the Messners' only hope of survival lay in retreat down the long, easier, but unknown, slopes of the Diamir Face.

It was a desperate descent, yet somehow Reinhold, out in front, managed to pick a way through the sérac walls and snow chutes down on to the Diamir Glacier. They had made the first complete traverse of the mountain. Messner had drawn ahead, there was running water to drink; he sat and waited for his brother. But Günther was never to arrive. An ice avalanche further back up the glacier was the inescapable evidence of how he had met his death. Even so Reinhold Messner scrabbled frantically at it with his bare hands and continued searching and shouting for another day and a night before admitting the worst and staggering emaciated, frostbitten and broken down to a high grazing camp of some local shepherds. It was an experience very few people would have survived physically or emotionally, but Messner's first experience of the Himalaya was to be a traumatic introduction to an increasingly challenging career in the world's highest mountains.

The French expedition to Makalu in the spring of 1971 was very different. Where Herrligkoffer's expedition ended in a savage flurry of legal

Reinhold Messner, left, after the traumatic experience of climbing his first 8000m peak. He was to go on to be the first man to climb Everest without oxygen, solo an 8000m peak (Nanga Parbat again) by a new route, solo Everest, climb two 8000m peaks in a continuous push and, finally, all fourteen eight-thousanders. Right, Günther Messner, who reached the summit of Nanga Parbat by its huge Rupal Face with his brother, only to be lost in an avalanche at the foot of the Diamir Face at the end of an epic descent involving an unplanned traverse of the mountain.

recrimination, the French worked happily together on the formidable West Buttress, with a good balance of seasoned climbers, like Lucien Berardini who had been on the first ascent of the West Face of the Dru, and upcoming younger stars like Yannick Seigneur who was one of the successful summit pair.

But in 1971 the attention of the climbing world was once more on Everest and the latest assault on its South-West Face by an international expedition of all the talents led by Norman Dyhrenfurth who had been so successful on Everest in 1963 and Colonel Jimmy Roberts. There were nineteen climbers from ten countries, the majority with impressive high-altitude credentials and expectations to match. Haston and Whillans were there, fresh from their success on Annapurna, and Uemura who had already reached the summit the previous year by the South Col. Like the Japanese, the international brigade gave itself two objectives and left it democratically to the climbers to decide whether they opted for the full West Ridge (a slight variation on the original American West Ridge route) or took up the challenge of the South-West Face.

At first all went well, but severe storm, viral infection and the death of the Indian member of the party brought home to them the over-extended nature of their enterprise. A vote was taken, as a result of which it was agreed that all their resources should now be concentrated on the South-West Face. At which point the Italian and French members, who had favoured a complete switch to the South Col, packed up and went home. On parting, Mazeaud is reputed to have said of the British, 'How can they expect me, a French Deputy, to work as a porter?' It was a rhetorical question on which the entente eventually fractured, leaving two Britons, two Japanese and two Austrians to push a route up the Great Central Gully.

This might have been enough to climb the face, though the Austrians were unable to get on with Whillans, complaining he was hogging the lead, and eventually retired. The two Japanese seemed content to remain in support, whether out of a disciplined courtesy, or genuine preference it is difficult to know. Whillans and Haston stayed out in front the whole time, sitting out any bad weather and inevitably using up the oxygen supplies. When they reached the Rock Band instead of going for the left-hand gully favoured by the Japanese the previous year, Whillans opted for a broad snow ramp leading up and to the right. But the monsoon was now getting close, everyone was tired, supplies coming up the face had dwindled to a trickle, the way above was steep and difficult, and they had run out of fixed rope. It was obvious they would not be able to make an effective bid for the summit, so they abandoned the attempt at 8300m, part way up a shallow gully stretching up through the Rock Band. The expedition had achieved a great deal, but any recognition of this was lost in the storm of acrimony that accompanied and followed it.

Dr Herrligkoffer was next in the queue in the spring of 1972. He invited Whillans and Haston to join him, presumably for their knowledge of the upper part of the face, but when Haston dropped out his place was taken by Hamish MacInnes, with whom Whillans had climbed the South-West Pillar of the Dru. Another Briton was Doug Scott, a newcomer to the big expedition game, but a powerful and accomplished climber who, over the years, had organised a series of enterprising low-budget expeditions to the Hindu Kush, Baffin Island and the Sahara, as well as climbing in North America, and putting up a series of very difficult artificial routes in Britain and the Alps. The expedition was no more successful than that of the previous year. This time it was the British who walked out, exasperated by Herrligkoffer's style and the attitude of their German partners.

In the autumn of 1972, I had my chance but with very little time to put the expedition together. At that time, no-one had reached the summit of an 8000m peak in the post-monsoon period. They had always been beaten by the savage winds and bitter cold of the Himalayan autumn. We had to take this slot, however, for the mountain was booked up for the pre-monsoon period for years ahead.

By the standards of previous South-West Face expeditions the team was quite compact, numbering seven lead climbers and four in a support role with twenty-four Sherpa high-altitude porters. The successful Anna-purna team provided a base, with Dougal Haston, Mick Burke and Nick Estcourt, plus Doug Scott and Hamish MacInnes from the previous year's bid. The notable omission was Don Whillans. His determination to stay out in front while others did the work, and my own doubts about being able to handle him combined to influence my decision to leave him out of the reckoning. Everest throws enough problems at a leader without him taking along his own pre-packaged.

In the event the expedition became a drawn-out battle of attrition with the savage winds in temperatures down to -40°F. We got no higher than the earlier attempts, but had become a good team and learnt a lot – not that we could put it to much use as the Japanese had permission for autumn 1973. They too were defeated by winter winds. Then we had our bit of luck. The Canadians cancelled a booking for 1975 and I immediately grabbed the slot.

The 1975 South-West Face expedition, sponsored by Barclays Bank, was the largest and best equipped ever to leave Britain. The team totalled nearly a hundred, with ten lead climbers, all in theory capable of reaching the summit, eight in support, and sixty-four high-altitude porters, a dozen cook staff and mail runners. It caused my newest and youngest climbing recruit, Peter Boardman, to observe mischievously that being invited on a Bonington expedition was the last great colonial experience.

Our Sherpas filled a vital role, doing the vast bulk of the carrying, though we had at least moved on from the 1920s, with the climbers being responsible for all their own personal kit and doing the odd carry. Pertemba, the sirdar or chief Sherpa, was a manager in a very modern sense. Only twenty-five years old, intelligent, a charismatic leader, he had been educated in Ed Hillary's school in Kunde and had visited Europe and the United States, yet remained in touch with his traditional culture and values. I consulted closely with him throughout the expedition. We had excellent, relaxed and friendly relations with our Sherpa team. Mike Thompson commented:

> As a 'support climber', I was aware that I was fortunate to have got as far as becoming the Camp 4 Commandant, responsible, in theory, for five face boxes, an equipment dump, nine Sherpas, and a variable number of 'lead climbers' in transit. I became obsessed with actually becoming a Sherpa and increasingly I resented the lead climbers who passed through on oxygen carrying just their personal equipment. I was quite ridiculously touched when, having managed to drag myself and my load up to Camp 5 without oxygen, Pertemba said, with what I now suspect was heavy sarcasm: 'You are a real Sherpa now'.

The morality of tempting Sherpas onto the mountains with the offer of high pay by Nepalese standards and inevitably exposing them to risk has been questioned. On Everest, ferrying loads day after day through the Icefall, they are arguably exposed to greater risk than any of the climbers who make as few journeys as possible through this danger area. By 1975, and increasingly today, however, the Sherpas do have alternative opportunities of earning good money guiding treks below the snowline at no risk to themselves, and yet they still join expeditions, in many cases I imagine from similar motivation to that of the visiting climbers – the excitement, the camaraderie, the desire for fame and an ambition to get to the top of the mountain. They understand the risks and accept them. This however does not relieve expeditions of a heavy responsibility for the safety of their Sherpas. We lost a young lad who fell into a glacier stream carrying a load up to Base Camp. We hadn't even reached the more tangible dangers of the mountain, but it didn't diminish our shock and grief. After heavy snowfall I always agonised over the decision whether to declare the route through the Western Cwm safe from avalanches and always erred on the side of caution.

Our expedition was a carefully planned siege, yet getting it right has its own satisfaction, particularly for a frustrated field-marshal like me who enjoys the task of planning and man-management. But whatever the logistics, nothing can detract from the thrill of having a turn out in front.

In 1975, the ascent of the Rock Band and the final push for the summit were immensely exciting for the climbers concerned and for those watching and waiting down below. It was Nick Estcourt and Tut Braithwaite who had the role of forcing the Rock Band. In doing this there was an element of sacrifice, for they knew that they were setting it up for another summit pair, but they also knew that their job was to find the solution to a problem that had now stopped five expeditions.

We had reverted to the line investigated by the Japanese in 1969 and 1970, the deep-cut gully to the left. It was still a gamble, for we had not managed to get hold of any photographs that showed its entire length, but this was the spot where the Rock Band was the least high, and there seemed a fair chance of success. In addition, we were in much better shape than any of the previous expeditions, who had all been on their last legs by the time they got to the Band.

It was 20th September when Nick Estcourt and Tut Braithwaite, supported by Mick Burke and myself, started up the deep-cut groove leading into what seemed the very heart of the mountain. Estcourt had already run out of oxygen, but he just kept going. Braithwaite ran out when still half-way up. The crux came at about 8230m on a broken snow-covered ramp beneath an overhanging yellow wall. It was Estcourt's turn to lead: 'I was getting desperate, goggles all misted up, panting helplessly I somehow managed to clear some of the snow behind the boss, using my fingers, while my arm still held my weight. I was losing strength fast. I think the others thought I was about to fall off, but whatever happened I wasn't going to give up. If I had, and let Tut do it, I'd have kicked myself for years.'

Estcourt didn't give up and in completing that pitch he solved the problem of the Rock Band and opened the upper part of the face for Doug Scott and Dougal Haston to make their bid for the summit from a camp above the Rock Band. Like John Hunt in 1953, I also took part in the carry to the top camp, with the instinctive desire of the leader to reassure himself that everything possible has been done, before handing over the outcome of the expedition to the summiting pair.

There was still a long way to go and Scott and Haston's first job was to run a line of fixed rope across the icefield below the South Summit. This would mean they could make faster initial progress on their summit day, safeguard their descent and make it easier for the next attempt. They went for the summit on 24th September, their progress slowing to a crawl in a gully below the South Summit where the snow was thigh-deep and unconsolidated. But they kept going, almost swimming up it, to reach the South Summit at 4.30 p.m. They had climbed the face but to reach the top they still had to negotiate the summit ridge. The snow was firmer. They were able to make reasonable progress as late afternoon crept into dusk. It was 6.30 p.m. when they reached the top of Everest. In Dougal Haston's words:

We were sampling a unique moment in our lives. Down and over into the brown plains of Tibet a purple shadow of Everest was projected for what must have been something like 200 miles. On these north and east sides there was a sense of wildness and remoteness, almost untouchability. Miraculous events seemed to be taking place in the region of the sun. One moment it seemed to dip behind a cloud layer lying a little above the horizon. End Game, thought we. But then the cloud dropped faster than the sun and out it came again. Three times in all. I began to feel like Saul on the road to Tarsus.

It was now too late to get back to the top camp in the dark, so they bivouacked in a snow hole at 8760m, shivering and hallucinating the night away. They ran out of oxygen at an early stage and only had enough fuel to melt snow for a couple of drinks of lukewarm water. It is a tribute to their physical condition that they came through the night without frostbite.

It is so tempting for a leader to close an expedition once success has been achieved, but in 1975 two more summit bids were planned and we

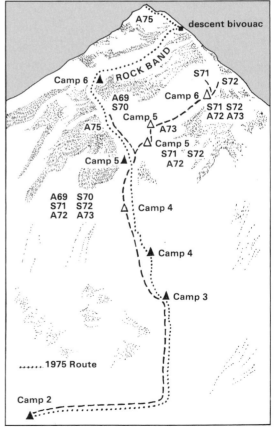

Mick Burke, climber and cameraman, who probably reached the summit of Everest alone in 1975 but disappeared in the blizzard on the descent. Right, the South-West Face of Everest, showing the progress of the six earlier attempts and the line of the successful 1975 ascent.
A69: autumn 1969, Japanese
S70: spring 1970, Japanese
S71: spring 1971, International
S72: spring 1972, Europeans
A72: autumn 1972, British
A73: autumn 1973, Japanese
A75: autumn 1975, British
(Note: the autumn 1972 and 1973 expeditions reached the height of Camp 6 at the right-hand foot of the Rock Band, but did not establish camp there.)

had the supplies to support them. The first was to be mounted by Mick Burke and Martin Boysen, who had worked so hard on Annapurna, then would follow Peter Boardman with Pertemba, our Sherpa sirdar, to honour a promise that at least one Sherpa should be given a summit chance. Even as they set out the weather was changing. Martin Boysen lost a crampon and his oxygen set gave out, so he retreated. Mick Burke also fell behind, leaving Peter Boardman and Pertemba to go to the summit together. As they returned, still above the Hillary Step, they were surprised to find a figure climbing towards them out of the mist. It was Mick Burke. He had been an hour slower than they, but was now only ten minutes from the summit. The others agreed to wait for him at the South Summit. It was the last time he was seen alive.

The weather began to deteriorate into a full-blown blizzard. Boardman and Pertemba waited for three-quarters of an hour for Mick Burke but he did not reappear and eventually Boardman was forced to take the agonising but realistic decision to retreat while it was still possible. They only just made it, being hit by an avalanche on the way down the South Summit gully and having great difficulty in finding the end of the fixed rope.

As for Mick Burke, who most probably did get to the summit, he took a well calculated risk, one Charles Evans declined on virgin ground in 1953, but one most of us would have taken in the circumstances of 1975 with the highest point on earth within reach, a line of tracks going all the way to the top and the knowledge that the difficult steps en route had fixed rope in position. The risk he took is the very essence of climbing and poignantly emphasises the fine balance between success and disaster that accompanies every expedition to the higher peaks.

Everest apart, there were plenty of other successful and demanding siege-style ascents. In the spring of 1972 Messner joined an Austrian expedition to the South Face of Manaslu (8156m/26,760ft). It is a huge complex face, of steep crumbling rock walls and chaotic icefalls. The only safe route was up a sheer rock buttress on the lower part of the face, followed by a serpentine traverse avoiding the dangerous upper rocks and sérac walls. The upper part of the climb over a series of long featureless snow slopes is not technically difficult. Messner, predictably, kept going alone to the summit when his partner, Jäger, turned back. Descending disorientated in thick cloud Messner heard Jäger calling but assumed he was safely at the top camp. He was not. Two other team-mates went out to look for him and one of these also failed to return. Inevitably there was criticism of

Messner for not escorting Jäger back to camp. But though one of the cardinal climbing school precepts is that the team should never split up, in the realms of extreme mountaineering such rules cannot always be applied.

In the explosion of activity through the mid-seventies a big part was now being played by Eastern European climbers. Ales Kunaver led the Yugoslavs on Makalu, reaching the top of its formidable South Face in 1972 and then returning in 1975 to complete the climb, putting seven on the summit. He went on to join the effort to climb the huge South Face of Lhotse in 1981 reaching 8300m, the highest point to that date. It was Yugoslav climbers who finally made it all the way to the top of the West Ridge of Everest in 1979. But most active were the Poles, who had a long tradition of climbing in their native Tatra and were at last being allowed out, albeit in a state controlled way that would have been the despair of the west but produced in them some rugged individualists, skilled at subverting all forms of bureaucracy in their own régime as well as in Asia. At the same time it gave them a strong sense of unity that enabled them to work effectively as teams in siege situations. Their background contributed to this. A network of local clubs was essential for the level of co-operation needed to go climbing in the Tatra, let alone abroad. The nature of the system led to a very controlled environment where a novice would rise through supervised graded courses until given permission to climb in the Alps, the Hindu Kush or the Himalaya. Before this the climbers had to turn steeplejacks, painting factory chimneys using climbing techniques, to raise expedition funds, and then become skilled fixers in order to acquire and stockpile scarce 'luxury' expedition food and gear destined for export or the more privileged members of the communist hierarchy. Working the system was as important a preliminary of Polish climbing as getting fit.

Andrzej Zawada led their first major Himalayan expedition in 1971, to Kunyang Kish (7852m), a complex mountain which had already defeated two expeditions in the 'sixties. Zawada evolved a system which was to stand the Poles in good stead in the years to come. There were no experienced high-altitude porters in that part of the Karakoram (the Poles rarely had enough funds to pay for them anyway) so they planned on doing all the carrying themselves. This approach has rarely been very successful with western expeditions, who tend to lack the stoicism and self-discipline needed to share the chores. He made a thorough reconnaissance, avoided the long and potentially dangerous lower part of the ridge by climbing a steep face, and succeeded in putting four people, including himself, on top of the

227

Left, Ales Kunaver, one of the foremost Yugoslav expedition leaders to Makalu and Lhotse. Right, Andrzej Zawada, a brilliant manipulator of the Eastern Bloc system, led eight successful Polish siege-style expeditions to challenging objectives that included the first winter ascent of Everest.

mountain. The mountain only had its second ascent in 1988 when a small British expedition, comprising five young climbers on their first visit to the Himalaya, poineered its North Ridge with Keith Milne and Mark Lowe reaching the top, a remarkable achievement by any standards. Zawada went on to lead eight successful expeditions which included the first winter ascents of Everest in 1980 and Cho Oyu in 1985. In this respect he was more successful than Messner, whose attempts on Cho Oyu and Makalu in winter both failed.

The Himalaya in winter takes on a savagery that is difficult to imagine, with winds of up to eighty mph and temperatures down to -40°F. This, combined with the effects of altitude, makes a deadly cocktail, creating a high risk of frostbite or death from hypothermia. The Poles particularly have had a very high success rate in winter, combined with a low casualty tally. The reason might be that winter climbing, quite apart from requiring well designed warm gear and very resilient climbers, demands a high level of teamwork, which in turn calls upon firm leadership particularly when siege tactics are employed, as has usually been the case. Within the former eastern bloc countries there has always been a strong incentive to achieve success as a team and for the individual to conform within it since this affects their chances of going on expeditions in the future. Though the climbing consensus in the west has now moved away from siege-style expeditions, the east Europeans' success at working together under a leader without losing their individualistic spirit must be one positive fruit of a totalitarian conditioning. Walking into a Polish base camp in the Himalaya is a happy experience, with a hospitable welcome and a great deal of fun.

This was also a period when Polish women began to take a more active part in expeditioning. Wanda Rutkiewicz is probably the most successful woman climber in the world. I met her in 1983 after a mountaineering conference in Delhi, and immediately recognised the drive and charisma which have led her into expedition organising. In 1975 she led her first Himalayan expedition to Gasherbrum II and III. It was meant to be a women's expedition but they allowed some men to tag along to help them through any difficulties they might encounter in a Muslim country. Wanda reached the summit of Gasherbrum III. She reached the top of Everest on the ubiquitous Herrligkoffer's expedition in 1978, Nanga Parbat in an all-women's expedition in 1985, and went to K2 in 1986, climbing it without oxygen, and becoming the first woman to reach the summit. She has also climbed Shisha Pangma (1987) and Gasherbrum II with Rhona Lampard in a British women's expedition, bringing her 8000m tally up to six.

Of women's climbing she comments, 'There is still a big difference between men and women climbers. The best woman climber is still not quite as good as the best male climber. It's like the Olympics where the fastest woman runner is not as fast as the fastest man. It is the same in the mountains.' This physiological fact is reflected in the history of climbing. No major first ascents that push back the thresholds have been completed by women. There has however been a steady increase in their involvement and their success, particularly in the sphere of rock climbing where the difference between the best women climbers and the best men is very slight.

Through the 'eighties there was no diminution in the international attention being paid to the 8000m peaks, mainly by siege-style expeditions. Today Everest has over a dozen different routes to its summit. Its last great face, the Kangshung, fell in 1983 to the Americans who used a petrol-driven winch to haul supplies up the steep rock buttress that guards the base. Climbers of all nations have shared in ticking off the routes and, besides the east Europeans, the Japanese and more recently the South Koreans have been very active.

The Russians came on the scene with the arrival of *glasnost*. Their collectivist culture has always favoured large groups, even when climbing alpine-style, and they had their own high mountains in the Pamirs on which to develop their big-expedition techniques. On their first expedition to the Himalaya in 1982 they made the first new route on the South-West Face of Everest since our British ascent in 1975, forcing an impressive line up the broken buttresses to the left of the Great Central Gully leading up to the West Ridge and getting eleven climbers to the summit. It was a notable achievement. They went on to make a highly organised grand traverse of Kangchenjunga with a team of thirty-two Russians and seventeen Sherpas in the spring of 1989 and the following year climbed the South Face of Lhotse, once again with a large expedition, using fixed ropes and bottled oxygen.

The Russians are finding, as we found in 1975, that if your team is big and well equipped enough and your planning is good, almost anything is possible. But having discovered that we, and other like-minded climbers, began to look elsewhere for our adventure. The old siege-style expedition with porters, fixed ropes, oxygen and pre-stocked camps is now the dinosaur of the climbing scene and, though not extinct, should be allowed to fade quietly away. The future of climbing lay in seeking out that quality of uncertainty that is the essence of adventure. This entailed climbing in smaller groups, even going alone on the highest and steepest places in the Himalaya.

CHAPTER THIRTEEN

THE ART OF SUFFERING

Extreme climbing in the Himalaya

•

They just had to pick up their sacks and start walking up the glacier. A month before our British expedition set out for its second and successful siege of the South-West Face of Everest, Reinhold Messner and Peter Habeler were about to attempt a new route in a daringly new way on an 8000m peak. Only a few months before, Messner had been part of a large Italian expedition, led by Riccardo Cassin, laying siege to the South Face of Lhotse. Bad weather and avalanches had undermined the morale of the team and they had abandoned the attempt, only confirming Messner's disillusionment with large expeditions. Now, just three months later, at the head of the Baltoro Glacier he had the chance of putting a cherished theory into practice and attempt to climb the North-West Face of Gasherbrum I (8068m/26,470ft) in genuine alpine-style.

His partner, Peter Habeler, was a guide from Mayrhofen in Austria who had climbed with Messner over a long period. In 1974 they had made a record ascent of the North Wall of the Eiger in ten hours, a reassuring sign that they could both move fast on difficult ground. They had also trained intensively. Like the modern rock climber who trains specifically for his craft, Messner undertook an intense schedule of distance running, exercises and diet to build up his stamina. His pulse rate was down to forty-two beats per minute and he could gain a thousand metres in height on his training runs in under an hour, all this at a time when British mountaineers regarded the act of climbing itself as sufficient training for the Himalaya.

In a traditional siege-style expedition, acclimatisation is taken care of by the procedures of the walk-in, the routine of taking turns out in front, establishing camps, and having rests at Base Camp. But the essence of an alpine-style push is to gain height fast, a precise prescription for altitude sickness. To avoid this, the climber needs to gain his acclimatisation on lower neighbouring peaks. There are different ideas about how this is best achieved, but in 1975 very little had been tested. Messner and Habeler contented themselves with a few reconnaissance climbs to around 6000m before setting out for the snow basin under the North-West Face.

Here they reduced their loads still further, throwing out spare food, and gaz cartridges, even the rope, on the grounds that climbing roped would slow them down and that the rock on the face looked so loose that a rope would only give them a false sense of security. They set out in the early hours of the pre-dawn, each man a self-sufficient unit, yet supported by the presence of the other.

The climbing was immensely serious, particularly in its upper part on steep yet badly broken rock. The steep section of the face ended at around 7000m on a shoulder where they bivouacked for the night. From there the North-West Spur swept more easily another thousand metres to the summit which they accomplished the following day. Not only was it the first 8000m peak to be climbed alpine-style, it was also by far the fastest ascent – just three days from Base Camp on a new route. It also made Messner the only man to have climbed three 8000m peaks.

In many ways this ascent was the most innovative of all Messner's climbs, bringing to technically challenging routes on the higher peaks of the Himalaya the same approach as used in the Alps, with the commitment, the freedom of movement and the sheer quality of adventure which this approach entails. It did not mean the end of siege-style climbing in the Himalaya, even by Messner himself. It is all too easy to become ensnared in semantics when talking about alpine-style. There are times when it just makes sense to use some fixed rope and one or two camps to reach a good launch pad for an alpine-style push carrying bivouac equipment.

In the spring of 1978 Messner and Habeler joined a party, led by Messner's old friend, Wolfgang Nairz, to climb Everest by the South Col route. It was to be a conventional expedition, using fixed camps, supplementary oxygen and porters, for Messner and Habeler needed the framework of a siege-style expedition to allow them to make a quantum leap into the unknown. They wanted to be the first climbers to reach the summit of Everest without oxygen. Back in 1924 Norton had reached a height of 8570m without oxygen and Messner himself had flown over Everest in a light plane without putting on an oxygen mask, but this was very different from actually climbing to the very summit. There were plenty of experts who said it was impossible and that they would almost certainly die in the attempt.

Reinhold Messner's historic photograph of himself on the summit of Nanga Parbat after he had made the first solo ascent of an 8000m peak.

Messner and Habeler played their part in making the route through the Icefall, the Western Cwm and up onto the Lhotse Face, in return for which they were allowed first crack at the summit, and at a second attempt on 8th May they succeeded in reaching the top of Everest without supplementary oxygen.

Only two months later, Messner was camped at the side of the lateral moraine below the Diamir Face of Nanga Parbat at almost the spot where he had waited with dawning horror for Günther to join him in 1970. Now he had just one other person for company, Ursula Grether, a medical student who had trekked into the Everest Base Camp that spring. His objective was a solo ascent of Nanga Parbat. This was something he had tried on two previous occasions, but he had not been ready and had barely started the climb before abandoning the attempt. He now had the right ingredients, the confidence and knowledge gained on his unroped ascent of Gasherbrum I, his strength on Everest without oxygen and the fact that on this visit to Nanga Parbat he had the emotional support of Ursula, as far as the side of the glacier at least.

He started early in the morning, cutting across the glacier, to turn the huge sickle-shaped sérac wall that guards the lower part of the Diamir Face on its right. He made good progress, gaining 1600m in six hours, and stopping before the heat of the day. The following morning, as he melted snow for a drink, the gentle roar of the stove was drowned by a rushing, roaring rumble that came from all around him. It was as if the entire mountain was on the move. He had chosen his campsite well, for the sérac wall above had saved him. Had he set out twenty-four hours later, he and Ursula would have been in the direct line of the huge avalanche. Much later he learned that this had been caused by an earthquake whose epicentre was in the knee-bend of the river Indus in its serpentine course through the mountains.

It never occurred to him to turn back. Neatly folding the tent, he set out once again in the bitter cold of the early morning, heading for the next barrier, a broken wall of rock and ice stretching down from the crest of the ridge. He was going more slowly now, each step taking a separate effort of will. There was no question of racing the sun, and once this crept over the shoulder the bitter cold changed to blazing heat and the snow soon turned into a treacherous morass. But still he kept going, and stopped just beneath the great trapezoid of rock that marked the summit block. He was now at a height of around 7400m, another thousand metres gained, another long afternoon to savour his isolation.

Intermittently he was hallucinating another presence. It was a girl at the extreme edge of vision. They talked. She reassured him that the weather would hold, that he would reach the summit the following day. Next morning the clouds were threatening, his body more weary and, with still 600m to go to the top, every step was a separate effort of will power. It was 4.00 p.m when finally he reached the summit, and he had achieved yet another major innovative first, the first 8000m peak solo. He still had to get down. The weather that had been threatening for the past twenty-four hours broke that night when he was back in his tent. He couldn't move the following day. Good visibility was essential. But the next day dawned fine and he was able to descend the steep slope, straight down an avalanche runnel, on the very brink of exhaustion.

In 1979 he climbed K2, his fifth 8000m peak, with a six-man expedition. His original objective was the South Buttress, by what he named his 'Magic Line', but there had been delays on the way in and they were badly shaken when a porter was killed at the bottom of the mountain, so Messner changed his objective to the Abruzzi Spur, reaching the summit with Michl Dacher. Not all his team were pleased with the change of objective. The Italian, Renato Casarotto came back to try the Magic Line once more in 1986 and was among those who died in that fateful summer on K2.

In 1980 Messner returned to Everest to link what he had learnt about his own capacity on Everest and on Nanga Parbat in 1978 by climbing the North Face of Everest solo. The pattern of his Everest attempt was in many ways very similar to Nanga Parbat. A friend, this time Nena Holguin from Canada, was his sole companion. He arrived at the foot of the Rongbuk Glacier in July at the height of the monsoon, but the weather was too unsettled, the snow too deep, and so he took off, wandering for a month in western Tibet gaining acclimatisation. On his return in mid-August the weather seemed to have settled and so he went straight up to Advance Base at the head of the East Rongbuk Glacier, did one carry towards the North Col and, the following day, made his push to the summit, bivouacking where the pre-war Everest expeditions had sited their Camp 6 at a height of around 7800m. The following day he crossed the North Face on a similar line to that followed by Norton, and then Shipton and Smythe, before the war, camping short of the couloir that had been the pre-war climbers' high point. He went for the summit on the 20th, pushing himself very near his limits: 'I could not manage the last few metres – I crawled on hands and knees. It was continual agony; I have never in my whole life been so tired as on the summit of Mount Everest that day.' But he got back to his tent that night and all the way down the following day.

This ascent was typical of the technique Messner had successfully evolved, focusing on a single objective at a time, acclimatising to around the 5500m level, at which height there is very little physical deterioration, choosing his weather window very carefully and then moving as fast as possible to the summit and back, spending the minimum number of nights on the mountain. To put his solo Everest ascent in perspective, there had been twenty successful expeditions to that date, none of them with less than a total of thirty climbers and Sherpas, none of them altogether without oxygen, and not one of these expeditions had taken less than a month to climb the mountain.

But what to do next? Messner claims that he only decided to go for all fourteen of the 8000m peaks in 1982, but he was focusing in upon them from a much earlier stage. The night before setting out to climb Gasherbrum I in 1975, he describes counting the 8000ers in his mind, as if the germ of the idea was forming. He has certainly climbed very few peaks beneath the magic height. One exception was in the autumn of 1981, when he climbed Chamlang (7317m) with Doug Scott, to acclimatise for an attempt on a complete traverse of Makalu, up the South-East Ridge and down the North-West Ridge, six-and-a-half miles over the fifth highest mountain in the world. It was the brainchild of Scott who had attempted it the previous year, feeling that these great traverses in a continuous alpine-style push, without any kind of support, fixed camps or ropes, were the next logical step in the development of Himalayan climbing. That year, as they waited for the right weather window, Messner was forced to rush back to Kathmandu on learning that he had just become a father, when his daughter was born prematurely to Nena Holguin, his companion on Everest.

Scott went on to make another attempt on the traverse in 1984 with the Chamonix-based climber, Jean Afanassieff, and the young American, Stephen Sustad. They nearly made it. In just four days they were close to the summit but the weather was threatening, they had only half a gaz canister left and Afanassieff, who was very tired, counselled retreat. Doug tried to persuade him it made better sense to finish the ascent and descend by the easier French route. 'By now however Jean had shot down twenty feet. I pleaded for two hours more climbing but with, "I go," he was gone. Stephen and I looked at each other, shrugged and followed.'

They had a desperate descent with a near miss from an avalanche, an exhausting crossing of a high cwm ending with a climb back on to the ridge at the end of it that very nearly finished them off. This traverse still awaits a complete crossing.

Messner was now fully committed to all fourteen 8000ers. In 1981 he climbed Shisha Pangma; in 1982, Kangchenjunga, Gasherbrum II and Broad Peak; and in 1983, Cho Oyu. He has been accused of abandoning the innovative approach of his earlier climbs in his drive to be first to bag all the 8000ers. While in the latter stages there is some justice in this comment, none the less, he still kept notching up the firsts and in 1984 even repeated two of the peaks he had already climbed in order to explore yet another concept, a traverse of two 8000m peaks in a continuous progression without a descent to Base Camp.

The only pair of peaks which he considered feasible were Gasherbrum I and II. He made the traverse with fellow South Tyroler, Hans Kammerlander, with whom he was to climb seven of his 8000m peaks and with whom he has had the most amicable of all his climbing partnerships. They spent seven days mostly above 7000m, covering a lot of ground that was not technically difficult, but still fraught with objective danger, climbing Gasherbrum II first, down into the huge Gasherbrum valley and then all the way up Gasherbrum I. It was an amazing and very imaginative achievement.

In 1985 he started with Annapurna and went on in the same spring season to climb Dhaulagiri. The pressure was on, but he chose the challenging unclimbed North-West Face of Annapurna with a team of four, two of whom had recently climbed the North Wall of the Eiger in a mere five hours. They used fixed ropes on the lower part and then Kammerlander and Messner made a push for the summit with two bivouacs in the teeth of a storm, reaching it on the 24th April. As if that wasn't enough, the pair moved on to Dhaulagiri with the minimum of rest to climb the original route in a single four-day push.

That left just two peaks to climb, Makalu and Lhotse. Messner is insistent that he wasn't racing and that the concept of a race was built by media hype. The latter is undoubtedly true, but he was just as determined to be the first to climb all fourteen 8000m peaks without the use of oxygen. After giving up on Makalu in the winter, Messner and Kammerlander went for it in September 1986 and a couple of weeks later also climbed Lhotse, both by their normal routes. Racing or not, he had just beaten his closest rival, the Polish climber, Jerzy Kukuczka, to it.

He had over the years also been to the highest point of all but one of the continents. He had collected these quite casually, but selectively, with a new route where feasible on each. He climbed the Carstensz Pyramid in New Guinea, highest point of Australasia, in 1971, made a new route up the South Face of Aconcagua solo in 1974, one on Mount McKinley in 1976, and the first ascent of the Breach Wall of Kilimanjaro in 1978. Everest he climbed solo. It's difficult to find an interesting way up Mount Elbruz in the Caucasus, the highest point of greater Europe, so he just walked up it. Which left Mount Vinson in Antarctica, which he contrived a way of getting to in 1986. Climbing Vinson gave him the inspiration for his next challenge, for Messner is a man who needs challenges. The great empty wastes of Antarctica and the scope they offer for long journeys across the ice led to a crossing of Antarctica on foot with one companion – another first.

In his book, *All 14 Eight Thousanders*, Messner deplores the peak-bagging obsession of many modern climbers with the 8000m peaks, yet it was undoubtedly his own obsession that has encouraged this trend. Inevitably, fame and success has unleashed plenty of criticism of Messner who has been accused of being motivated solely by a hunger for fame or money. He certainly enjoys both. He lives in an exquisitely renovated castle on top of a hill above the Val Venosta in the Süd-Tyrol. His home is filled with artefacts collected from all over the world on his mountain travels. This provides another clue. Messner is a collector, of pictures, of Buddhist art, of books, of sculpture, of bits of rock, and a collector of mountains. Like any compulsive collector, he must try to attain as complete a collection as possible. This no doubt is why, over a period of years, he quietly added his highest points of each continent as a small side collection, but never really showed any interest in the 7000m peaks – there were too many of them.

He undoubtedly enjoys the position he has attained and is extremely sensitive to criticism or any threat to this. He has never forgiven Peter Habeler, for instance, for implying that he reached the summit of Everest first, when in fact it was Messner who was out in front. He is also a person of focused drive. He has lost interest in rock climbing and alpinism, perhaps now that he has completed his 8000m peaks he will forswear the Himalaya, his energies taken up with the challenge of long ice walks. He seems to need the superlative for the scale of the challenge it offers and the lure of the unknown. But light-heartedness does not often come into his vocabulary and this is perhaps one reason why he has abandoned one aspect of his sport as he has moved onto the next. The person who climbs for the fun of climbing is more likely to continue in all aspects of the sport, irrespective of how good he is at them.

Although Messner has dominated the mountain arena in the last twenty years, there have been other trends in high-altitude climbing that in the long term may well have as great an influence in the development of mountaineering. After our 1975 Everest expedition we all felt the need of a change of focus from the big battalions, none more so than Peter Boardman who had had to cope with the remorseless media attention paid to his own ascent, coupled with his decision not to wait any longer for Mick Burke on the South Summit. The invitation to his next expedition came from Joe Tasker. Slightly built, wiry, with a dry, cutting sense of humour, he had a fierce determination, honed by a seminary education. While Boardman had been climbing Everest, part of a massive well funded expedition, Joe Tasker and Dick Renshaw, who was as quietly determined and perhaps even more ascetic than his partner, were pitting themselves against the South Ridge of

Peter Boardman, left, and Joe Tasker, a formidable pairing on Changabang, Kangchenjunga, K2, Kongur and the North-East Ridge of Everest.

Dunagiri (7066m) in the Garhwal Himalaya. They had driven out in a battered old Ford Thames van, walked up to the foot of the ridge, and slowly fought their way up it. It was in the same spirit as Messner's ascent of Gasherbrum I. True, it was lower and they were less experienced, but the technical difficulty was more continuous. They only just came through the experience, six days up and five days down and Dick Renshaw was badly frostbitten. But even in extremis, Joe could not help wondering at the magnificent, sheer, ice-veined rock wall of the West Face of Changabang (6864m) across the valley.

This was the objective proposed to Pete by Joe. Dependent solely on each other, they tackled this huge face; it was the Himalayan equivalent of that first attempt on the West Face of the Dru by Guido Magnone and his party in 1951, but with the vital difference of altitude and isolation. There were no friendly lights to be seen, no prospect of rescue if either of them were injured and, creeping into the Himalayan autumn, it was considerably colder than an alpine summer. They were trying to do something that no-one had ever done before, and which most of the pundits, myself included, had dismissed as impossible.

They had to work out their own system. From a tent on the col at the foot of the face, they started running 1700 ft of fixed rope up the face, seeking out the easiest line up what seemed the near impossible. The angle was unremitting. Boardman describes this rate of progress.

> A sloping, uneven ramp, a foot wide, stretched upwards across the leaning Wall. It was plastered by white ice that was stacked along it, smoothing it flush against the Wall. Leaning out on the piton I started trying to smash the ice off with my axe. It was hard work. I hacked until my arms were exhausted and I could hardly open my fingers or lift the adze, panted until some strength returned, then started again. Eventually the hard ice at the back of the ramp came away and I managed to place a piton in it. This I pounded in as hard as I could, then used it to gain some height. Two more pitons higher up, the ramp stopped for a couple of feet and then bulged out again. Holding myself in balance with one foot on the ramp and one braced against the Wall, I reached across to where the ramp started again.

They used up their rope and now had no choice but to start climbing alpine-style, like snails, carrying their homes with them as they crawled up the face. This entailed hauling their sacks and sleeping cocooned in hammocks at night. They were warm enough in their sleeping bags, but the process of cooking was a desperately slow, cold business. There had built up between them an outwardly jokey, but very real, sense of competition, in which neither was prepared to admit weakness. Occasionally this exploded in emotion, as when a struggling Pete resented the camera-clicking that recorded his desperation:

> What was he going to do with the pictures? Give a lecture on 'How I took Boardman up Changabang'? In the heat of suspicion I gasped as loudly as I could, 'If you take another picture like that, I'll thump you.'
> As soon as I had said it, the balloon of my ego deflated. When I reached Joe, I tried to explain. He was cold, perhaps shocked. I wished I hadn't bothered explaining, I lost respect. So I hardened – we had to stay within our shells to do this climb. Joe was astounded and appalled by the incident.

But they kept going, went back down to their Base for a rest and returned, hacking a ledge in the ice to pitch a tiny tent, hauled up all the rope they had put in place on the lower part of the face to fix the stretch above, and made their push for the summit. They had been on their own, isolated in this harsh demanding world for forty days. They were making their own rules in the face of almost insuperable odds, and battled through, establishing another precedent for high standard unsupported technical climbing on the big Himalayan walls. Pete and Joe had also forged a powerful yet perhaps vulnerable partnership, based on an unspoken competitiveness, where neither was prepared to admit weakness to the other.

Other members of the Everest team were also seeking a more individual style of climbing. That same year Doug Scott and Dougal Haston made a challenging new route up the South Face of Mount McKinley and then

Scott went on to make another new route on Baffin Island. This was typical of his vast appetite for climbing in wild places on unknown ground. In 1977 I was one of five people he invited to attempt the Ogre, a magnificent and very steep unclimbed peak of 7285m (23,900ft). It was intended to be an alpine-style holiday with the six climbers using Base Camp as they would the Chamonix campsite, and working as three separate pairs, choosing their own routes and doing their own thing on the mountain. Though we reached our summit, the fact that Doug slipped and broke both legs just metres below the top, at the start of our descent, turned our holiday into an epic retreat.

It would have been impossible to have carried Doug all the way back down the mountain. We helped him as far as we could, digging steps and carrying his gear, but he had to make it under his own steam, and he did so, crawling all the way back to Base Camp. The Ogre has maintained its reputation and, in spite of several attempts, has still not had a second ascent.

In 1979 Doug Scott, Peter Boardman, Joe Tasker and the French climber, Georges Bettembourg, came together to make a bold new route on the north side of Kangchenjunga, once again using a modified alpine-style approach with fixed rope and even some Sherpa support on the lower part of the mountain to establish a sound base from which to make their push, with Scott, Boardman and Tasker reaching the top. Although alpine-style was the ideal of most of the leading climbers of this period, practicality frequently dictated modification with the core ethic being a small expedition, using the minimum of fixed rope and a rejection of bottled oxygen. That same autumn Doug Scott made the first ascent of the North Face of Nuptse climbing alpine-style with George Bettembourg, Al Rouse and Brian Hall, while Peter Boardman helped put together a capsule-style ascent of the south summit of Gauri Sankar. This entailed carrying sufficient rope to fix between two camps, ferrying supplies between them, then picking up the ropes, and starting the same process all over again. It means the team can carry supplies with them, but it is inevitably a slower and more cumbersome process than the pure alpine-style push.

Whilst the eastern Europeans have been particularly successful in sieging the big walls and ridges, a number were now beginning to assert their individualism by turning to the small expedition and alpine-style climbing. As their travel regulations relaxed, a particularly fruitful Polish-British alliance developed in which the British provided the currency and the Poles the food and gear. It started with an expedition to the Hindu Kush in 1977 organised by Zawada. The British contingent were five young hot shots loosely based on Leeds. A last minute addition was Alex MacIntyre, dirty Alex to his friends, a law student who had already made a name for himself in the Alps. One team member, John Porter, described it as 'the first East/West alpine-style big-peak-bashing affair; five capitalist yahoos teamed up with six socialist aristocrats. The anarchistic approach we shared in common.'

One of the Polish team members was Voytek Kurtyka who had followed the classic eastern European line from the Tatra, to new routes in the Alps, to Norway (where he made the first winter ascent of the Troll Wall), to the Hindu Kush and then the Himalaya as a member of large siege-style expeditions on the South Face of Lhotse and the North-East Ridge of K2, but he was never happy in that environment. He, perhaps more than any other Polish climber, was totally committed to the alpine-style ethic as an expression of his own individuality and mountain adventure. In Alex MacIntyre he found a kindred spirit, and once in the Hindu Kush he proposed they ignore their permit to the Mandaras valley and go instead to Koh-e-Bandake, which boasted an unclimbed wall of 2500m. It gave a terrifying six-day alpine-style ascent, under a constant stone bombardment.

In the autumn of 1979, Alex MacIntyre received a postcard on one side of which was a picture of a mountain, its face obscured by a mass of lines, spot heights, arrows and exclamation marks. The reverse side read:

> Dear Alex,
> Great chance for great days on the face. See you in Kathmandu, March 10th.
> Love Voytek
> PS Bring a partner.

It was an invitation to the unclimbed East Face of Dhaulagiri. Alex spent Christmas in Chamonix, 'waging climb' against the North Wall of the Grandes Jorasses. Afterwards, 'Down in the bar I put my card on the table, photo side up, picture still obscured by a mass of lines, dots, question marks and spot heights that still only made sense to their author. We pondered the thickest black lines. I resolved to ask René along. He accepted on the strength of a hot wine, the postcard and an assurance that it was bound to be a giggle. Perhaps inside every Franco-Italian there is an Englishman trying to get out?'

And so the team was complete with René Ghilini, a Franco-Italian guide, and Ludwik Wilczynski, musician and classical philologist. They climbed the East Face of Dhaulagiri alpine-style, without any preliminary reconnaissance, taking three days in a fierce storm, with three desperate bivouacs to reach the crest of the North-East Ridge at around 7500m. They could be forgiven for descending the ridge to recoup and then, a week later, returned to complete the classic original route to reach the summit.

MacIntyre and Kurtyka joined forces the following spring to try the formidable West Face of Makalu, but were stopped at around 6800m. They returned in the autumn with Jerzy Kukuczka and this time reached 7600m before being turned back by a smooth rock wall which probably would have required bolting. Kukuczka displayed his restless drive by going on to solo a new route up to the Makalu La and then went on to the summit itself by the original French route. This was his third 8000m peak. In 1982 MacIntyre joined an expedition to Shisha Pangma which included Doug Scott, and Roger Baxter-Jones, who had taken part in an impressive alpine-style ascent of Jannu (7709m), with Al Rouse, Brian Hall and Rab Carrington in 1978. It was an interesting and at times stressful combination – the forceful, even abrasive young MacIntyre, a laid back but very competent Baxter-Jones, and the older introspective Scott. But they were united in wanting to climb the South Face of Shisha Pangma in pure alpine-style, and they did so in just three days after a long wait for the right weather, traversing the summit and descending the South Ridge.

Just two months after getting back from Shisha Pangma, MacIntyre was off again to Annapurna with two well tried companions, René Ghilini and John Porter, to attempt an alpine-style ascent of a new line on the South Face. Ghilini and MacIntyre made two attempts, getting about half-way up the face on the second, before being stopped by sheer compact rock. It was near the bottom that MacIntyre was hit by a solitary stone and killed instantly. It was the kind of accident that could have happened almost anywhere to anyone near the bottom of any face in the Alps or the Himalaya. Every climber exposes himself to objective risk from the stray stone, avalanche, or hidden crevasse which ninety-nine times out of a hundred occurs in a place where it isn't lethal. But the extreme climber is not only taking more risks, he is also putting himself at risk on so many more occasions, twice, three times a year in the big mountains and, while he knows the statistical odds against him are shortening, it is not something he is going to dwell on or allow to influence his climbing. Just a few months earlier Peter Boardman and Joe Tasker had made their bid to complete the unclimbed section of the North-East Ridge of Everest and had vanished high on the Pinnacles. It had been a terrible year.

Ghilini and MacIntyre's line on the South Face of Annapurna was finally climbed in the autumn of 1984 by two young Catalans, Nil Bohigas and Enric Lucas. It was a remarkable achievement by two unknown but superbly capable climbers, taking just five days in contrast to the eight weeks of struggle with fixed ropes and camps on the route we climbed in 1970 – a sign of how far climbing had developed and an indication that almost any face, however steep, can succumb to alpine-style tactics.

Kurtyka, Kukuczka and MacIntyre had been planning an ambitious programme in the Karakoram for 1983. Now there were just the two of them, they didn't try to replace MacIntyre. That summer they camped below the Gasherbrums, proving happily that, among the flood of trekking and climbing activity, you could still achieve solitude in the Himalaya sometimes. 'We stayed on in the mountains totally alone for almost a whole month: just Jurek and me without anyone else to listen or talk to. The only voices were those of echoing avalanches.' Although linked by climbing ability, they were in many ways a disparate pair. Lightly built with tense yet expressive features, Kurtyka has an elfin quality, combined with a sharp mind and a philosophical bent. Kukuczka, on the other hand, was solidly built, quiet to the point of shyness, his very real warmth co-existing with

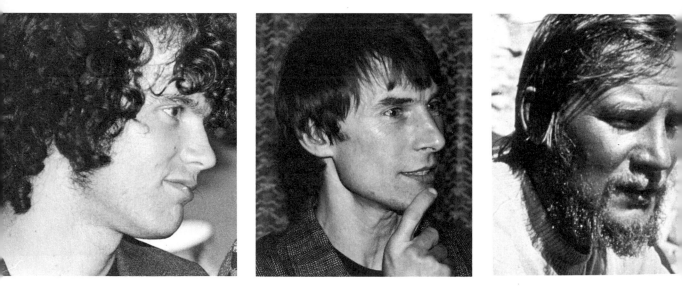

Left and centre, Alex MacIntyre and Voytek Kurtyka, kindred spirits in the Hindu Kush, on the South Face of Changabang and on Dhaulagiri East Face. Right, Jerzy Kukuczka who completed ascents of all fourteen 8000m peaks soon after Messner. All but one were by new routes or winter ascents.

a dogged determination. He smoked heavily, enjoyed his food and did not go in for an intensive training routine — a refreshing indication that you don't have to be an Olympic-style athlete to reach the top of 8000m peaks without oxygen. He was also a family man, happily married with two children.

Their objective was the remote and potentially dangerous South-West Face of Gasherbrum I, but they first made a remarkable traverse of Gasherbrum II just as a warm up. Then followed twenty days of unsettled stormy weather. It would have tested the determination of anyone. It is never easy to remain inactive, particularly when there are only two of you. But they sat it out. The weather at last showed signs of clearing on the day their porters were due to return to evacuate their camp. They decided to go for it anyway, burying their money and passports and leaving a piece of paper with a picture of Gasherbrum and the figures of two climbers on it with an arrow pointing to the summit, in the hope the porters would understand and wait. It was an immensely long dangerous route. They bivouacked the first day at 7400m, the next day they were stopped by the steep rock of the headwall and, as they began to find a way round it, Kurtyka's crampon fell off, tumbling down out of sight below. To have only one crampon so far from safety was desperately serious, but they decided to keep going for the summit anyway, had another bivouac, and then the following day, while descending to reach a traverse line to the crest of the ridge, Kukuczka stumbled over the missing crampon. The fates were looking after them this time; they managed to reach the summit ridge and completed the climb.

The following summer the pair returned to the Karakoram to make the traverse of all the tops of Broad Peak, which entailed making the first ascent of its North-West Face. But now their paths began to diverge. Kurtyka had long been intrigued by the great triangular face of Gasherbrum IV, focus of attention for all who walk up the Baltoro Glacier, but at 7980m it was just below that magic height of 8000m and Kukuczka already had the 8000m collection in his sights. He had climbed six of them, compared to Messner's ten, so opted the next year to go for Dhaulagiri, Cho Oyu and Nanga Parbat. He was successful with the first winter ascent of Dhaulagiri by its North-East Ridge, and new routes on the South Pillar of Cho Oyu and the South-East Pillar of Nanga Parbat — an impressive year by any standards.

And so Kurtyka had to find another partner, ending up in the summer of 1985 with the Austrian climber, Robert Schauer. Several parties had already tried Gasherbrum IV, but they had all gone for the centre and had been stopped at about half height. Kurtyka and Schauer chose a line further to the right up a couloir which, though dangerous, enabled them to move more quickly into the middle of the face. Here, however, their pace slowed and it took them six days to pick their way up the smooth marbled walls of the upper part of the face, bivouacking on tiny ledges, often running out complete rope-lengths with neither belays nor runners. They were at last in sight of the top, the main difficulties surmounted, when they were engulfed in a storm and trapped for two nights and a day. They had nearly run out of food and fuel and were being forced off their ledge by the continuous torrent of spindrift pouring down the face. There was no question of retreat, since they did not have enough pitons for abseil anchors to get all the way down. Their only escape was over the top.

They were at last able to move again on their eighth day on the face, reaching the left-hand end of Gasherbrum IV's chisel-shaped summit ridge. Exhausted as they were, there was no question of going that last short stretch to the very top; it was all they could do to get down the difficult North-West Ridge. To this day, it is probably the most consistently technically difficult climb of this height and size to be achieved in the Himalaya alpine-style and yet Voytek described it as his greatest disappointment, feeling that a Himalayan route had to finish with the complete symmetry of the summit.

Kukuczka that year had already made the first winter ascent of Kang-chenjunga with Krzysztof Wielicki, who made the first winter ascent of Everest and has since emerged as the strongest winter climber in the world. Kukuczka went on to join a Herrligkoffer expedition to K2 in that fateful summer of 1986, when nine expeditions were on the mountain at the same time, two major new routes were completed, twenty-seven people reached the top, and thirteen died. Kukuczka with his partner, Tadeusz Piotrowski, went for the unclimbed South Face, making a bold new route using two fixed camps, the top one at only 6400m, and then going for it alpine-style with five bivouacs. They reached the summit in a storm but on the way down Piotrowski slipped and fell to his death.

Kukuczka now had only three more 8000m summits to climb – Manaslu, Annapurna and Shisha Pangma – while Messner still had two, Lhotse and Makalu, both of which were higher and more demanding. Though each denied he was racing, the media were entranced and the material stakes were high. Kukuczka was now sponsored by western companies and, for the first time, had the freedom to climb wherever and with whomever he chose.

In the autumn of 1986, Voytek Kurtyka climbed for the last time with Kukuczka in an attempt on Manaslu. With avalanches pouring down on all sides, Voytek felt that his friend was ignoring obvious dangers and this drive to be first to capture all the 8000m summits, not only led to a level of risk-taking he felt was unacceptable, but it was attacking the very essense of what he gained from mountaineering. He deplored the growing obsession with numbers, be it the 8000m peaks race, or speed climbing on a mountain not for safety but for records. He spoke of this split saying, 'Our climbing partnership is like a broken marriage. We no longer find each other attractive', and so he left the expedition.

Kukuczka stayed on and some weeks later reached the top by a new route from the north-east, after everyone else but one climbing partner had gone home. By this time Messner had completed the fourteen 8000ers but Kukuczka was only just behind, climbing Annapurna in February 1987, its first winter ascent, and in the spring making the first traverse of the long West Ridge of Shisha Pangma, ski-ing from the summit. His was an amazing achievement. He came into the race comparatively late, climbing his first 8000er, Lhotse, in 1979. This also was the only peak that wasn't a first, either as a new route or a first winter ascent. Whatever the ethical arguments about competing to collect 8000m peaks, there is no denying each one of his climbs was a major ascent in its own right. He and Messner were honoured with Silver Medals at the Winter Olympics at Calgary in 1988. One wonders what a climber has to do these days to gain a Gold.

Messner has not climbed another 8000m peak since finishing his collection on Lhotse, but Kukuczka continued his extreme climbing. In the autumn of 1989, when leading an expedition to the South Face of Lhotse, he slipped and fell to his death when very nearly above the difficulties. The statistics of risk had finally caught up with him as well.

Kurtyka found new partners in the Swiss climber, Erhard Loretan, and the Frenchman, Jean Troillet. They had developed a tactic of very fast ascents of 8000m peaks on K2 and Dhaulagiri and in 1986 climbed Everest by the North Face and Hornbein Couloir in thirty-one hours from base to summit and an incredible three and a half hours back down again, most of it in a sitting glissade! They were not speed climbing for records, but simply found this the most effective way of reaching the tops of high mountains, as well as the safest because it minimised the time spent at over 8000m.

In the summer of 1988 Loretan and Kurtyka made a particularly elegant ascent on the Trango (Nameless) Tower. It is little more than a midget by Himalayan standards, a mere 6237m, and yet almost every mountaineer who has walked up the Baltoro Glacier has been captivated by this slender spire of warm brown granite. Joe Brown with Mo Antoine, Martin Boysen and Malcolm Howells, had made the first ascent in 1976 and, with the increasing popularity of Baltoro granite through the 'eighties, more routes were made on it and the neighbouring rock spires and walls. The line Loretan and Kurtyka chose was very much in the modern idiom, the seemingly blank East Face of the Tower, taking eight days of extremely difficult climbing to reach its top.

In arguments over just how much can be achieved alpine-style and where siege tactics may always be inevitable, the length of time spent over 8000m seems the vital factor. This was brought out in the autumn of 1988 when four Slovak climbers, Ducan Becík, Peter Bozík, Jozef Just and Jaroslav Jasko made an attempt on the South-West Face of Everest. Becík and Just had already climbed Lhotse a fortnight earlier by the South Col route. Now they set out from Base Camp on 12th October, spent the night at the traditional Advance Base in the Western Cwm, and the next day started up the face, reaching a height of 8100m, below the Rock Band. The following day they had a shock, finding the gully and ramp, first climbed by Braithwaite and Estcourt, very much harder than they had expected. As a result they only just managed to get beyond the Rock Band and spent their second night on the face at around 8400m. It took them all day to cross the upper snowfield and they had a third night just below the South Summit. Only Just was strong enough to make it to the summit on the morning of 17th October. He rejoined the others on the South Summit and they started down at about four o'clock in the afternoon. They had a radio and at 5.30 p.m. reported reaching 8300m, which would have been in the region of the South Shoulder, but were showing signs of altitude sickness and having trouble with their eyes. This was the last time they were heard, and it can only be assumed they slipped and fell down the Kangshung Face. It highlighted the risk of spending more than one night above 8000m without oxygen.

Although Everest has now been climbed several times without oxygen, the casualty rate has also been considerable, with a high risk of frostbite thrown in. In 1984 a small Australian expedition put a superb new route up the North Face of Everest, with Tim McCartney-Snape and Greg Mortimer reaching the summit without oxygen, but Andy Henderson, whose crampon broke near the top, got severe frostbite trying to refit it and lost all his fingers. The same thing happened to Ed Webster in 1988, when Stephen Venables was the first Briton to climb Everest without using bottled oxygen after making a new route from the Kangshung Glacier to the South Col. Webster had been taking photographs ungloved high on the South-East Ridge and also got badly frostbitten in the process.

The mid-eighties saw the arrival on the climbing scene of the man who was to revolutionise Himalayan climbing. Tomo Česen, a shy, withdrawn thirty-year old from Kranj in Slovenia, started climbing at the age of sixteen, graduating from his local mountains to the Alps, the Andes and the Pamirs, before his first visit to the Himalaya with a Yugoslav expedition in 1985. Their objective was the North Face of Yalung Kang, the west summit of Kangchenjunga. It was a siege ascent up a complex face of icefalls divided by steep rock walls. Česen, using oxygen and his partner, Borut Bergant, going without, reached the summit but on the way down, Bergant slipped and fell, leaving Česen to bivouac alone without equipment at 8300m, and then make a desperate solitary descent. 'In seven days, the Yalung Kang changed my life.'

The following year he joined an expedition with permission for Broad Peak and Gasherbrum II, but after easily soloing Broad Peak, he couldn't resist having a try at K2, so slipped past the crowded international tented village below the mountain and made his bid, climbing the South-South-East Spur to the side of the Abruzzi Spur, a line whose lower part was explored by Al Rouse and Roger Baxter-Jones in 1983. On reaching the shoulder, however, the weather seemed to be breaking up, so he returned down the fixed ropes on the Abruzzi Spur, all in the course of a couple of days, and quietly left without anyone having seen him.

Having found that he could move quickly and with confidence at altitude, he decided to build up his personal resources by soloing increasingly difficult routes in the Alps, particularly in winter, before following the same theme on the big walls of the Himalaya. He started with the same series of solo linked ascents of the three great north faces of the Jorasses, Eiger and Matterhorn that Christophe Profit had made with extensive media coverage, being carried from peak to peak by helicopter and parapenting from the summits. Česen drove from mountain to mountain, climbing back down on foot. Other climbs followed; hard modern routes climbed solo for the first time, and in winter; No Siesta on the flank of the Walker Spur, the direttissima on the Red Pillar of Brouillard, Modern Times on the South Face of the Marmolada.

This was all aimed as a preparation for the North Face of Jannu, a face steeper and technically more difficult than anything so far attempted of this size and height in the Himalaya. He arrived at Base Camp at the foot on 22nd April 1989. There were just three in his support team, Janni, the doctor, who accompanied him almost by chance, the liaison officer and a cook. He spent a week reconnoitring the foot of the face, getting different views of it and acclimatising, then on the afternoon of the 27th he set out, carrying the minimum of gear: a lightweight bivvy sack and sleeping bag, food for a couple of days, his ice tools and a length of light rope.

He climbed the lower dangerous part of the face, which is swept by stonefall and blocks of ice throughout the day, in the chill of the night. He had reached the start of the consistently steep climbing by dawn. Icy grooves, flanked by smooth, almost sheer granite slabs, swept ahead of him. There was no let up, no chance to relax.

> At the end of the rock, there was always ice: hard, black, green, sometime crumbling but always very steep. At one point I had to pendulum – a narrow ice gully had lost itself in blank granite slabs, with vertical rock above, left and right. I noticed a tiny crack above me and climbed slowly and carefully almost to the tip of this fragile ice tongue, taking care not to break it. I hammered in a piton, threaded the rope, and started to swing, thus managing to reach the continuation of the ice gully to the left.

At 2.30 p.m. he reached the summit ridge. The climbing would have been fast and hard by alpine standards, but this was on a peak of 7710m. A sea of clouds was lapping against the wall beneath him, tendrils drifting up to him. He struggled the last few metres to the top, reaching the summit at 3.30 p.m. and then hurried, as far as exhaustion would let him, back down a less demanding route established by the Japanese.

The following year he tackled something with an even more formidable reputation, the South Face of Lhotse. This was *the* face for the last great problem connoisseurs. There had been twelve attempts on it over some fifteen years. Messner had failed on it twice and proclaimed it was the face for the twenty-first century. Ales Kunaver, Česen's countryman and one of the most successful expedition leaders of the post-war era had been on it and Kukuczka had died on its upper reaches only the previous year.

Česen had done his homework, carefully examining previous accounts:

> To me it seemed that the crux of the climb would be the middle section, which was tried in 1981 by the Yugoslavs led by Ales Kunaver. For twenty years he had dreamt

of this face and studied it carefully. Two months prior to the main expedition in 1981 he sent a small reconnaissance team to the foot of the face to monitor everything that happened on it. They produced a photograph which showed the path of every single snow and rock avalanche and the safest line. Looking at this photo I couldn't figure out why later no one (except for the French team of Michel Fauquet and Vincent Fine in the autumn of 1985) tried this line. The attempt by these two French climbers, who reached 7400m in alpine-style, was sufficient proof for me that a solo ascent, alpine-style, was feasible. I gleaned much useful information from the climbers on the 1981 trip, and lastly, in 1987 I spent two months on the South-East Ridge of Lhotse Shar – to the right of Lhotse. From there, the South Face can be studied as closely as the palm of your hand.

This time he had one more companion than the previous year, Janni, his friendly doctor, and Tomaz Ravnihar, a cameraman, plus the inevitable liaison officer and cook. They set up camp on 15th April. He spent a week acclimatising, making four sorties up the long relatively easy lower slopes of Lhotse Shar, reaching a high point of around 7200m. On 22nd April he was ready to go, packed the same kind of gear as he had used on Jannu, and set out in the late afternoon to climb the dangerous couloir reaching up into the face, climbing on through the night. He stopped at a sheltered spot at around 7500m in the early morning before the sun hit the face and loosened the daily rock bombardment. He started climbing once again in the early afternoon and by late evening had reached 8200m, the foot of the sheer pillar that he knew was going to provide the crux of the climb. That night he couldn't sleep for the cold and worry of what the morning would bring, but the weather held and it was another perfect day. He left all his spare gear on the bivvy and started out. His description of the climbing is very bald.

> A snowy ramp led to a steep step. Most of it was rock but sometimes there was snow and sometimes ice of dubious quality. Climbing this at 5000m would have been no problem, but here, above 8000m it would require a supreme effort. I spent a good three hours just climbing 50-70m using pitons. Putting my Yalung Kang experience to good use, I fixed a part of the rope at the top of the step to safeguard my retreat.

The main difficulties were over but he still had a long way to go. The afternoon cloud had closed in, and it started snowing. There was also a fierce wind, but he just kept plodding on and, at last, at 2.20 p.m. he reached the summit of Lhotse. But he still had to get back down. He opted to return the way he had come, rather than try to drop down to the South Col, abseiling from his bivouac down the buttress on which the Yugoslavs had fixed rope in 1982. The ropes had been swept away but the pitons were still in place.

It had been an incredible achievement and perhaps it was inevitable that there would be doubters. This was particularly strong in the French climbing press, after Česen's nomination for membership of the exclusive Groupe de Haute Montagne was deferred until he produced better photographic evidence of his solo climbs. One of the problems of the solo climber is that he has no witnesses. Messner has always been careful to take extensive photographs, but Tomo Česen's photographic evidence is more skimpy and his major climbs have all been solo ascents. The following year two French climbers, Christophe Profit and Pierre Béghin, made separate solo attempts on the face but turned back, while a huge Russian expedition, using fixed ropes and oxygen, sieged the face and claimed the first ascent, denying that Česen could possibly have got up, and claiming discrepancies between his description of the summit ridge and the views he described.

But the body of climbers believe him. I certainly do, having met and talked with him. It all comes down to trust and a measure of the person in question. Reinhold Messner felt the same. In 1971 Walter Bonatti dedicated his autobiography, *The Great Days*, 'to Reinhold Messner, last youthful hope of the great tradition of mountaineering'. In his turn Messner has created an award which he calls his Snow Lion. It is given 'in recognition of the ecologically purest and most creative alpine achievement' and Messner nominated Tomo Česen as its first recipient. In doing so he has passed on his mantle to a young climber who has undoubtedly taken alpine-style climbing to an extreme which questions if any route on any mountain can any longer be declared impossible.

ALWAYS A LITTLE FURTHER

As it is now and as it might be in the future

•

Climbing has come a long way since Paccard and Balmat made those first tentative steps into the mysterious unknown represented by the top of Mont Blanc, but I suspect the essential motives for climbing remain very much the same. For them there was the challenge of discovery, the excitement of risk, competition to be there first, and a sense of wonder made all the more piquant by that edge of fear and commitment, and the beauty of the mountains around them. There must also have been that sense of physical well being, of sensuous pleasure, as they picked their way through the icefalls or up the final summit ridge; the vast satisfaction gained from pushing one's body to the limit, achieving a goal, and then resting afterwards in the full knowledge of that achievement. There was also the first glimpse, in the controversy that followed, of the problems that sponsorship, media interest and money can bring.

If the heart of climbing is trying to achieve an objective that has never been gained before, be it a summit, a new facet of a mountain, or just a stretch of rock, the climber has to be prepared to stake his life on his judgement as he moves up into the unknown. And it is here that so many of the ethical arguments are rooted. The desire to be sure of success tempts the climber to limit uncertainty of outcome by increasing his resources with improvements in equipment, larger teams, use of fixed ropes and camps, or ladders of bolts on rock walls. This goes hand-in-hand with a desire for survival. Climbing at its purest as an adventure game is undoubtedly solo climbing, but most of us prefer to hedge our bets, climbing with a partner, linked by a rope which we hope will save us from injury in the event of a fall.

Paccard and Balmat had the world at their disposal. The Victorian mountaineer in the 1860s might have bemoaned the fact that almost all the 4000m peaks in the Alps had been climbed but he was easily able to find fresh ground on the lower steeper peaks and the unclimbed faces or ridges of mountains that had already been climbed. The Himalaya has gone through the same sequence as each generation not only wants to venture into the unknown in terms of terrain, but to prove itself also in terms of difficulty, to climb something that is harder, steeper, more committing than has been tackled before. In the Himalaya this has led to many climbers concentrating on the 8000m peaks, so that Everest has a dozen different routes to its summit, while there are still many hundreds of unclimbed peaks in the 6000m bracket, ignored by all but a discerning minority.

But let us look at the full sweep of climbing activity today, starting with what I feel is its foundation, the rock climbing we can pursue the year round, for it is near our homes. To bring it up to date we need to return to where I left Joe Brown and Don Whillans at the end of the 'fifties. Climbing standards developed steadily through the 'sixties, with a widening base of talented climbers, but the actual character of the routes being tackled was still in the same idiom and Joe Brown was still at the forefront, climbing with the stars of the day such as Pete Crew, intense and fiercely competitive, Martin Boysen, who had an almost slothlike approach to climbing, or Allan Austin who for a time dominated the Lakeland scene. In hand with the steady increase in climbing standards was the continual development of equipment. The inserted pebble was replaced in the early 'sixties by the drilled-out nut (of nuts and bolts), and was then refined into shaped alloy wedges of different dimensions to suit different crack sizes. The refinement has continued to this day with a bewildering array of different shapes, curves and, more recently, mechanically adjustable camming devices which will fit almost any crack.

But the next big leap forward was the introduction of systematic training for climbing in the early 'seventies. The man primarily responsible was Pete Livesey. Thin, wiry, bespectacled, with a shock of frizzy, now thinning, grey hair, he looks like a cross between the mad professor and some kind of prophet. Son of a builders' merchant, he was born in Barnsley in 1943, showed promise as an athlete in school, and was in the British junior squad for cross-country running. He came relatively late (in his early thirties) to serious climbing via caving, but applied to it the competitiveness and athletic disciplines he had developed in his earlier activities. He refined the use of traverses on brick or stone walls to build up stamina and in the early 'seventies took the crags by storm, first on Yorkshire limestone and then venturing further afield to the Lakes and Snowdonia, taking the

Pete Crew, top left, a leading member of a new early 'sixties generation who pushed forward the next step in climbing after the 'fifties breakthrough of Brown and Whillans. Top right Johnny Dawes, who put up the first E9 on Indian Face, Master's Wall in 1986. Above, Peter Livesey, principal initiator of systematic training for rock climbing, on Wellington Crack, Ilkley Quarry, Yorkshire.

standard of climbing to a new high. His ascent of Footless Crow on Goat Crag in Borrowdale caused a special stir and was typical of the routes he pioneered. It called for boldness, since the protection was thin, particularly with the gear available at the time. It also needed stamina and great finger strength, the two latter acquired by training. There were many other climbs and the Right Wall up the seemingly blank book-end face to the right of Cenotaph Corner on Dinas Cromlech was one of his finest. The new style of climb differed from those of the past in a steepness that verged on the continuous overhang, and in the number of consecutive moves on very small holds. To climb at this standard you had to train.

In 1973 Livesey was one of the first leading British rock climbers of this new wave to make the pilgrimage to Yosemite in California. He was not so much interested in the big wall routes on El Capitan as the shorter but very difficult lines with which the valley abounds. There was a cross-fertilisation of techniques, ideas and ethics throughout the 'seventies which continues to the present day.

Whereas Brown and Whillans had been out in front on their own for some ten years, the pace and competition was now hotting up. Ron Fawcett started his partnership with Livesey almost in the role of apprentice. Also from Yorkshire, of farming stock, he is twelve years younger, tall and lean, with powerful muscles in his upper torso and a huge pair of hands with large muscular fingers. Easy going, even shy, he is very different from Livesey. He is not so much competitive, as supremely good at his craft, and loves the long hours of training on boulders, which produces a superbly attuned physique for hard climbing. One difference between them is that Livesey gave up climbing once he felt he had reached his high point and sought out other sports in which he could excel, first fell running and then orienteering. I have a feeling that Fawcett will always climb, untroubled by a drop in standard as age creeps up on him. Livesey often joked, 'I knew from when I first climbed with him that Ron was better than me. The thing was, not to let Ron know that.'

Fawcett went on to dominate the climbing scene in the late 'seventies and early 'eighties, surpassing the routes put up by his mentor. But he wasn't alone. Each climbing area had its experts, all of them pushing the limits. Based on the Lake District was Pete Whillance, lean, quietly spoken, almost dour in manner, who put up a series of climbs in the Lakes, Wales and Scotland that were technically very hard and bold. Dave Cuthbertson was pushing the limits in his native Scotland while in the West Country was

28 *(previous page): The chisel-headed Gasherbrum IV (7980m) climbed by Voytek Kurtyka and Robert Schauer in 1985 and still one of the most consistently difficult feats of technical climbing achieved alpine-style at that altitude.*

29 (facing): Kurtyka on Gasherbrum IV.
30 (left): The ropes of many previous expeditions clutter popular routes on 8000m peaks like the Abruzzi Spur of K2 and were removed in 1990 by a controversial clean-up expedition. 31 (below): The highest rubbish tip in the world, the South Col of Everest.

32 (facing inset): Jerry Moffatt making the winning move at the first international climbing competition in Leeds, 1989. 33 (facing): Moffatt, seen here on L'Horla (E1), a superb traditional climb on Curbar Edge, is one of the most outstanding rock climbers of the 'eighties, and earns a living competition climbing on the top European circuits. 34 (above): Ron Fawcett, here on Gordale Right-Hand, dominated the adventurous traditional climbing scene in the late 'seventies and early 'eighties. 35 (left): Sport climbing which means safe climbing with bolt protection: Martin Atkinson on Chouca (E8 6C) at Buoux, Provence, photographed at the crux.

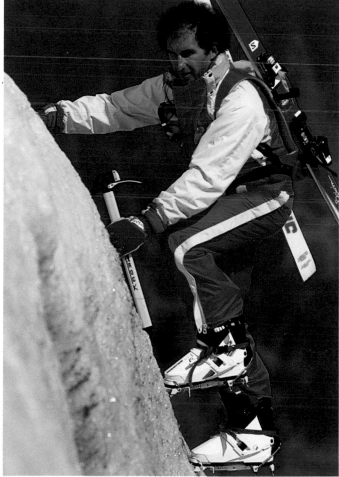

The sheer athleticism of the French style of rock climbing is exemplified by Patrick Edlinger, 36 (facing above), a beautifully graceful climber and major exponent of competition climbing, and by Christophe Profit, 37 (facing below), who made an impressive series of linked ascents of the north faces of the Jorasses, Eiger and Matterhorn. 38 (above): Benoit Chamoux's international L'Esprit d'Equipe under contract on the summit of Shisha Pangma which they had just climbed by a new route for their sponsors. 39 (left): Jean-Marc Boivin, a brilliant climber and extreme skier who parapented from the summit of Everest in 1988.

40 (overleaf): Though the 8000ers are over-visited, there are, happily, range upon range of challenging 6000–7000m climbs still to be sought out in the Himalaya where the pleasure of exploration combines with high standard climbing. One impressive example is the Golden Pillar of Spantik (7027m), climbed alpine-style by Mick Fowler and Victor Saunders.

Pat Littlejohn who specialised in the beetling sea cliffs of Cornwall, Devon and Pembroke, or John Redhead, a wild-haired artist who perhaps had the edge in North Wales. Amazingly, new routes are still found on our crowded crags and new crags are developed, but they are getting smaller and smaller and it is difficult, if not impossible, to find the great bold lines so beloved by Don Whillans.

Rock climbing was becoming more and more a separate sport in its own right. There had always been so-called rock gymnasts who preferred to nurture their high standards not at altitude but on any increasingly challenging rock they could find throughout Europe and in the States. Rock climbing was becoming a cosmopolitan game, and contact with Europe was to have a profound effect on British climbers and climbing.

It was in the 'seventies that the French 'discovered' free climbing, but it was a very different style from that practised in Britain. On the continent rock climbing had been considered much more as training for the Alps than it had been in Britain, so the ethics had always been less strict, particularly on the question of pitons, which had been freely used on the outcrops, both as belays and running belays.

With the opening up of the magnificent limestone walls that abound in southern France bolts were used from a very early stage for protection, particularly on the blank faces where there were no cracks for piton placements. The accepted ethic was for the first ascensionist to abseil down, drilling holes and hammering in the bolts where he judged they were necessary, and then make the climb without any direct aid – hence the description 'free' – but clipping into the bolts for protection. The climbing was intensely athletic without the distraction of danger, since the pre-placed bolts ensured that there was no risk of a long fall. It also meant that the climber could venture almost anywhere with the knowledge that the worst he could suffer was the indignity of a fall.

Patrick Edlinger was the star of this style of climbing. A beautifully graceful climber, he became a major exponent of the newly formalised competition climbing. This had started in the Soviet Union but for a long time was ostracised by western climbers. The original competitions had been speed climbs, protected by a top rope. But in the early 'eighties they were modified to come closer to 'real' climbing, and introduced into Italy and France. The competitor led climbs of increasing difficulty, clipping into bolt runners. It was unlikely the climber would hurt him or herself in the event of a fall but, none the less, the falls could be dramatic and the competition had the appeal of combining the challenge of supremely difficult climbing with a time constraint. Competition climbing was further encouraged by the introduction of artificial indoor climbing walls which made sport climbing a year round activity with, for its extroverts, a uniform of dayglo lycra tights and, for a better grip, a flurry of gymnast's chalk.

Competition climbing has shown graphically how close women climbers are coming to the men in technical ability. The difference between men and some of the best women climbers, Lynn Hill from America and Isabelle Patissier from France, is very narrow indeed. At the International Grand Prix championship held at Lyon in 1989, Lynn Hill came third over all. This is particularly impressive when one considers the degree of sheer athleticism involved and the gap between men and women's performance in track and field events.

A new generation of British climbers was now becoming attracted to bolt-protected sport climbing and also to climbing competitions. Perhaps most outstanding was Jerry Moffatt who had put up a series of very hard and committing rock climbs in the early 'eighties of which Master's Wall on the East Buttress of Clogwyn Du'r Arddu was one of the finest.

Cloggy is the crucible of British rock climbing for the long and serious quality of many of its routes, the richness of its history and its classic proportions – the steep and angular East Buttress, capped by the triangular mass of the Pinnacle, the overlapped slabs of the West Buttress, and then, like the flanking cavalry of an eighteenth-century army, the Far East and West Buttresses, all towering above the quiet dark waters of Llyn Du'r Arddu. Nearly every climber of merit in Britain has placed his mark on Cloggy and the focus of the crag, almost the benchmark of modern British climbing, is Master's Wall, a seemingly blank sweep of rock in the very centre of the East Buttress.

It was first seriously attempted by Joe Brown in the 'fifties with a route that crept up the flank, but he had rationed himself to two pitons for a pitch, used his allocation and retreated with dignity. Peter Crew finally climbed it in 1962, naming his line The Great Wall, but used six points of aid. Local hard man, John Redhead, tried a more direct route up the centre, put in a bolt for protection and retreated. Jerry Moffatt inspected the line by abseiling, decided he could do without the bolt and chopped it, then, using a secret weapon, a pair of specially sticky-soled rubber shoes that have now become the norm, climbed it in bold style in 1983 naming it Master's Wall. He also soloed the Great Wall – an extreme exercise in the game of risk!

But Moffatt was attracted to the sheer athleticism of the French style of climbing. At a certain level of difficulty you can't hang around to slot in natural protection. He also liked the look of competition climbing, which incidentally offered a means of earning a living around his sport, for competition climbing has always been professionally based with cash prizes and sponsorship deals. Moffatt and a small group of top British rock climbers began to take part on the continental circuits and it was inevitable that both bolt-protected climbing and competitions would come to England, but not without opposition. When a competition was proposed at Malham Cove, to be covered by BBC Grandstand, it had the climbing world in an uproar which Colonel Strutt may have been orchestrating in heaven, and it was stopped by the energetic action of the British Mountaineering Council.

Why all the fuss? Firstly, it meant putting yet more bolts into a fine stretch of limestone, but the traditionalists saw it as the beginning of the end, an admission that formalised competition was part of the sport. There was still a significant number of climbers wanting to pursue it and so a compromise was reached. Competitions should only be held on man-made climbing walls, keeping the competitors, with their bolts, crowds of onlookers and the media circus off the crags, and demonstrating that the event had nothing to do with the unstructured freedom of traditional climbing.

The first international event was held in the spring of 1989 in Leeds on a scaffold-supported wall, bristling with overhangs. It was a lovely spring day and I can remember driving over resentfully, muttering to myself that I would have preferred to spend the day rock climbing in the sunshine, but once at the competition I was riveted. It was exciting to watch the grace and fluidity of movement on tiny holds up this fifteen metres of inverted overhanging staircase, and experience the rising tension of competition in a super final between Simon Nadin, a complete newcomer to competition climbing, Didier Raboutou, one of the top French climbers, and Jerry Moffatt. Nadin was first and got over half-way up, Raboutou went higher but was stopped by a square-cut roof overhang at about three-quarters height. It was up to Moffatt. He started badly, wobbling and very nearly falling off on the bottom holds, but somehow kept going, reached Raboutou's high point and rested, if you can rest hanging on a finger-hold. Then, like an uncoiling spring, he leapt out under the overhang, grasped the hold on the lip of the roof, swung out and up, and was away to the rapturous applause of the audience. It could have been the climax of a hard run race in the Olympics, but somehow was even more exciting. Competition climbing is very different from the lonely but totally fulfilling personal experience on a mountain crag, but it is fun to watch and represents a superb level of physical fitness and control on the part of the contestants. Simon Nadin, the outsider, went on to win the World Championship in 1989 and Moffatt came third.

But sport climbing, with its bolt protection on natural crags, began, and is still developing independently from competition climbing. It started appearing on certain limestone crags, at the bottom of Malham Cove, at Cheedale in Derbyshire, and in the smooth dark slate quarries of Llanberis, as well as the smaller leafier ones of the Lake District. The excursions are seen as the wedge in the door by traditional climbers who fear the challenge of natural lines is about to be destroyed by bolting and much heat is still generated by the topic in climbing pubs and press. Those seeking another point of compromise say why can't the sport climbers do their thing on the blank walls between the natural lines? But a tenuous line winding its way up a complex crag can only offer its full challenge if those blank, seemingly holdless walls on either side don't present an escape line. Furthermore they might only be holdless to this generation. Climbing standards are still increasing. The seemingly impossible is still being achieved.

Johnny Dawes is an example of this. He extended the bounds of the possible on Clogwyn Du'r Arddu in 1986 when he made the first ascent of Indian Face up the one very blank space remaining on Master's Wall. Had bolt protection become acceptable, this would have been an obvious spot for it, and Dawes' route would have been eliminated. He climbed it with the minimum of protection and, had he fallen, would probably have been killed, certainly badly injured.

> I went for the crux. The motion startling me like a car unexpectedly in gear in a crowded parking lot. I swarm through the roundness of the bulge to a crank on a brittle spike for a cluster of three crystals on the right; each finger crucial and separate like the keys for a piano chord. I change feet three times to rest my lower legs, each time having to jump my foot out to put my other in. The finger holds are too poor to hang on should the toes catch on each other. All those foot changing mistakes on easy moves by runners come into my mind. There is no resting, I must go and climb for the top. I swarm up towards the sunlight, gasping for air. A brittle hold holds under mistreatment and then I really blow it; fearful of a smear on now non-sticky boots I use an edge and move up, a fall now fatal. But the automaton stabs back through, wobbling but giving its all, and I grasp a large sidepull and tube upward, the ropes dangling uselessly from my waist.

There is a dynamic energy about Dawes and a lot of fun. He climbs for the joy of it and seems to bounce up a crag like an energetic rubber ball, with a series of 'dynos', almost leaping for holds. He threw down the gauntlet when he gave his route the grade of E9, for a lead without any pre-inspection, (the Extreme or E grades had been subdivided initially from E1 to 5 in the mid-seventies and by 1986 had crept up to E7). No-one has yet summoned up the courage to repeat the route and challenge the grade.

And so adventurous traditional climbing and modern sport climbing co-exist, but it is an uneasy relationship and certainly a growing number of young climbers who started on artificial climbing walls and have naturally progressed to high-standard bolt-protected routes in this country and abroad, have little patience with traditional methods. They lack the background and perspective of men like Moffatt who have served their apprenticeship and played the risk game to the full. There is a fear that conflict between the two schools of thought may develop in a fight for territory, the sport climbers wanting to place their bolts on the higher mountain crags that are the home of the traditional climber. We see this on the rocky spires of the Mont Blanc massif where climbers change into sticky rubber shoes at the bergschrund, climb fast with the minimum of gear and abseil back down on bolt anchors.

But the excitement of risk and the aesthetic desire to leave the crags in their natural state, are deep-seated in so many climbers, that I am confident the traditionalists in Britain will prevail and the sanitised quality of sport climbing will pall for many. This has already been seen in the case of Parisian, Catherine Destivelle, one of the most talented, and certainly best known, women in competition climbing in the late 'eighties. She has turned her back on sport climbing, recently made an alpine-style ascent of the Trango Tower with the brilliant American climber, Jeff Lowe, and went on to solo the South-West Pillar of the Dru. Even more remarkable, in June 1991, she made a solo first ascent of a route on the West Face of the Dru, taking ten days without any kind of support to complete it. Hauling a 30kg load (she only weighs 54kg herself), she fought her way through rain, hailstorms and heavy snow, had her ropes cut by a falling stone, was frostbitten and yet kept going. This ascent ranks with the hardest climbs being done by anyone in the Alps and has certainly nailed the belief that women don't go in for extreme adventure climbing. It will be interesting to see if women's achievements in the Himalaya follow a similar path.

In many ways, modern alpinism has gone the same way as rock

climbing. Although new routes are still being discovered, the great natural lines have now all been climbed and this has encouraged top climbers to explore other ways of expressing their individuality by climbing solo, by climbing solo in winter, or by linking climbs together. Renato Casarotto, who was to lose his life attempting to solo the South Buttress of K2 in 1986, spent fifteen days in February 1982 on his own on the south side of Mont Blanc, climbing the West Face of the Dru, the Gervasutti Route on the Aiguille Blanche de Peuterey and finishing up with the Central Pillar of Frêney. Chistophe Profit of France made a series of very impressive solo and linked ascents, while Jean-Marc Boivin combined these with parapente descents. He was a brilliant climber and extreme skier and went on to parapente from the summit of Everest in 1988. All these climbs were amazing athletic achievements with a high level of risk, but I can't help wondering whether something of the romance and savourability of mountaineering was lost in the headlong pursuit.

One disturbing development in the Himalaya is the relaxation by the Pakistan and Nepalese authorities of the regulations which used to limit one expedition to one mountain. The 8000ers were 'booked' for years ahead. Then, at the urging of the climbing community, they allowed more than one expedition, provided that they were on separate routes. But more recently they seem to have abandoned all restrictions, allowing any number of expeditions on a mountain. An immediate result is the turning of each 8000er base camp into a giant rubbish tip, as Charlie Houston, Sigi Hupfauer and I discovered with disgust at Nanga Parbat. No one expedition is going to accept responsibility for the state of a shared campsite and where some refuse has accumulated, more follows.

A more serious consequence of an overfree hand with the permits was however demonstrated on K2 in 1986, when there was a total of nine expeditions officially on the mountain and, as we have seen, despite two major new routes being completed, thirteen people died in a series of accidents. A prolonged storm hit the mountain during the second week of August, trapping seven climbers above 8000m at the top camp on the shoulder of K2. But though this was the direct cause of the subsequent tragedy, the reason they were in such a vulnerable position needs examining. Only one of the expeditions, the South Koreans, was a conventional old-fashioned siege-style expedition. They were highly organised, put a line of fixed ropes and camps up the mountain and on 3rd August made a successful summit bid using oxygen. Three separate parties also used their fixed ropes to reach the site of the top camp: Al Rouse, who had been the leader of an unsuccessful British expedition on the West Ridge, had paired up with the Polish climber Dobroslawa 'Mrufka' Wolf; Kurt Diemberger, now seeking his sixth 8000er, was climbing with Julie Tullis, from Britain, after her second; and there were three members of an Austrian guides' expedition. It is arguable that the presence of the ropes put in place by the Koreans gave them an illusory sense of confidence. Once the storm broke, some of these climbers were not only already exhausted but their ad hoc alliances meant there was no support system to shore up a retreat. Only the two oldest, Diemberger and Austrian Willi Bauer, both over fifty, survived to make a desperate solo descent out of danger.

The mountains are not only aesthetically much more appealing when you have them to yourself, they are also safer. A small group, totally reliant on its own efforts to reach a high point on a mountain, is much more likely to get back down again in the face of emergency. Equally, a small group arriving alone at the foot of a mountain is much more likely to clear its rubbish and leave the spot in the unspoilt state they found it.

The ascents of most of the main lines on the world's highest peaks has led climbers to seek out in the Himalaya the same kind of novelty climbs that have become popular in the Alps. There have been a growing number of speed ascents, not so much now for safety as for the record books. In September 1988 Marc Batard climbed Everest from Base Camp to the summit by the South Col in twenty-two-and-a-half hours, his third attempt in a matter of fourteen days.

There has already been a mountain marathon from the Everest Base Camp, and a Russian, Alexander Shevchenko, who is apparently something of a maverick in Russian climbing circles, is planning a race to the top! Climbers are also thinking of attempting all fourteen 8000m peaks in the course of a single year, and sooner or later someone, I am sure, will achieve this. Both the Russians and the Japanese have examined the possibility of making a grand traverse of the Everest horseshoe, up the West Ridge of Nuptse, on to Lhotse, across to Everest and down its West Ridge. This would almost certainly entail a massive expedition, using dumps placed by support teams on the way round, and the use of oxygen for the traversing team. Another great challenge is the traverse of Lhotse Shar and Lhotse, with an intriguing unclimbed top in the middle between the two peaks. This is something that Doug Scott had been planning to try alpine-style and, inevitably, without the use of oxygen.

Commercial sponsorship has also increased its influence and in some instances has dominated expeditions, shaping the way climbs have been tackled. This was the case in a series of ascents in the late 'eighties organised by the French climber, Benoit Chamoux, who has specialised in fast ascents of 8000m peaks, climbing K2 in 1986 in twenty-three hours from Base Camp and Nanga Parbat the following year in the same time. Chamoux persuaded the computer company Bull to sponsor his concept of *L'Esprit d'Equipe* which involved a programme of six expeditions to 8000m peaks by an international team of mountaineers. The aim was to promote team-work and, through this high profile demonstration, act as a public relations exercise for Bull.

Alan Hinkes was the British representative. The entire team was put under contract, paid a fee for each climb and took part in pre- and post-expedition promotional activities. They attempted Everest by its North Ridge, climbed Annapurna and Manaslu by their South Faces, and Shisha Pangma by a new route. Sponsorship is nothing new. Most big expeditions since the Second World War have depended upon different levels of commercial sponsorship, but the climb has always come first and the sponsorship has been fitted to suit the climb. What Benoit Chamoux was doing was creating projects specifically tailored to the sponsorship. Many climbers are undoubtedly disturbed by this trend. Not only in expeditioning but also in alpinism, with climbs that have become media events, and in rock climbing, with the competition circuit, they fear commercial interests could dominate the sport, weakening the key element of unfettered adventure. There are certainly grounds for concern, but I believe that the adventurous drive and individuality of climbers is sufficiently strong not to be diverted.

We are watching a process in which the great ranges of the Himalaya and Karakoram are becoming a giant version of the Alps. A climbing guide book with graded routes has already been produced for Everest and soon, no doubt, there will be a series for the entire region. The comparatively easy ways up the 8000m peaks are already becoming *voies normales* with heavy traffic repeating what are becoming classic routes. Guided climbing is becoming increasingly popular, with commercial guided expeditions to peaks ranging from the smaller trekking peaks of Nepal to Everest itself. At the moment the guides tend to come from Europe or the United States but an increasing number of Sherpas are taking over this role and this trend should continue.

In the spring of 1991 the first all-Nepalese expedition climbed Everest, with Sherpas going to the summit, and on the north side an English/New Zealand/American group, attempting both the North-East Ridge and the North Ridge, laid down a policy that only the Sherpas should be allowed to use oxygen. None of the 'Sahibs' managed to make it to the top but two of the Sherpas, using oxygen, were successful.

For the leading players, like Béghin and Cesen, there are endless opportunities for difficult solo or alpine-style climbs on the steepest and biggest faces. The West Face of Makalu is still virgin and I am sure could be climbed solo or in alpine-style. But the day of the siege-style expedition is not over. There are still plenty putting up new routes using siege tactics to give themselves a greater chance of success or to avoid the extreme commitment of an alpine-style push. The ethical argument, no doubt, will continue but, more to the point, as solo and alpine-style ascents increase, the kudos gained from a first ascent using siege tactics will be less and the more adventurous style may become the norm.

But while all too many climbers still seem obsessed with 8000m peaks, there are countless unexplored ridges, faces and glaciers awaiting the discerning at between 6000-7000m. So far only a select number of climbers are enjoying a style of mountaineering that combines the challenge and excitement of modern high-standard climbing and the joy of exploration amongst empty, little known mountains.

One of the most outstanding of these is a London-based tax collector called Mick Fowler. In his own way, he is as remarkable as Reinhold Messner, but has never bothered to chase the conventional records, making instead an extraordinary collection of new routes whose common denominator is immense seriousness and individuality. He pioneered extreme chalk climbing on the south coast of England, using the same techniques as those employed on steep ice with crampons and ice tools, to climb the precarious white cliffs of Dover and others in the area. He has put up a series of rock climbs on traditional crags like Clogwyn Du'r Arddu, as well as on sea cliffs and the big vegetated walls of terrifyingly loose rock and in the Scottish Highlands. He and a small group of London climbers have taken pride in leaving London after work on a Friday night, driving up to the far north of Scotland, and snatching from the resident Scottish hard men some of the best unclimbed winter lines in Scotland. He has left his mark in the Alps with a new route on the Grand Pilier d'Angle, in Peru on the South Face of Taulliraju and in the Himalaya on the Golden Pillar of Spantik, a buttressed wall of light brown granite veined in snow, leading to a 7027m summit. He and like-minded Londoner, Victor Saunders, succeeded, despite bad weather and a time-span limited by the length of their annual holiday. Their alpine-style climb did not have the glamour or scale of a Gasherbrum IV or a Lhotse South Face, but it had all the ingredients of adventure. There were long sections without any form of protection; retreat would have been impossible, for there were no anchor points from which to abseil, and there was no certainty of being able to reach the summit. Looking into the future, there are thousands of climbs like this just waiting to be done. It is not mountaineering that makes national press headlines, but there is an almost limitless scope for pioneering adventure.

There is also the question of risk. High-altitude climbing is a dangerous game with a very high casualty rate among the top players. It is a chilling thought that of the four companions who went to the top of Kongur, Al Rouse, Peter Boardman, Joe Tasker and I, only I am left. Doug Scott has the same experience. All those who went with him to the tops of the three 8000m peaks he has climbed subsequently died on the mountains. The fact that we are alive can be ascribed to luck rather than greater skill.

Charlie Houston commented on how his generation in the 'thirties, and even the early 'fifties, regarded this level of risk as unacceptable. Reaching the summit was of a lower level of importance than it is in today's more pressured atmosphere and yet on K2 in 1953 the survivors were extremely lucky to come out of it alive. A factor today is not just that the climbing is both bolder and more difficult, it is the sheer number of times the modern climber puts himself at risk, with two or even three Himalayan expeditions in a single year. If we compare the number of people climbing in the Himalaya in any one season in the 'thirties with how many are climbing there today, the proportion of fatalities has hardly changed.

One of the great attractions of climbing is that addictive thrill of risk. We all kid ourselves that we are good at risk assessment, but when close to a summit, ambition, curiosity about the unknown, the need to test ourselves to the limit or just the joy of the experience, can egg us on beyond the bounds of prudence. Just going into the mountains is dangerous. Ian Clough, one of the safest and most cautious of climbers, was killed at the foot of the South Face of Annapurna at the very end of the expedition, as was Alex MacIntyre after following the prudent course of retreating.

But perhaps the greatest challenge facing every climber, as on a global scale it faces mankind, is how we treat our mountain environment. Many

Mick Fowler, left, and Victor Saunders, partners on the totally committing first ascent of the Golden Pillar of Spantik, represent the best tradition of adventure climbing.

of the problems may seem beyond the climbers' control, such as over-population in the valleys leading to deforestation, and inappropriate development among the mountains themselves, like the hotel being built below Nanga Parbat. Could the Himalaya go the way of the Alps, with its enchainment of *téléfériques*, ski developments and network of mountain huts? What we climbers can do is treat the mountains with respect and restraint, take our rubbish away with us, encourage others to do so, and climb in a manner that does not leave permanent traces of our presence. The most important issue facing us today is not so much the ethics of siege or alpine-style expeditions, large or small, fast or slow, or the number of treks. It is the impact we make on the vulnerable mountain environment. If climbers can successfully take up this challenge, they will then be in a much better position at least to try to influence the outcome of some of the wider issues affecting the well-being of the mountains.

The history of climbing is wonderfully rich – it is not so much a matter of hanging on to tradition and distrusting new developments, for these must occur as they do in all forms of human development. The argument about ethics, the use of bolts, the effect of competitions will continue to rage, as ethical arguments have done from the earliest days of the sport. But the essential motives and drive to climb are timeless; the feeling of wonder at the sheer beauty of ice, snow, rock and sky, the thrill of risk, a giant curiosity about the unknown, the satisfaction at goals achieved and the strength of shared friendship, these don't change. But if we want to go on enjoying something that is so much more than a sport, we must start taking better care of those very mountains that once we thought were so vast and immutable.

A BRIEF HISTORY OF MOUNTAINEERING
compiled by *Audrey Salkeld*

218 BC · Hannibal crossed the Alps with some 9000 men and mounts, and 37 elephants.

126 AD · Emperor Hadrian scaled Mount Etna to view the sunrise.

1492 · Antoine de Ville and eight companions in the service of Emperor Charles VIII of France clambered up Mont Aiguille near Grenoble with the help of ropes and siege ladders. (The climb was not repeated until 1834.)

1555 · Conrad Gessner climbed the Gnepfstein.

1624 · Jesuit priests become the first Europeans to cross the Himalaya. They cross the Mana La (5600m/ 18,400ft) into Tibet.

1786 · First ascent of Mont Blanc by Dr Michel Paccard and Jacques Balmat ended 20 years of fruitless attempts. Both climbers came from Chamonix.

1798 · In Wales, the East Terrace of Clogwyn Du'r Arddu was ascended by two botanists, Rev William Bingley and Peter Williams. This was the earliest recorded British rock climb.

1809 · Among the party to accomplish the seventh ascent of Mont Blanc was the first woman to climb the mountain, Marie Paradis of Chamonix.

1811 · Brothers Johann Rudolf and Hieronymus Mayer from the Oberland climbed the Jungfrau with Valais chamois hunters Alois Volker and Josef Bortis.

1821 · First company of mountain guides founded in Chamonix.

1829 · The Finsteraarhorn was first climbed by F.J. Hugi and party.

1830 · Alexander Gardiner crossed the Karakoram on his way from Chinese Turkestan (Sinkiang) to Kashmir. Later in the decade G.T. Vigne visited Kashmir, Ladakh and Baltistan. From Skardu he reached the snout of the Chogo Lungma Glacier.

1848 · Pillar Rock in the Lake District was climbed by a Lt. Wilson of the Royal Navy.

1851 · Albert Smith made his ascent of Mont Blanc which formed the basis of his celebrated illustrated lectures at the Egyptian Hall in London.

1852 · From distant observations, the Survey of India calculated that their Peak XV was the highest in the world, and named it Everest after an illustrious former Surveyor General. Six years later they computed the height of K2 – but again, only from afar.

1854 · This year, in which Sir Alfred Wills climbed the Wetterhorn and the Smyth brothers claimed the second highest summit in the Alps, the Dufourspitze, is often taken as the start of the 'Golden Age of Mountaineering'. In the 11 years till 1865 180 great peaks were first climbed, more than half of them (all the big prizes) by British parties.

1856 · The German Schlagintweit brothers travelled extensively in the Himalaya, Adolf penetrating the

Baltoro and reaching one of the Muztagh Passes; Hermann and Robert crossed the Karakoram Pass.

1857 · The Alpine Club was founded in London, first of all alpine clubs. Two years later it published the first volume of *Peaks, Passes and Glaciers*, forerunner to the *Alpine Journal*. Guidebooks began appearing from 1863. *Ball's Alpine Guide* was the first.

1858 · The Eiger first climbed by Charles Barrington with Christian Almer and Peter Bohren. The same year Prof John Tyndall soloed the Dufourspitze.

1861 · Sir Leslie Stephen and party climbed the Schreckhorn, Tyndall the Weisshorn, and Edward Whymper Mont Pelvoux.

· In the Himalaya the surveyor Lt Col H.H. Godwin-Austen penetrated the heart of the Karakoram, exploring the Baifo and Baltoro Glaciers and sighting K2.

1864 · First ascent of the Aiguille d'Argentière by Whymper and A. Adams Reilly with M. Croz, M. Payot and H. Charlet; the Marmolada (Dolomites) was climbed by P. Grohmann and the Dimai brothers.

1865 · First ascent of Matterhorn, the Hörnli Ridge, by Whymper with Charles Hudson, Douglas Hadow, Lord Francis Douglas, Michel Croz, and the old and young Peters Taugwalder. The climb, from which four did not return, is usually considered to mark the end of the Golden era. The Italian Ridge of the Matterhorn (Cresta Leone) was climbed in the same year by Jean-

Antoine Carrel, Jean Baptiste Bich, Ame Gorret and Jean-Augustin Meynet.

1865 · A.W. Moore, George Mathews and the Walkers, father and son, climbed the Brenva Spur with Melchoir and Jakob Anderegg, one of the first serious ice climbs.

1868 · Matterhorn Traverse, following Hörnli and Italian Ridges, by Tyndall and party. First ascent of the Grandes Jorasses by H. Walker with Melchoir Anderegg and J. Jaun.
· D. Freshfield, A.W. Moore and C.C. Tucker climbed the lower east summit of Mount Elbruz, the highest mountain in Europe (5630m/18,480ft).

1871 · Lucy Walker was the first woman to climb the Matterhorn.

1876 · First guideless ascent of the Matterhorn by A. Cust, J.B. Colgrove and A.H. Cawood earned them stern rebukes from *The Times* and other newspapers.

1877 · First ascent of the main summit of the Meije (Dauphiné) by the Baron Emmanuel Boileau de Castelnau (aged 20) with Pierre Gaspard and son. (Its Pic Centrale had been climbed in 1870 by W.A.B. Coolidge and his aunt, Miss Brevoort.) The first guideless ascent was made by the Pilkington brothers and F. Gardiner in 1879.

1878 · First ascent of the Aiguille du Dru by Clinton Dent's party with Alexander Burgener.

1879 · Zmutt Ridge of Matterhorn climbed by A.F. (Fred) Mummery, Alexander Burgener, Johan Petrus and Augustin Gentinetta. The mountain's West Face was climbed in same year by Willian Penhall, Ferdinand Imseng and Ludwig Zurbriggen (via Penhall Couloir).

1880 · Mummery and Burgener climb Matterhorn's Col du Lyon.

1883 · W.W. Graham visited the Indian Himalaya with two Swiss guides. Though there remains doubt over which peaks were scaled, this is regarded as the first sport-climbing expedition to the great ranges.

1885 · Death of the great Viennese climber Emil Zsigmondy in a fall from the South Face of the Meije.

1886 · W.P. Haskett Smith's ascent of Napes Needle is generally accepted as the start of rock climbing as a sport in Britain.

1887 · The 17-year-old Georg Winkler soloed the Eastern Vajolet Tower (Torre Winkler), but was to disappear shortly afterwards in an attempt on the Weisshorn.
· Young subaltern F.E. Younghusband crossed the Karakoram mountains from China, discovered the Shaksgam valley and crossed the old Muztagh Pass into the Baltoro.

1888 · Mummery with the guide Heinrich Zurfluh visited the Caucasus where he climbed Dych Tau.

1890 · Norman Neruda with Christian Klucker climbed the Piz Roseg and Lyskamm North Faces, still considered serious ice routes today.

1892 · W.M. Conway led an exploratory expedition to the Karakoram, visiting the Hispar, Biafo and Baltoro Glaciers and climbing 'Pioneer Peak' (6890m/22,376ft), a subsidiary of Baltoro Kangri ('Golden Throne'). A world altitude record for the time.

1893 · Klucker, with Emile Rey and Dr Paul Gussfeldt, climbed the Peuterey Ridge of Mont Blanc.

1895 · Mummery's death with two Gurkhas in the course of the first expedition to Nanga Parbat in the Himalaya.

1898 · Wilhelm Paulcke made first solo ascent of Matterhorn.
· In Scotland, Raeburn's ascent of the gully on Lochnagar that now bears his name marked the beginning of serious Scottish winter climbing.

1902 · The Anglo-German climber Oscar Eckenstein led an international expedition for the first attempt on K2. His team included the notorious satanist Aleister Crowley.

1905 · Crowley led a disastrous attempt on the world's third highest peak, Kangchenjunga (8598m/28,208ft).

1907 · Ascent of Trisul (7120m/23,360ft) by Tom Longstaff, the Brocherel brothers and a Gurkha, Karbir – the first 'seven-thousander' to be climbed.
· The first women's mountaineering club, which later became the Ladies Alpine Club, was founded as a section of the Lyceum Club in London.

1908 · Oscar Eckenstein introduced 10-point crampons and the short ice axe to European climbing. Two years later pitons and karabiners made their appearance.

1909 · The Duke of the Abruzzi brought a large expedition up the Baltoro to attempt K2. They also reached (7500m/24,600ft) on Chogolisa, a height record.

1911 · The Laliderer North Face (Karwendel) was climbed by the Meyer brothers with the Dolomite guides Angelo Dibona and Luigi Rizzi. Paul Preuss soloed the West Face of the Totenkirchl in the Wilder

Kaiser and traversed the Guglia di Brenta in the Dolomites, climbing by the East Summit Face. (Two years later he was killed attempting a difficult solo climb on the Mandlkogel in Gosaukamm.)

· British climber Geoffrey Winthrop Young and Josef Knubel climbed the Mer de Glace Face of the Grépon with H.O. Jones and his two guides Henri Brocherel and R. Todhunter; and an Austrian dentist, Karl Blodig completed climbs of all the then known 4000m peaks in the Alps. As new measurements revealed others, he added these to his tally.

1912 · The indefatigable husband and wife team William Hunter and Fanny Bullock Workman, whose well-publicised travels had already taken them to the Lesser Karakoram and Nun Kun and gained for Fanny the women's world altitude record, this year visited the Siachen Glacier, crossing the Bilafond La.

1913 · Mount McKinley in Alaska (6187m/20,300ft) received its first ascent by H. Stuck, H. Carstens and R. and W. Harper.

1914 · In Britain, Siegfried Herford climbed the Central Buttress on Scafell, a route well ahead of its time.

1921, 1922 · First reconnaissance expedition to Mount Everest through Tibet, led by Col Charles Howard-Bury, thoroughly explored that side of the mountain, climbed the North Col and discovered a feasible route to the summit. A second expedition the following year attained 27,300ft (8320m), but seven porters were lost in an avalanche on the slopes of the North Col.

1924 · Fritz Riegele and Willo Welzenbach made the earliest use of ice pitons in their first ascent of the Wiesbachhorn North-West Face (Hohe Tauern).

· George Mallory and Andrew Irvine were lost on Mount Everest. When last seen above the highest camp they were 'going strong for the top'. To this day no-one knows if their attempt was successful.

1925 · Civetta North-West Face climbed for the first time by Emil Solleder and Gustl Lettenbauer. Welzenbach seized the North Faces of the Eiskogele and Grossglockner and the North-West Face of the Klockerin, and with Eugen Allwein makes direct ascent of the Dent d'Herens North Face, which included a tensioned rope traverse.

1927 · Piggott's climb on the East Buttress of Clogwyn Du'r Arddu (named after its leader, Fred Piggott of Manchester) ushered in years of intense activity on the popular crag, soon to become universally known as 'Cloggy'. J.L. Longland led his famous eponymous climb on the West Buttress the following year, then went on to climb Javelin Blade in Cwm Idwal, Britain's first 'Extreme' and probably the hardest UK rock climb put up before Second World War.

· In the Alps Frank Smythe and T. Graham Brown climbed the Sentinelle Rouge on the Brenva Face of Mont Blanc, following this the next year with the covetable Route Major. In 1933 Brown returned with guides A. Graven and Josef Knubel to climb a third route on the face, the Via della Pera.

1928 · Erwin Schneider with Karl Wien and Eugen Allwein, members of a Russo-German expedition led by W. Rickmer Rickmers, made the first ascent of 7134m (23,400ft) Pik Lenin in the Pamirs.

1929 · The Italian Duke of Spoleto carried out reconnaissance and geographic studies around K2. His young geologist Ardito Desio went

on to lead the expedition that eventually climbed the mountain 25 years later.

1930 · First ascent Jongsong Peak (7473m/24,510ft) by Schneider and H. Hoerlin on an international expedition led by Prof G.O. Dyhrenfurth.

1931 · Paul Bauer led a German team to Kangchenjunga, the third expedition to attempt the mountain in three years. It reached (7700m/25,263ft) by the Eastern Spur. Frank Smythe's small expedition climbed Kamet (7756m/25,447ft), the highest summit attained to that date, though higher altitudes had been reached on Everest.

· In the Alps, the Matterhorn North Face was climbed by Franz and Toni Schmid.

1932, 1934 · Willy Merkl's German-American expedition to Nanga Parbat attempt the Rakhiot Face, gaining a height of 6949m (22,800ft). His second (Austro-German) attempt two years later ended with the deaths of four Germans and six Sherpas in a protracted retreat.

1933 · Italians Emilio Comici and the Dimai brothers climbed the North Wall of the Cima Grande di Lavaredo, the first Dolomite climb in which pitons provided a systematic aid.

1935 · Rudolf Peters and Martin Maier climbed the Central or Croz Spur of the Grandes Jorasses North Face. Max Sedlmayer and Karl Mehringer were lost on the first attempt of the Eigerwand. Riccardo Cassin and Vittorio Ratti climbed the North Face of Cima Ovest.

1936 · Giusto Gerevasutti made first solo of Matterhorn's Italian Ridge of winter. Four more climbers died on the Eiger, including the young Bavarian soldier Toni Kurz.

1936 · British climbers experienced disappointment on Everest, but a small Anglo-American team made first ascent of Nanda Devi (7816m/25,645ft).

1937 · Cassin, Ratti and Gino Esposito climbed the North-East Face of Piz Badile in the Bregaglia during blizzards which killed two other contenders from Como.

· In Scotland Bill Murray experimented with a short ice-climbing tool (a slater's pick); his winter climb of Crowberry Ridge (Garrick's Shelf Route) with W.M. Mackenzie was an early modern Scottish ice climb.

1937, 1938 · On Nanga Parbat seven Germans and nine Sherpas were engulfed in a huge avalanche at their Advance Base at the foot of Rakhiot Peak. There were no survivors. The following year Paul Bauer's well-equipped party almost gained the Silver Saddle.

1938 · First ascent of the Eiger North Face by Anderl Hinterstoisser, Ludwig Vorg, Heinrich Harrer and Fritz Kasparek; and of the Walker Spur on the Grandes Jorasses by Cassin, Esposito and Ugo Tizzoni.

1938, 1939 · Charles Houston's American K2 expedition attained a height of c.7925m (26,000ft) via the Abruzzi Ridge, and the following year Fritz Wiessner climbed to 8382m (27,500ft) with Pasang Lama, but his expedition turned into a fiasco, resulting in the deaths of Dudley Wolfe and three Sherpas.

1939–45 · The Second World War did not put a total stop to climbing. Indeed the formation of mountain training units by the Services introduced many new recruits to climbing, and intensively developed certain areas, such as the Cornish sea cliffs by the Commandos and

Sonamarg in Kashmir by the RAF. The technological impetus as a result of the war also had its spin-off for mountaineers, the advent of nylon revolutionising outdoor clothing and climbing ropes.

· In the Alps, though there were few advances, new routes continued to be made, notably by such climbers as Giusto Gervasutti, Raymond Lambert, Lionel Terray, Louis Lachenal and Gaston Rebuffat. In 1942 Hermann Buhl with Wastl Weiss and Hans Reichl climbed the West Face of the Mauk, the hardest route to date in the Wilder Kaiser.

· The British Mountaineering Council, a voluntary federation of climbing clubs, was founded in 1944, largely at the instigation of Geoffrey Winthrop Young.

1946 · In North America climbers were quick to pick up where they had left off. Fred Beckey, in particular, maintained a steady stream of new routes, including Kate's Needle and Devil's Thumb in Alaska's remote Coast Range with R. Craig and C. Schmidtke.

1947 · In the Yosemite Valley, California, John Salathé and Anton Nelson made the first complete ascent of Lost Arrow Chimney in five days. Salathé, an émigré Swiss blacksmith, developed a series of hard-steel pitons suitable for even the narrowest of granite cracks. This led to a great surge in Yosemite big wall climbing.

· Earl Denman, an accentric Canadian, made a secret attempt on Everest. He climbed to just above the North Col with his Sherpas, Tenzing Norgay and Ang Dawa.

1949 · Nepal, hitherto closed to outsiders, began allowing foreign expeditions to explore and climb.

1950 · Chinese armies invaded Tibet. It was to remain closed to mountaineers for thirty years.

· Annapurna (8091m/26,545ft) was climbed by a French expedition, led by Maurice Herzog. First of the fourteen eight-thousanders to be climbed.

· H.W. (Bill) Tilman was also exploring in the Annapurna Himal. With a small party, including Jimmy Roberts and Dr Charles Evans, he followed the Marsyandi valley and unsuccessfully attempted Annapurna IV (7525m/24,688ft), as well as making reconnaissances of Manaslu and Himalchuli. Back in Kathmandu, Tilman joined Dr Charles Houston, his father and two companions, for a trip to Sola Khumbu. They were the first European party to approach Everest from the south.

· In the Andes, Dave Harrah and James Maxwell, with an American student expedition, climbed Yerupaja (6632m/21,755ft), a fierce peak in the Cordillera Huayhuash which had defeated several previous parties.

1951 · Eric Shipton led a reconnaissance expedition to the southern approaches of Everest.

· A French expedition, led by Roger Duplat, attempted a traverse of the two summits of Nanda Devi. In the summit region Duplat and G. Vignes were lost.

1952 · During the winter of 1951–2 a French expedition climbed Cerro Fitzroy (3375m/11,040ft), a ferocious ice-coated granite monolith in the Patagonian Andes. Reports of their climb were instrumental in attracting other climbers to this remote cluster of peaks bordering the Patagonian Ice Cap. The summit was reached by Lionel Terray and Guido Magnone. Both went on to have further successes that same year. Terray climbed Huantsan (6395m/20,980ft) in the Andean Cordillera Blanca, Magnone was one of the team to make the first ascent of the West Face of the Dru, an Alpine face of 600m plus which required eight days of siege tactics to achieve.

· Swiss mountaineers mounted two expeditions to Everest. The spring assault, led by Dr Wyss-Dunant, climbed the Geneva Spur to the South Col, from where Raymond Lambert and Tenzing Norgay reached a high point of 8595m on the South-East Ridge. The autumn attempt failed to get beyond the South Col and suffered one fatality.

· British mountaineers, led by Eric Shipton, went to Cho Oyu (8153m/26,750ft) by way of a trial of men and equipment for Everest the following year. The expedition failed at 6850m.

· At home the productive rock climbing partnership of Joe Brown and Don Whillans had already yielded a number of fine new routes, such as Cemetery Gates. They were popularly known as the 'hard men' and were influential in bringing new impetus to British climbing. Cenotaph Corner was climbed by Joe Brown and Dave Belshaw.

1953 · First ascent of Everest (8848m/29,028ft) by a British expedition, led by John Hunt. The South Summit was reached by Dr Charles Evans and Tom Bourdillon on 26th May and the main summit by Ed Hillary (NZ) and Sherpa Tenzing Norgay three days later. Oxygen apparatus was used.

· Another eight-thousander was climbed a few weeks later when Hermann Buhl (Austria) struggled to the summit of Nanga Parbat (8125m/28,660ft). His forty-hour solo climb from Camp 5 (still four miles and nearly 1000m below the summit) to the top and back astounded mountaineers the world over.

· On K2, the world's second highest mountain (8611m,28,253ft), Dr Charles Houston's American expedition reached 7770m when bad weather forced a retreat.

1954 · First ascent of K2 by a large Italian expedition led by Professor A. Desio. The summit was reached 31st July by Lino Lacedelli and Achille Compagnoni.

· Another 8000er, Cho Oyu, was climbed, by contrast, by a very small expedition organised by Herbert Tichy (Austria).

· In Alaska, H. Harrer, F. Beckey and H. Maybohn made first ascents of Hunter (4442m/14,575ft) and Deborah (3822m/12,540ft).

· The very steep South Face of Aconcagua (6960m/22,868ft), highest peak in the Americas, was climbed by a lightweight French expedition led by R. Ferlet. The first big difficult wall to be climbed at high altitude.

1955 · Kangchenjunga (8598m/28,208ft), the world's third highest peak – first ascent by a nine-man British expedition, led by Dr Charles Evans. George Band and Joe Brown climbed to within a few feet of the summit, 25th May, followed next day by Norman Hardie and H.R.A. Streather. The summit itself was untrodden in deference to the wishes of the Sikkimese people.

· Makalu (8481m/27,825ft) received its first ascent in the same month. A French expedition, led by J. Franco, put three groups on summit on three consecutive days: J. Couzy and L. Terray; J. Franco, G. Magnone and Gyalzen Norbu; J. Bouvier, S. Coupe, P. Leroux and A. Vialette.

· In the Alps, Walter Bonatti (Italy) made the first ascent of the South-West Pillar of the Petit Dru, a remarkable solo climb taking six days.

1956 · Lhotse (8511m/27,923ft) – first ascent by Ernst Reiss and F. Luchsinger with a Swiss expedition which also made the second ascent of Everest, led by A. Eggler. Japanese climbers, led by Y. Maki, scaled Manaslu (8156m/26,760ft).

· In the Karakoram, four British climbers visited the striking

pyramid of Mustagh Tower (7237m/23,743ft). Following the short, steep North-West Ridge, Joe Brown and Ian McNaught Davis climbed the West Summit and next day Tom Patey and Jon Hartog reached the main East Summit. A French expedition reached the top by the longer South-East Ridge five days later.

· Gasherbrum II (8035m/26,360ft) was climbed by an Austrian expedition led by F. Moravec.

· Collective climbing was preferred in Russia. V. Abalakov led a large party to the summit of Pobeda (7439m/24,407ft), or Victory Peak, highest point in Tien Shan range. A Sino-Russian expedition climbed Muztagh Ata (7546m/24,757ft) in the Aghil range of Tibet.

1957 · Broad Peak (8047m/26,400ft) – first ascent by four-man Austrian team: Markus Schmuck (leader), Fritz Wintersteller, Kurt Diemberger and Hermann Buhl.

· In South America Pumasillo (6070m/19,915ft) was climbed by a British student expedition, led by S. Clarke; and Jirishanca (6126m/20,098ft), the Peruvian Matterhorn, by Austrians Toni Egger and S. Jungmaier; German climbers (leader G. Hauser) made the first complete ascent of Alpamayo.

· The Nose route on El Capitan was completed over eighteen months by the persistence of Warren Harding and companions, using such unconventional aids as 'stove legs', 'Dolt cart', now folklore. The North-West Face of Half Dome was climbed by Royal Robbins, V. Gallwas and M. Sherrick.

· In the Alps, the East Face of the Grand Pilier d'Angle was climbed by Walter Bonatti and T. Gobbi, and a route on the Civetta, Punta Tissi by W. Phillip and D. Flamm, considered the hardest free climb of its day in the Dolomites.

1957 · Scottish ice climbing was undergoing a period of development. Zero Gully on Ben Nevis was climbed by Tom Patey, Hamish MacInnes and Graeme Nicol.

1958 · Another eight-thousander, Gasherbrum I (or Hidden Peak, 8068m/26,470ft), was climbed by American mountaineers, P. Schoening and A. Kauffman (leaders: R. Schoening and N. Clinch). Gasherbrum IV (7925m/26,000ft) was climbed by Walter Bonatti and Carlo Mauri with an Italian expedition under Riccardo Cassin; Rakaposhi (7788m/25,550ft) was climbed by British climbers, Mike Banks and Tom Patey, with a British-Pakistani Forces expedition, led by Banks; and Haramosh (7406m/24,298ft) by H. Roiss, S. Pauer, F. Mandl of an Austrian expedition.

· In the Alps, where the absolute 'direttissima' was the ultimate ideal, four Germans – L. Brandler, D. Hasse, J. Lehne and S. Löw – climbed the North Face Direct of Cima Grande.

1959 · First ascent of Cerro Torre (3128m/10,262ft) in Patagonia – claimed by Cesare Maestri (Italy). He reported he reached the summit with Toni Egger (Austria), who was fatally injured during the descent. Maestri was incoherent when found. As years passed, people questioned whether the two could really have been to the top. The route seemed way ahead of its time and there was no photographic evidence. It remains one of mountaineering's great enigmas.

1960 · Dhaulagiri (8167m/26,795ft), which had proved a most stubborn eight-thousander, was finally climbed by a Swiss expedition led by M. Eiselin. Eight men reached the summit.

· The Chinese climbed Everest, the first ascent by the North Col route. The summit was reached by Wang Fu-Chou, Konbu and Cho Yin-Hua in darkness. Few details, no photographs.

· Many seven-thousanders were climbed, including: Annapurna II by the British Indian Services expedition, led by Jimmy Roberts (summit reached by Chris Bonington, Dick Grant and Ang Nyima); Distagil Sar (7885m); Himalchuli; Masherbrum; Noshaq. A period of great activity throughout the Himalaya, Karakoram and Hindu Kush.

1961 · Nuptse (7879m/25,850ft) in the Everest group was climbed by a British expedition led by Joe Walmsley. The summit was reached by Dennis Davis and Sherpa Tashi; then by Chris Bonington, Les Brown, Jim Swallow and Sherpa Pemba.

· Ama Dablam (6856m/22,493ft), a shapely pyramid on the approach to Everest, was first climbed by an Anglo-American-NZ team. Mike Gill, B. Bishop, Mike Ward and W. Romanes reached the top.

· Political tension closed Baltoro Karakoram to climbers until 1974.

· On Mount McKinley (6194m/20,322ft), Alaska, a mixed climb of over 3000m was put up by Riccardo Cassin and party (Italy) in two weeks of siege climbing. (Nowadays the route is usually climbed alpine-style and has been soloed.) In Yosemite, the Salathé Wall on El Capitan, a natural line described as the greatest rock-climbing route in the world, was climbed by Chuck Pratt, Tom Frost, Royal Robbins (US).

· In the Alps, the coveted Central Pillar of Frêney on Mont Blanc was finally climbed by Chris Bonington, Ian Clough, Don Whillans and Jan Djuglosz (Poland).

1962 · A French expedition climbed Jannu (7710m/25,296ft), fiercest of Kangchenjunga's satellites; the summit was reached by R. Desmaison, P. Keller, R. Paragot and Gyaltsen Mikchung.

· Meanwhile on Nanga Parbat a second route was climbed, this time on the Diamir Face, again by an expedition led by Dr Karl Herrligkoffer. Toni Kinshofer, Siegi Löw and Anderl Mannhardt climbed to the summit via the Bazhin Gap; Löw died during the descent.

· Winter ascents were becoming popular in the Alps. Matterhorn North Face received its first winter ascent by P. Etter and Hilti von Allmen, the Eigerwand having been climbed the previous winter by Toni Hiebeler, Toni Kinshofer, Anderl Mannhardt and W. Almberger.

1963 · Everest – a powerful American expedition, led by Norman Dyhrenfurth, put six men on the summit and achieved the first traverse of the mountain.

· American climbers were also making their mark in the Alps: John Harlin and Tom Frost made the first ascent of the Hidden Pillar on the Frêney Face of Mont Blanc, and, with Garry Hemming and S. Fulton (GB), climbed Aiguille du Fou.

· Eiger North Face was soloed for the first time by Swiss guide, Michel Darbellay. Walter Bonatti climbed the Grand Pilier d'Angle with C. Zapelli, and the same pair made first winter ascent of the Walker Spur.

1964 · Final eight-thousander climbed by Chinese – Shisha Pangma (or Gosainthan, 8046m/26,398ft).

· North America Wall on El Capitan – first ascent by Yvon Chouinard, Tom Frost, Chuck Pratt and Royal Robbins.

1965 · Mountains of Nepal closed to mountaineers until 1969.

· In Norway the impressive North Face of Trollryggen, the Troll Wall, was climbed by British climbers A. Howard, J. Amatt, B. Tweedale with five bivouacs.

· In the Alps a direct West Face route was made on the Dru by John Harlin and Royal Robbins (US); Walter Bonatti soloed the Matterhorn North Face in winter by a new direct route.

1966 · Eiger Direct – a new North Face climb in winter. Siege tactics over thirty-eight days ultimately brought success to Anglo-American-German climbers, but only after John Harlin, one of the leaders, had been killed. Now known as Harlin Route.

· The highest peak in Antarctica, Vinson Massif (5140m/16,863ft), was first climbed by an American expedition, led by Nick Clinch.

1968 · A long-cherished problem on the Grandes Jorasses, the Shroud, was finally climbed in winter by R. Desmaison and R. Flematty. A second, solo, ascent was made soon afterwards by P. Desailloud. The first solo ascent of the Walker Spur route was made by the young Italian climber, A. Gogna.

· In Yosemite, Royal Robbins soloed the Muir Wall on El Capitan (ten days), and took part in the ascent of a new route on Half Dome's North-West Face, Tis-Sa-Ack (eight days, 110 bolts). Robbins was instrumental in putting up all four routes that existed to date on this face.

1970 · Chris Bonington led a British expedition to Anapurna (8091m/26,545ft) to climb the impressive South Face. The summit was reached by Dougal Haston and Don Whillans on 27th May and the era of Himalayan big wall climbing had begun.

· The precipitous Rupal Flank of Nanga Parbat was the ambitious

objective of another expedition led by Dr Karl Herrligkoffer. Reinhold and Günther Messner were first to the summit, followed next day by Felix Kuen and Peter Scholz. By descending the Diamir Face the Messners made the first complete traverse of the mountain. But Günther was killed by an avalanche at the foot of the face, Reinhold severely frostbitten.

· Lhotse Shar (8398m/27,553ft), a subsidiary of Lhotse in the Everest group, was first climbed by a small Austrian party described as 'Old Timers'! (Leader: S. Aeberli, summit reached by Sepp Mayerl and K. Walter.)

· The Wall of Morning Light on El Capitan was climbed by W. Harding and D. Caldwell over a period of twenty-six and a half days. 330 drilled anchor bolts were used.

· On the Eiger, Japanese climbers established a new direct route on the North Face.

1971 · Cesare Maestri returned to Cerro Torre and, in a theatrical gesture to confound those critics who discounted his 1959 climb, bolted his way up the South-East Ridge, employing a pneumatic drill.

· Polish mountaineers climbed the difficult Karakoram peak of Kunyang Kish (7852m/25,761ft).

· French climbers, led by Robert Paragot, succeeded on the formidable West Ridge of Makalu with Yannick Seigneur and Bernard Mellet reaching the summit; but an international attempt on the South-West Face of Everest brought only discord.

· On Mount Kenya (5199m/17,058ft) the main problems of the celebrated Diamond Couloir were overcome by I. Howell and P. Snyder. (Two years later Snyder extended the climb through the Gate of the Mists to the summit with African climber P. Thumbi. Yvon Chouinard added a direct finish in 1975. The Diamond Couloir has

become one of the world's most celebrated difficult ice climbs.)

1973 · Two Japanese climbers reached the summit of Everest by the South Col route during an un-successful attempt on the South-West Face. The first post-monsoon ascent.

1974 · Changabang (6864m/22,920ft) – first ascent by Indian-British team led by Balwant Sandhu and Chris Bonington. Six climbers reached summit: Sandhu, Bonington, Martin Boysen, Dougal Haston, Doug Scott and Sherpa Tashi.

· In the Alps, the partnership of Reinhold Messner and Peter Habeler produced swift ascents of the North Faces of the Matterhorn and the Eiger.

1975 · Two women climbed Everest. The first was Junko Tabei with the Japanese Ladies' expedition, led by E. Hisano. She reached the summit via the South Col/South-East Ridge on 16th May with Sherpa Ang Tsering. A very large Chinese expedition climbing the northern slopes had as its deputy leader a Tibetan named Phantog. She was one of nine to reach the summit.

· A post-monsoon British expedition, led by Chris Bonington, finally met with success on the South-West Face route on Everest, which had been attempted repeatedly since 1969. After discovery of a ramp, which solved the problem of the Rock Band, Doug Scott and Dougal Haston reached the summit 24th September. Peter Boardman and Pertemba reached it two days later.

· Dhaulagiri IV (7661m/25,135ft), which had defeated several previous expeditions and claimed a number of lives, was finally climbed (twice) by Japanese climbers.

· Hidden Peak climbed by 2-man team of Reinhold Messner and Peter Habeler alpine-style.

· On nearby Gasherbrum III (7952m/26,090ft), at the time the world's highest unclimbed mountain, Polish mountaineers led by Wanda Rutkiewicz were busy. Mrs Rutkiewicz reached the summit with Januscz and Alison Onyskiewicz and Krzysztof Zdzitowiecki. Gasherbrum II was climbed by the same expedition by a new route.

1975 · Joe Tasker and Dick Renshaw (GB) made the first ascent of the South Face of Dunagiri (7066m/23,182ft) in six days during October. The descent by the same route took a further five days.

· Yalung Kang, the west summit of Kangchenjunga, was climbed by an Austrian/German expedition led by S. Aeberli, all nine climbers reaching the summit.

1976 · Trango's Nameless Tower was climbed by a British team – Joe Brown, M. Howells, Martin Boysen and Mo Anthoine made the summit.

· On Changabang Peter Boardman and Joe Tasker (GB) climbed the tough West Face, one of the hardest routes to date in the Himalaya. Elsewhere in the Garhwal, Americans, L. Reichardt (climbing leader), and John Roskelley, climbed a new North Ridge route on Nanda Devi. The expedition was co-led by H. Adams Carter and Willi Unsoeld. His daughter, Nanda Devi Unsoeld, died in Camp 3, prior to a second summit bid.

· The South-West Ridge of Nanga Parbat was climbed in lightweight style by four Austrians: H. Schell (leader), R. Schauer, H. Sturm and S. Gimpel.

1977 · K2 – second ascent by a large Japanese team, following the original Abruzzi Ridge route.

· A small British team climbed the Ogre (7285m/23,901ft) during which Doug Scott and Chris Bonington made an epic retreat from the summit – Scott crawling with two broken legs, Bonington suffering broken ribs.

· George Lowe and M. Kennedy (US) make a new route on the south Face of Mount Foraker, Alaska.

1977–8 · Y. Ghirardini (France) soloed all three big Alpine North Faces in winter, the Matterhorn, Eiger and Grandes Jorasses.

1978 · Having in the spring climbed Everest without oxygen with Peter Habeler, Reinhold Messner went on within weeks to launch a successful solo bid on Nanga Parbat.

· On K2, a British expedition, led by Chris Bonington, abandoned an attempt on the West Ridge after the death of Nick Estcourt in an avalanche. Later, American climbers (leader J. Whittaker) were successful in putting two ropes on the summit by the North-East Ridge to 7700m, then picking up the Abruzzi Ridge: L. Reichardt and J. Wickwire reached the top on 7th September, R. Ridgeway and John Roskelley followed the next day, having made the total ascent without oxygen.

· Kangchenjunga South (8490m/27,855ft) – first ascent by Polish climbers, E. Chrobak and W. Wroz; Kangchenjunga Central (8496m/27,875ft) – climbed on the same Polish expedition by W. Branski, A. Heinrich and K. Olech.

· The East Face of nearby Jannu (7710m/25,294ft) was climbed alpine-style by four British climbers: Rab Carrington, B. Hall, R. Baxter-Jones and Al Rouse.

· China began to readmit outside expeditions to mountains within China and Tibet, including Everest.

· First ascent of Changabang South Buttress by Anglo-Polish expedition of V. Kurtyka, Alex MacIntyre, J. Porter and K. Zureck. A technically difficult climb, undertaken alpine-style.

1979 · Kangchenjunga – a four-man expedition put three on the summit

after a semi-alpine-style climb of a difficult new route: Peter Boardman, Doug Scott, Joe Tasker. No oxygen, no porters.

· Guari Sankar (7150m/23,458ft), twin-topped peak in Rolwaling Himal long on 'forbidden list', was eventually climbed in spring by an American/Nepali team led by A. Read and Pertemba. In the autumn Peter Boardman climbed the South summit with Tim Leach, Guy Neithardt and Pemba Lama.

· Everest. The long West Ridge from Lho La was climbed to the summit by Yugoslav expeditions (Americans had joined in at the West Shoulder in 1963). Five climbers went to the top, using oxygen higher up. Ang Phu was killed on the descent.

· The North Face of nearby Nuptse was climbed by Doug Scott, Georges Bettembourg, B. Hall and Al Rouse.

1980 · The Nepalese authorities conceded a new 'winter' climbing season. For the first time a permit was granted and Everest ascended in winter (South Col route by a Polish expedition, leader A. Zawada). The Poles returned in the spring to make a new route on the South Pillar of Everest.

· During the monsoon period Reinhold Messner climbed Everest solo from the north (Tibetan) side.

· A major new Himalayan climb, the East Face of Dhaulagiri was achieved by Alex MacIntyre, R. Ghilini, W. Kurtyka and L. Wilczyczynski in poor conditions during May. The summit itself was gained by the North-East Ridge.

1980–83 · Partly as a result of the spread of artificial climbing walls, a new athleticism was revolutionising rock climbing. Specialised training was no longer considered affected, but essential. As early as 1980 John Redhead led the very bold The Bells,

The Bells (E7, 6b) on North Stack, Angelesey, but it was in 1982 when Ron Fawcett freed The Prow (E6 6b), an old bolt route on Raven Tor, Derbyshire, that the new dawn could truly be said to have arrived. It was Fawcett, again, who claimed the coveted Master's Edge (E7 6c) on Millstone the following year. In Europe, the spectacular limestone crags of Verdon Gorge and Buoux became essential places of pilgrimage for top rock athletes.

· There was development, too, in ice-climbing. Throughout the seventies frozen waterfalls had been attracting increasing attention, particularly in North America. Often brittle, invariably steep, and sometimes hanging clear of any rock support, these transitory pillars demanded a delicate ice technique and the highest levels of concentration. Climbs like Bridalveil, Widow's Tears and Weeping Wall captured the imagination; now similar routes can be found anywhere that boasts cold, damp winters.

1981 · A Yugoslav expedition led by Ales Kunaver climbed the steep and avalanche-prone South Face of Lhotse, reaching the West Shoulder (8100m) after establishing six camps/snowholes.

· A Polish expedition (leader Ryszard Szafirski) climbed a new and extremely difficult route on the South Face of Annapurna which they dedicated to Pope John Paul II (five camps).

· Japanese climber Hironobu Kamuro completed an alpine-style solo ascent of Dhaulagiri without oxygen via the North-East Ridge, the normal route.

1982 · British climbers Roger Baxter-Jones, Alex MacIntyre and Doug Scott made the first ascent of the South-West Face of Shisha Pangma (8046m/26,398ft) climbing from the Nyanang Phu Glacier in

three days alpine-style and reaching the summit on 28th May.

1983 · In the Himalaya an American post-monsoon expedition climbed the formidable East or Kangshung Face of Everest to reach the summit on two consecutive days. They employed no mountain porters. The summiters were Carlos Buhler, Kim Momb, Lou Reichardt, Jay Cassell, George Lowe and Dan Reid. Climbing alpine-style, Dave Breashears and Jeff Lowe (US) put up a new route on the Hungo (North) Face of Kwangde; rated Grade VI overall, it is technically one of the hardest climbs ever accomplished on a major Himalayan peak. Pierre Béghin (France) soloed Kanchenjunga by its South-West Face.

1984 · Catalan climbers, Enric Lucas and Nil Bohigas, climbed the South Face of Annapurna's Middle Summit without fixed ropes or pre-placed camps (9 days up and down.) A route of sustained difficulty, it was the one being attempted in 1982 by Alex MacIntyre and René Ghilini when MacIntyre was killed.

· Five young Australians climbed a difficult new direct line on Everest's North Face, taking in the Great Couloir. The summit was reached by Tim Macartney-Snape and Greg Mortimer. Andrew Henderson suffered serious frostbite injury to his hands.

1985 · After three earlier unsuccessful attempts, 55-year-old American millionaire Dick Bass finally made it to the summit of Everest (accompanied by David Breashears and Ang Phurba) and became not only the oldest man to have stood on top, but also the first person to climb to the highest points of all seven continents. Two other North American climbers completed all seven later the same year: Pat Morrow (Can.) and Gerry Roach (US).

1986 · In March Yugoslav climber Tomo Česen became first man to 'enchain' the three great North Faces in winter, alone, when he accomplished the Eigerwand, the Shroud (Jorasses) and the Matterhorn in four days.

· The summer of 1986 will long be remembered for its tragic toll on K2. Thirteen died – including some of the world's most skilful mountaineers, seven perishing in a last all-out, multi-expedition push for the summit when extended storms trapped all those high on the mountain.

· Elsewhere in the Baltoro, all five members of a young British team led by Andy Fanshawe succeeded in making first complete traverse of Chogolisa's two summits.

· On Everest, Erhard Loretan and Jean Troillet ascended an unprepared Hornbein Couloir, reaching summit after only 31 hours of climbing, and glissading to the foot of the mountain again in ony three and a half hours.

· With ascents during the summer of Makalu and Lhotse, Reinhold Messner became the first person to climb all fourteen of the world's 8000m peaks. All of them accomplished without supplementary oxygen.

1987 · Jerzy Kukuczka of Poland became the second person to have scaled all fourteen 8000ers. All but one of his climbs were by new routes or as winter ascents. The exception was Lhotse, and it was whilst attempting the difficult and unclimbed South Face of that mountain in 1989 that he met his death.

· Karakoram activity included new rock route on the West Pillar of Trango's Nameless Tower by Patrick Delale, Michel Fauquet, Michel Piola and Stephane Schaffter; and later in the summer a first ascent of the Golden (NW) Pillar of Spantik (7027m/23,053ft) in the Hispar

Karakoram ('twice as high as the Eigerwand') by Mick Fowler and Victor Saunders (GB).

1988 · Voytek Kurtyka (Poland) and Erhard Loretan (Switzerland) made first ascent of difficult technical route on East Face of Trango Nameless Tower in 8 days. Later in the season the route was climbed free by Germans Wolfgang Gullich and Kurt Albert.
· US climbers Paul Piana and Todd Skinner successfully free-climbed Salathé Wall on Yosemite's El Capitan, surviving a freak accident near the summit when rockfall severed their ropes.
· A four-man Anglo-American-Canadian expedition put

up a new route on the East (Kangshung) Face of Everest, joining the South-East Ridge route on the South Col. The summit was reached without oxygen by Stephen Venables (GB).
· Jean-Marc Boivin climbed a new line to the right of the Walker Spur in the Alps, which he called Extreme Dream. A winter climb, this involved sustained 90 degree stretches over mixed ground.

1989 · Remarkable solo first ascent of North Face of Jannu by Yugoslav climber Tomo Česen. The direct 2700m route took 23 hours of climbing and merits a 'VI' grading in the central portion of the face and the final overhanging wall.

· A post-monsoon Anglo-American team to the Makalu area climbed 17 six-thousanders; Victor Saunders and Steve Sustad made the first ascent of West Face of Kangchungtse, also known as Makalu II (7640m/25,066ft). Pierre Beghin of France soloed South Face of Makalu (8463m) over 5 days in October. He survived two avalanches during the descent.

1990 · Tomo Česen soloed the very difficult South Face of Lhotse (8501m) in three days of climbing during April. The face had been considered one of the 'Last Great Problems' of the Himalaya, and was described by Reinhold Messner as a route for the Year 2000.

GLOSSARY

A
abseil method of descending a rock face by sliding down a rope, usually doubled so that the rope can be pulled down afterwards.

acclimatisation process of physiological adaptation to living and climbing at high altitude.

aid climbing using equipment such as pitons, ice screws, bolts, directly to assist progress; also called artificial climbing.

alpine-style climbing at high-altitude in one continuous push from the foot to top of the mountain, carrying minimum gear, bivouacking en route as necessary, but not returning to base to restock, nor using fixed camps or fixed ropes.

anchor the point to which a fixed abseil or belay rope is anchored; either a natural feature or a piton, bolt or nut.

arête a sharp ridge of rock or snow.

artificial climbing see aid climbing.

B
belay a method of safeguarding a climbing partner from falling by tying oneself to a firm anchor from which one can pay out or take in the rope. A lead climber may safeguard himself with a running belay (runner) by putting in a piton, nut or, in earlier days, placing a rope loop over a natural rock spike or round a chockstone, then letting his rope run through a karabiner (or sling and karabiner) attached to it.

bergschrund the gap or crevasse between the glacier proper and the upper snows of a face.

bivouac to spend a night in the open or in a snow hole on a mountain, or in a minimal bivvy sack or tent, as

opposed to a proper tent or fixed camp.

bolt an anchor point hammered into a hole drilled in the rock, which expands to create a friction grip.

bouldering exercising or training by climbing boulders that require a high level of technical expertise.

C
capsule-style a method of climbing between siege-style and alpine-style in which ropes are fixed where necessary on part of a climb, a bivouac established, and then all ropes and gear from below brought up to the new high point to use for the next upward push, usually to the next camp.

chimney a fissure in the rock or ice wide enough to climb up inside.

chockstones stones found wedged in a crack or placed there specially to hold a running belay, or belay, the natural precursors of manufactured wedges and nuts.

climbing roped climbers rope together on difficult or dangerous ground for safety, and can either all move together or move one at a time, leaving the other member(s) of the team constantly belayed.

col a pass or dip in a ridge usually between two peaks.

cornice an overhanging mass of snow projecting over the edge of a ridge, formed by prevailing winds.

couloir an open gully.

crampons steel spiked frames which can be fitted to boots to give a grip on ice and firm snow slopes.

crevasse a crack in a glacier surface which can be both wide and very deep, made by the movement of the glacier over the irregular shapes in its bed, or by bends in its course.

cwm a deep rounded hollow at the head or side of a valley, formed by glacial action.

D
direttissima the most direct natural line up a face.

E
étrier portable rope and metal or webbing loop ladders of a few rungs used in aid climbing.

F
face a steep aspect of a mountain between two ridges.

fifi hook a metal hook attached to a thin cord, used in artificial climbing.

fixed ropes on prolonged climbs up steep ground the lead climber, having run out the full length of rope, ties it to an appropriate anchor, and subsequently all climbers move independently up and down the fixed rope, clipped on to it, using it either as a safety line or, on very steep ground, for direct progress. The rope

is left in place for the duration of the climb.

free climbing climbing rock using only natural holds and not pulling on any of the running belays.

front pointing climbing straight up steep snow or ice by means of kicking in the front points of crampons and supporting balance with an ice axe, or, on steep ground, using the picks of an ice axe and ice hammer in either hand.

G
gendarme a rock pinnacle obtruding from a ridge, often surrounded by snow.

grades systems of stating the degree of difficulty of a climb. The terminology varies between climbing nations. Britain started with descriptive grades of Easy, Moderate, Difficult, Very Difficult, Severe, Very Severe (VS). VS was the top standard in England and Wales until the Second World War and the Scots held on to it until the 1960s. In the 1950s the grade Extremely Severe (ES) was added. Standards increased once again in the mid-seventies and the Extreme grade was sub-divided from E1 to E5. Today there is even an E9–Indian Face on Clogwyn Du'r Arddu, climbed by Johnny Dawes. The rest of the world employed a variety of numerical grades. Numerical technical pitch ratings have also been introduced.

H
hanging glacier a glacier part of the way up a mountain which connects to the main glacier at the foot by ice cliffs or an icefall.

headwall steep rock barrier at head of a valley.

I
icefall where a glacier falls steeply and creates a series of crevasses and pinnacles of ice.

J
jumar clamps devices which lock on a fixed rope to support a climber's weight when subjected to downward

force, but which can be slid up the rope as a method of climbing, or jumaring, it.

K
karabiners oval metal snap-links used for, among other things, attaching rope to an anchor.

L
la pass (Tibetan).

M
monsoon the monsoon reaches the Himalaya and climbing is impossible by the middle of June, so expeditions are made in the pre-monsoon season (mid-May to mid-June) or the post-monsoon season (mid-September to mid-October). The Karakoram is not affected by the monsoon in this way.

moraine accumulation of stones and debris carried down by a glacier.

N
nuts originally were nuts (of nuts and bolts) with the thread drilled out, but progressed to alloy wedges. Used in cracks to support belays.

O
oedema a high-altitude illness in which water accumulates in the brain (cerebral oedema) or the lungs (pulmonary oedema). Immediate and swift descent is imperative for survival.

off-width cracks too wide to fist jam, too narrow to take more than an arm and leg. Difficult to protect.

P
pitch section of climbing between two stances or belay points.

piton a metal peg hammered into a rock crack to support a belay.

powder-snow avalanche caused by freshly fallen snow on steep surfaces before it has had time either to thaw or freeze; one of the most spectacular and dangerous avalanche conditions.

protection the number and quality of running belays used to make a pitch safer and psychologically easier to lead *prussiking* a method of directly ascending a rope with the aid of prussik knots, or friction hitches, with foot loops.

Q

quick-draws short slings linking two karabiners, mainly for connecting wired nut runners to the rope.

R

ridge the line along which two faces of a mountain meet.

runner (running belay) an intermediate anchor point between the lead climber and the main belay, when the climbing rope runs through a karabiner attached to this anchor, thus reducing the distance a leader would fall.

S

sérac wall, pinnacle or tower of ice, often unstable and dangerous.

siege-style the method by which the 8000m summits were first climbed which involves establishing fixed camps up a mountain, connected by fixed ropes. These camps are stocked by porters and/or climbers who move up in relays, taking turns out in front making the route and establishing the next camp, then returning to Base Camp to rest while another team moves up to continue from the new

high point. The use of supplementary oxygen on the higher 8000m peaks and using large porter teams is another regular feature of siege-style climbing.

Sherpas an ethnic group of Tibetan stock, living in the Everest region, who have obtained an effective monopoly of high-altitude portering in Nepal.

sirdar head Sherpa on an expedition.

sling a loop of rope or nylon tape used for belays or in abseiling.

solo climber by himself on a climb or mountain.

spindrift loose powder snow carried by wind or small avalanche.

sport climbing where the element of risk is eliminated by use of bolt runners, and the emphasis is on technical and gymnastic skills.

spur rock or snow rib on side of mountain.

stance place where climber makes his belay, ideally somewhere comfortable to stand or sit.

step vertical or short steep rise in a gully or ridge.

T

top rope a rope secured from above.

traverse to move horizontally or diagonally across a rock or snow slope. Also the ascent and descent over a mountain by different routes.

tsampa barley flour, a staple of Sherpa diet.

U

undercut low horizontal crack or pocket with lip on its upper surface around which a hold or pinch grip can be attained.

V

voies normales the most regularly climbed routes.

W

wedge made from wood and used for hammering into wide cracks for belays or runners.

white-out condition of driving snow and mist with a snow background which makes it impossible to judge distance or distinguish between solid ground and space.

windslab avalanche occurs when a snow layer formed by wind-compacted snow settles insecurely on top of old snow and descends in enormous blocks or slabs.

A SELECT BIBLIOGRAPHY

•

Certain books stand out as classic or comprehensive narratives and will be found relevant to more than one chapter in this book. Among these are Walt Unsworth's *Everest* and Kenneth Mason's *Abode of Snow*.

The *Alpine Journal*, first published in March 1863 and annually since 1969, is a primary source for the flavour and excitement of the nineteenth-century pioneers and is quoted by permission of the Alpine Club.

Among the magazines that have proliferated over the past decades with the popularising of climbing, *Mountain* stands out for its high level of accuracy and photography.

GENERAL REFERENCE

Baume, Louis, *Sivalaya: the 8000m peaks of the Himalaya*, Gaston-West Col, 1978

Dyhrenfurth, G. O., *To the Third Pole*, Werner Laurie, 1955

Engel, Claire Eliane, *Mountaineering in the Alps, an Historical Survey*, Gau, 1971

Irving, R. L. G., *The Romance of Mountaineering*, Dent, 1935

Keenlyside, F., *Peaks and Pioneers*, Elek, 1975

Lunn, Arnold, *A Century of Mountaineering*, Allen & Unwin, 1957

Mason, Kenneth, *Abode of Snow: a history of Himalayan exploration and mountaineering*, Diadem, 1987

Mehta, Soli and Kapadia, Harish, *Exploring the Hidden Himalaya*, Hodder & Stoughton, 1990

Neate, Jill, *High Asia, an illustrated history of the 7000m peaks*, Unwin Hyman, 1989

Scott, Doug, *Big Wall Climbing*, Kaye & Ward, 1974

Unsworth, Walt, *Encyclopaedia of Mountaineering*, Penguin, 1976
Everest, Oxford Illustrated Press, 1988

CHAPTER ONE
A JOURNEY BACK IN TIME
Mummery's first ascent of the Grépon

Mummery, A. F., *My Climbs in the Alps and Caucasus*, 1895, Blackwell, 1946.

CHAPTER TWO
A MOUNTAIN PRIZE
The first ascent of Mont Blanc, 1786

Unsworth, Walt, *Savage Snows: the story of Mont Blanc*, Hodder & Stoughton, 1986

CHAPTER THREE
THE GOLDEN AGE
The heyday of Victorian alpinism

Alpine Club, *Peaks, Passes and Glaciers*, separate editions, 1862, 1926, 1932

Clark, Ronald, *The Victorian Mountaineers*

Whymper, Edward, *Scrambles Amongst the Alps*, John Murray, 1871

CHAPTER FOUR
A NEW BREED
Alpine climbing up to the First World War

Clark, Ronald, *The Victorian Mountaineers*, Batsford, 1953

Mummery, A. F., *My Climbs in the Alps and Caucasus*, 1895, Blackwell, 1946

CHAPTER FIVE
FIRST STEPS IN THE HIMALAYA
Himalayan forays up to the First World War

Crowley, Aleister, *The Confessions of Aleister Crowley*, Routledge & Kegan Paul, 1986

Longstaff, Tom, *This My Voyage*, John Murray, 1950

CHAPTER SIX
PROFANED WITH SPIKES
Aid climbing and north faces between the wars

Cassin, Riccardo, *50 Years of Alpinism*, Diadem, 1981

Harrer, Heinrich, *The White Spider*, Palladin, 1989

Roberts, Eric, *Welzenbach's Climbs*, West Col, 1980

Young, Geoffrey Winthrop, *On High Hills*, Methuen, 1927

CHAPTER SEVEN
EVEREST, A BRITISH PRESERVE
The earliest expeditions of the 1920s

Bruce, C. G. (and other expedition members), *The Assault on Mount Everest, 1922*, Edward Arnold, 1923

Finch, C. G., *The Making of a Mountaineer* (new ed. with biographical foreword), Arrowsmith, 1988

Holzel, Tom and Salkeld, Audrey, *The Mystery of Mallory and Irvine*, Cape, 1986

Howard-Bury, Charles (and other expedition members), *Mount Everest, the Reconnaissance, 1921*, Edward Arnold, 1922

Howard-Bury, Charles and Mallory, G. L., *Everest Reconnaissance* (new ed. with biographical foreword), Hodder & Stoughton, 1991

Noel, J. B. L., *Through Tibet to Everest*, Hodder & Stoughton, 1989

Norton, E. F. (and other expedition members), *The Fight for Everest, 1924*, Edward Arnold, 1925

Somervell, T. H., *After Everest*, Hodder & Stoughton, 1936

Younghusband, Sir Francis, *The Epic of Mount Everest, 1926*, EP Publishing, 1974

CHAPTER EIGHT
THE INVISIBLE BARRIER
Attempts on the 8000m peaks in the 1930s

Bauer, Paul, *Himalayan Campaign: the attack on Kangchenjunga*, Blackwell, 1937
Himalayan Quest: the German expeditions to Siniolchum and Nanga Parbat, Nicholson & Watson, 1938
Kangchenjunga Challenge, Kimber, 1955
Bechtold, Fritz, *Nanga Parbat Adventure*, John Murray, 1935
Roberts, Eric, *Welzenbach's Climbs*, West Col, 1980
Ruttledge, Hugh, *Everest, 1933*, Hodder & Stoughton, 1934
Everest, the Unfinished Adventure, Hodder & Stoughton, 1937
Smythe, F. S., *The Kangchenjunga Adventure*, Gollancz, 1930
Camp Six: an account of the 1933 Mount Everest Expedition, Hodder & Stoughton, 1937

CHAPTER NINE
COULD WE HAVE MADE IT?
Himalayan attempts to the outbreak of the Second World War

Bates, Robert H (and others), *Five Miles High: the story of an attack on the second highest mountain in the world by members of the first American Karakoram expedition*, Robert Hale, 1940
Cranmer, Chapel and Wiessner, Fritz, 'The Second American Expedition to K2', *American Alpine Journal* vol IV, 1940
Houston, Charles, and Bates, Robert, *K2, Savage Mountain*, Mountaineers/Diadem, 1979
Roberts, David, 'The K2 Mystery', *Outside*, October 1984
Rowell, Galen, *In the Throne Room of the Mountain Gods*, Allen & Unwin, 1977
Shipton, Eric, *The Six Mountain-Travel Books*, Diadem, 1985
Tilman, H. W., *The Seven Mountain-Travel Books*, Diadem, 1983
Webster, Ed, 'The Life and Climbs of Fritz Wiessner', *Climbing*, December 1988

CHAPTER TEN
THE LAST OF THE CLASSIC LINES
Post-war alpinism in Europe

Bonatti, Walter, *On the Heights*, Diadem, 1979
The Great Days, Gollancz, 1974
Bonington Chris, *I Chose to Climb*, Gollancz, 1966, 1985
The Next Horizon, Gollancz, 1973, 1986
Brown, Joe, *The Hard Years*, Gollancz, 1967, Penguin, 1975
Desmaison, René, *Total Alpinism*, Granada, 1982
Haston, Dougal, *The Eiger*, Cassell, 1974
Heckmair, Anderl, *My Life as a Mountaineer*, Gollancz, 1975
Jones, Trevor and Milburn, Geoff, *Welsh Rock*, PIC Publications, 1986
Magnone, Guido, *The West Face*, Museum Press, 1955
Mazeaud, Pierre, *Naked Before the Mountain*, Gollancz, 1974
Messner, Reinhold, *The Seventh Grade*, Kaye & Ward, 1974
Big Walls, Kaye & Ward, 1978
Reinhold Messner, Free Spirit, Hodder & Stoughton, 1991
Peascod, Bill, *Journey After Dawn*, Cicerone Press, 1985
Rebuffat, Gaston, *Between Heaven and Earth*, Nicholas Vane, 1965
Starlight After Storm: the ascent of the six great north faces in the Alps, Dent, 1956
Terray, Lionel, *Conquistadors of the Useless*, Gollancz, 1975
Whillans, Don, and Ormerod, A. *Portrait of a Mountaineer*, Heinemann, 1971, Penguin, 1973

CHAPTER ELEVEN
LADDERS INTO THE SKY
The first ascents of the 8000m peaks

Buhl, Hermann, *Nanga Parbat Pilgrimage*, Hodder & Stoughton, 1981
Diemberger, Kurt, *Summits and Secrets*, Hodder & Stoughton, 1991
Evans, Charles, *Kangchenjunga, the Untrodden Peak*, Hodder & Stoughton, 1956
Herrligkoffer, Karl M, *Nanga Parbat*, Elek Books, 1954

Herzog, Maurice, *Annapurna*, Paladin, 1985
Hillary, Edmund, *High Adventure*, Hodder & Stoughton, 1955
Nothing Venture, Nothing Win, Hodder & Stoughton, 1975
Coronet, 1977
Hornbein, Tom, *Everest: the West Ridge*, Allen & Unwin, 1971
Hunt, John, *The Ascent of Everest*, Hodder & Stoughton, 1953
Noyce, Wilfrid, *South Col*, Heinemann, 1954
Shipton, Eric, *The Six Mountain-Travel Books*, Diadem, 1985
Terray, Lionel, *Conquistadors of the Useless*, Gollancz, 1975
Tichy, Herbert, *Cho Oyu: by favour of the gods*, Methuen, 1957
Whillans, Don, and Ormerod, A. *Portrait of a Mountaineer*, Heinemann, 1971, Penguin, 1975

CHAPTER TWELVE
BIG WALLS – BIG TEAMS
Himalayan sieges of the 1970s and 1980s

Bonington, Chris, *Annapurna, South Face*, Cassell, 1971
Everest, South-West Face, Hodder & Stoughton, 1973
Everest the Hard Way, Hodder & Stoughton, 1976
The Everest Years, Hodder & Stoughton, 1986
Haston, Dougal, *In High Places*, Cassell, 1972
Mazeaud, Pierre, *Naked Before the Mountain*, Gollancz, 1974
Miura, Yuichiro, *The Man Who Skied Down Everest*, Harper & Row, 1978
Steele, Peter, *Doctor on Everest*, Hodder & Stoughton, 1972
Thompson, Mike, 'Out With the Boys Again', *Mountain*, 5.

CHAPTER THIRTEEN
THE ART OF SUFFERING
Extreme climbing in the Himalaya

Bettembourg, Georges and Brame, Michael, *The White Death*, The Reymond House, Seattle, 1981
Boardman, Peter, *The Shining Mountain*, Hodder & Stoughton, 1978
Sacred Summits, Hodder & Stoughton, 1982

Česen, Tomo, 'Jannu-Lhotse Solo',
Mountain, 134
Child, Greg, 'The Art of Suffering',
Climbing, 115
Curran, Jim, *K2, Triumph & Tragedy*,
Hodder & Stoughton, 1987
Kurtyka, Voytek, 'The Gasherbrums
are lonely', *Mountain*, 97
MacIntyre, Alex, 'Broken English',
Mountain, 60
Messner, Reinhold, *The Challenge:
two men alone at 8000m*, Kaye &
Ward, 1977
Everest, Expedition to the Ultimate,
Kaye & Ward, 1979

*The Crystal Horizon: Everest, the first
solo ascent*, Crowood Press, 1989
All 14 Eight Thousanders, Crowood
Press, 1988
Reinhold Messner, Free Spirit,
Hodder & Stoughton, 1991
Porter, John, 'Reverse Polish',
Mountain, 60
Scott, Doug and MacIntyre, Alex,
The Shishapangma Expedition,
Granada, 1984
Tasker, Joe, *Savage Arena*, Methuen,
1982
Everest, the Cruel Way, Eyre
Methuen, 1983

CHAPTER FOURTEEN
ALWAYS A LITTLE FURTHER
*As it is now and as it might be in the
future*

Jones, Trevor and Milburn, Geoff,
Welsh Rock, PIC Publications, 1986
Saunders Victor, *Elusive Summits*,
Hodder & Stougton, 1990
Williams, Paul, *Clogwyn Du'r Arddu*,
Climbers' Club Guides to Wales,
1989

PICTURE CREDITS

Colour
John Beatty: pic 34; Peter Boardman: pics 14, 15, 16; Chris Bonington: pics 1, 2, 5, 6, 8, 10, 12, 23, 31; Sylvie Chappaz: pics 20, 36, 37, 39; John Cleare: pics 18, 24, 27; Leo Dickinson: pics 7, 22; Chris Gore: pic 35; Alan Hinkes: pics 17, 25, 38; Tim Greening, Karakoram Experience: pic 4; Jerzy Kukuczka: pic 21; Alex Lowe: pic 9; Galen Rowell/Mountain Light: pic 13; Victor Saunders: pic 40; Robert Schauer: pics 3, 28, 29, 30; Doug Scott: pic 11; Ian Smith/High Magazine: pic 32; Ian Smith: pic 33; Stephen Venables: pics 19, 26.

Black and white
Nat Allen: p 159 (inset); Alpine Club: pp 21 (left), 35 (left and right), 39 (left and right), 51 (left), 61 (right), 72; Fritz Bechtold: p 122; Walter Bonatti:

p 177; Chris Bonington: pp 21 (right), 88, 217 (left above and below and right), 239 (left and right), 244 (centre); John Cleare: pp 183 (above left), 255 (above left and below); Leo Dickinson: p 85 (inset); Ed Douglas: p 267 (right); Jim Duff: p 183 (below left); Norman Dyhrenfurth: pp 117 (right), 211; Ludwig Gramminger: p 85 (main picture); Charles Houston: pp 135, 137, 138; Marcel Ichac/ Fédération Française de la Montagne: p 187 (left and right); Trevor Jones: p 255 (above right); Tim Greening, Karakoram Experience: p 123; Jerzy Kukuczka Collection: p 244 (right); Longland Collection: p 91; Guido Magnone: p 163; Mansell Collection: p 32; Reinhold Messner: pp 219 (left and right), 233; Peter

Müllritter: p 125 (main picture), 128; Noel Collection: pp 94, 109; Noel Odell/Alpine Club: p 113; Steve Roper: p 153; Royal Geographical Society: pp 61 (left), 69 (right), 95, 99, 103, 189 (above left and right and below), 191, 192, 195, 197, 199, 208; Salkeld Collection: pp 29 (left and right inset), 69 (left), 78 (right), 87, 206 (left); Doug Scott: pp 201 (right), 224 (left); Vittorio Sella, courtesy Fritz Wiessner family: p 146; Edgar Siddall: p 159 (main picture); Swiss National Tourist Office: p 41 (left and above right); Herbert Tichy: p 206 (right); Terry Tullis: pp 244 (left), 267 (left); Audrey Whillans: p 160; Ken Wilson/Diadem Archives: pp 183 (right), 214–15; 228 (left and right); Keiichi Yamada: p 225.

INDEX

•

Abbreviations: Aig. Aiguille(s); exped. expedition; asc. ascent; Gl. glacier